HEALING IN THE
RELATIONAL PARADIGM

HEALING IN THE RELATIONAL PARADIGM

The Imago Relationship Therapy Casebook

Edited by
**Wade Luquet, M.S.W., and
Mo Therese Hannah, Ph.D.**

USA	Publishing Office:	Taylor & Francis
		1101 Vermont Avenue, NW, Suite 200
		Washington, DC 20005-3521
		Tel: (202) 289-2174
		Fax: (202) 289-3665
	Distribution Center:	Taylor & Francis
		1900 Frost Road, Suite 101
		Bristol, PA 19007-1598
		Tel: (215) 785-5800
		Fax: (215) 785-5515
UK		Taylor & Francis Ltd.
		1 Gunpowder Square
		London EC4A 3DE
		Tel: 0171 583 0490
		Fax: 0171 583 0581

HEALING IN THE RELATIONAL PARADIGM: The Imago Relationship Therapy Casebook

1 2 3 4 5 6 7 8 9 0   B R B R   9 0 9 8

A CIP catalog record for this book is available from the British Library.
⊗ The paper in this publication meets the requirements of the ANSI Standard Z39.48-1984 (Permanence of Paper)

Library of Congress Cataloging-in-Publication Data
Healing in the relational paradigm: the imago relationship therapy
    casebook / Wade Luquet, and Mo Therese Hannah, editors.
        p.   cm.
    1. Marital psychotherapy–Case studies.   I. Luquet, Wade.
II. Hannah, Mo Therese.
RC488.5.H415   1998
616.89' 156–DC21   97-45130
                                                    CIP

ISBN 0-87630-861-2

CONTENTS

CONTRIBUTORS

All contributors are Certified Imago Relationship Therapists.

Dale Bailey, Th.D., has been in private practice as a licensed psychologist in San Francisco for 33 years. A graduate of the Harvard Divinity School; Manchester College, Oxford; and the Claremont School of Theology, he is an ordained Presbyterian minister.

Homer Bain, Ph.D. (Religion and Psychological Studies, University of Chicago), is the director of graduate studies at San Antonio's Ecumenical Center for Religion and Health. He and his wife, Irma Coronado Bain, M.A., conduct bilingual pastoral and relationship training in the United States and Latin America.

Bonnie Bernell, Ph.D., is in private practice in Palo Alto and San Jose, Calif., and is also an adjunct professor at the Institute for Transpersonal Psychology and at Santa Clara University. She recently coauthored the chapter "Couples Therapy with Sexual Disorders" for the book *Library of Current Clinical Techniques*, Irving Yalom, M.D., Editor.

Gary Brainerd, Ph.D., the director of the Brainerd Psychological Association in Pasadena, Calif., developed the Couples Garden program, a couples resource center used by many churches in Southern California.

Betsy Chadwick, M.S.W., M.Div. (Yale Divinity School), is the coordinator and marketing specialist for Associates in Counseling and Development in Lewisburg, Pa.

Bonnie Eaker Weil, Ph.D. is in private practice in New York City. She is the author of *Adultery: The Forgivable Sin*, which was adapted for a Lifetime Television movie, *The Silence of Adultery*.

Jill M. Fein, M.S.W., is in private practice in Chicago and is a founding member of the Institute for Imago Relationship Therapy of Greater Chicago.

Mo Therese Hannah, Ph.D., is Associate Professor of Psychology at Siena College in Latham, N.Y. She has published extensively in the field of clinical psychology and is coeditor of *The Journal of Imago Relationship Therapy* and of *The Handbook of Preventative Approaches in Couples Therapy* (Brunner/Mazel, 1998).

Kathleen Kelly, R.N., M.F.T., is in private practice in Philadelphia, Pa., where she specializes in counseling and in running workshops for couples in which one or both partners have been diagnosed with attention-deficit disorder.

Lisa Kelvin Tuttle, M.A., is a freelance writer and editor specializing in medical and mental health issues. She resides in Wynnewood, Pa.

Sharon Kleinberg, M.S.W., is in private practice in New York City. With her partner, Patricia, she leads couples workshops for gay and lesbian couples. She has written articles on the influence of homophobia on gay and lesbian relationships and is a contributing author to *Lesbians and Psychoanalysis: Revolutions in Theory and Practice.*

Maya Kollman, M.S.W., a Master Trainer on the faculty of the Institute for Imago Relationship Therapy, presents workshops for gay and lesbian couples and trains professionals in conducting Imago therapy.

Marianne Luquet, M.S.W., is in private practice in North Wales, Pa. A Certified Parent Educator, she specializes in working with couples affected by attention-deficit disorder.

Wade Luquet, M.S.W., is on the faculty of the Institute for Imago Relationship Therapy. He has written numerous professional articles and chapters and is the author of *Short-Term Couples Therapy: The Imago Model in Action* (Brunner/Mazel, 1996).

Donna M. Ritz, M.S.W., is in private practice in Princeton, N.J. She worked as a therapist in the Ryan White program for early HIV intervention, and helps conduct spiritual retreats for persons affected by HIV.

Cora Thompson, Ph.D., is the author of *Emotions Seek to Heal* and *The Pride of Slavery: An Explanation of the Emotional Heritage.* She has been a mental health practitioner for 13 years in the Kansas City, Mo., area.

Patrick Vachon, M.S.W., is in private practice in Houston, Texas. He specializes in working with gay and lesbian couples, including those affected by HIV and AIDS.

Helen Weiser, Ed.S., is the director of Midtown Psychological Services in Kansas City, Mo. She developed the minority counselor training program at Pioneer College.

Bruce A. Wood, M.S.W., is in private practice in New York City and has extensive experience in working with individuals and couples with addictions. He is past president of the Association for Imago Relationship Therapy.

Patricia Zorn, R.N., M.S.N., is in private practice in New York City. With her partner, Sharon, she leads workshops for gay and lesbian couples. She also writes about gay and lesbian relationships, and is a contributing author to *Lesbians and Psychoanalysis: Revolutions in Theory and Practice.*

PREFACE

Every day, as new ideas emerge within a given discipline, the established theories shift, sometimes radically, to make room for new paradigms. Often, a paradigm shift in one discipline (e.g., biology, physics) has a ripple effect in other disciplines (e.g., religion, psychology). In recent years, for example, discoveries in the field of quantum physics have changed our thinking about the ways human beings function. The resulting paradigm shift holds that all things, animate and inanimate, operate within relationship. This casebook invites readers into the process to witness Imago Relationship Therapy's (IRT) contribution to that paradigm shift as it becomes manifest in the field of couples therapy.

A new paradigm requires propagation if it's to survive, ways to demonstrate the usefulness of its tenets and to attract a variety of pioneers who can validate its technology. Imago Relationship Therapy, derived from the work of Harville Hendrix and described in his book, *Getting the Love You Want: A Guide for Couples* (Holt, 1988), represents a synthesis of Western psychological thought, Eastern spiritual traditions, mythical literature, and new scientific discoveries. Recast and integrated into a methodology that enables couples to use their relationship to promote growth, healing, and spiritual development, these multiple perspectives give Imago a unique flexibility and potential for wide ranging application. Since its introduction in 1988, IRT has been adopted by thousands of practitioners, who have attested to its effectiveness and who have modified its procedures for use in accordance with their clinical needs.

This book provides a glimpse into the work of therapists who conceptualize couples' problems in terms of the relational paradigm. The cases presented here offer anecdotal evidence of the potency of IRT, and provide a springboard for more systematic research on IRT's effects.

The book opens with a chapter by Wade Luquet on the relational paradigm. Relational thinking might require a psychological leap on the part of many practitioners as most did not learn this in graduate school. Luquet's chapter provides a general overview of the relational paradigm; the subsequent chapters open the doors to the therapy room as the therapists use relational thinking and processes in working with specific clinical cases. All of the discussions include a transcript of the couple in dialogue, vividly demonstrating the healing potential of Imago's primary clinical intervention and revealing its subtle power. The editors' commentaries, which follow the chapters, revisit the specific cases in order to relate them to the book's broader theme of the relational paradigm.

Imago Relationship Therapy's conceptualization of romantic attraction is explored in Chapters 2 through 5. Imago theory poses that romantic partners are drawn to one another on the basis of their having been wounded at the same or a similar developmental stage of childhood. The chapters on attachment-, exploratory-, identity-, and competency-wounded couples consider the ways in which children are wounded during the various phases, how defensive adaptations develop, and how such adaptations become manifest in adult romantic relationships.

Subsequent chapters show how Imago therapy can be applied with specific populations and couples issues. There are more populations and issues than we could fit into a dozen books, but we have selected the types of cases that seem to show up most frequently in the offices of couples therapists.

All of our authors are Certified Imago Relationship Therapists. We solicited their contributions based on their experience and interest in working with particular types of couples. Some of these therapists moved into Imago work after years of doing couples therapy according to the individual or systems paradigms. Their clinical astuteness, their eloquence, and their compassion represent, we believe, the clinical profile of the larger community of Imago therapists.

When you read the transcripts of the dialogues, you might feel moved by the intimacy, the almost poetic nature of the couple's sharing. This is not merely the result of good editing; it reflects what we observe in our offices everyday. When couples engage in safe and empathic dialogue, their authentic selves emerge. Authenticity is what makes a good novel or movie scene hit us between the eyes. It is also what makes dialogue between partners so touching.

These transcripts also reveal that not all the couples end up "living happily ever after." Imago therapy does not claim to cure a couple's every ill. What it does do is give couples the knowledge and the tools they need to participate in each other's journey toward growth and healing. Even when the end result is separation or divorce, if a couple has worked toward becoming more conscious, the outcome can be less tumultuous than it would otherwise have been. In this approach, becoming conscious is the essential theme, taking precedence over a single motion of success.

If the therapist helps the couple to create emotional safety by engaging them in an empathic dialogical process, the partners will change. Personal growth is never easy, and it is not easy for the couples you are about to meet. But when couples hold hands while walking the high road toward self-development and healing, the journey gets just a little bit easier.

Wade Luquet
Mo Therese Hannah

ACKNOWLEDGMENTS

Thanks especially to our editor, Suzi Tucker, for sticking with us until the end. She and the Brunner/Mazel staff at the old New York office have always been a pleasure to work with.

Thanks to Lisa Kelvin Tuttle for helping several contributors edit their work into finely crafted chapters.

To Will Hannah and Marianne Luquet, our spouses and fellow Imago Therapists, who endured our hundreds of phone calls without complaining, because they believe in this work too. They are deeply loved.

Thanks to Harville Hendrix, Ph.D., for planting the seeds of Imago Therapy in our minds and hearts.

Above all, thanks to our contributors for sharing their clinical talents with us and our readers. It is they who inspired this book.

Chapter 1

THE RELATIONAL PARADIGM

Wade Luquet

Whatever the year and the place of our birth, we arrive in a culture that has its own unique view of reality—of how things are and how they should be. Socialization embeds in each of us the dominant world view of our time, teaching us appropriate behavior, language, and thought processes. We have, at best, only a faint notion that our version of reality might be specific to our time, and we rarely consider that one day this view might be looked back upon as quaint and naive. Think, for example, of the medieval notion that angels push the sun, planets, and stars around the earth—which now seems amusing, if not ludicrous. Likewise, more enlightened ideas about reality, new paradigms, are certain eventually to replace our present way of thinking.

The science historian Thomas Kuhn first brought the notion of a "paradigm shift" to our attention in his 1970 release of *The Structure of Scientific Revolutions*. While focused primarily on shifts that occur in science—from Newtonian physics to quantum physics, for example, or from cathode rays to x-rays—Kuhn's work applies equally well to political, cultural, and technological transitions in thinking. Over 30 years after Kuhn's ideas were accepted by the scientific community, we are seeing their relevance to the shifts occurring in our understanding of human behavior.

It was in this work that Kuhn coined the term "paradigm" to describe a way of seeing the world. If we wear pink sunglasses, for instance, it appears pinkish, and "pink" serves as the paradigm through which we interpret the world. Through a blue paradigm, the world appears blue. Because science is constantly evolving, usually several paradigms exist at once, and the adherents of each interpret the world according to their own paradigmatic perspective, upholding that paradigm until

1

one offering better explanations and more compelling evidence comes along. Then, and only then, can a paradigm shift occur. For Kuhn (1970), new paradigms must possess two qualities: "Their achievement was sufficiently unprecedented to attract an enduring group of adherents away from competing modes of scientific activity. Simultaneously, it was sufficiently open-ended to leave all sorts of problems for the redefined group of practitioners to resolve" (p. 10).

Kuhn adds that, when armed with a new paradigm, scientists begin to look in places they never thought to look before, and they even look in places in which they previously looked and discover new information: "It is rather as if the professional community had been suddenly transported to another planet where familiar objects are seen in a different light and are joined by unfamiliar ones as well" (p. 111). To those making the shift, the new ground may feel unstable, and yet be exciting to explore. To those whose paradigms are affected, the fact that former adherents have made such a shift might seem revolutionary or absurd.

SHIFTS IN THE MENTAL HEALTH PARADIGMS

The first paradigm shift in our understanding of human behavior occurred when Sigmund Freud dismissed the notion that people are the victims of original sin and demons. He maintained, instead, that all humans have built-in unconscious drives for food and sex, and, through transference and other elements of the psychoanalytic process, they can gain insight and consciousness, allowing them to control their neurotic thoughts and behaviors. We can think of Freud as ushering in the individual insight paradigm, having met both of Kuhn's requirements of paradigm shifts: Freud drew adherents away from competing modes of scientific activity, and his theory was open-ended enough to leave all sorts of problems for the emerging school of psychoanalysis to resolve.

A new paradigm is not meant to be orthodox in nature; rather, it provides a foundation—a way of seeing—on which those who ascribe to it can agree. From this foundation, scientists and thinkers can begin to branch off. Offshoots of Freud's insight-oriented paradigm began to emerge, such as the theories of Carl Jung, Karen Horney, Harry Stack Sullivan, and Margaret Mahler. Although their treatment modalities differed somewhat, all rested on the paradigmatic tenet that individuals can be restored to optimal functioning by working with thought processes and insights.

But like most paradigms throughout history, the individual insight paradigm began to exhibit inadequacies. As Kuhn said, "Scientific revolutions are inaugurated by a growing sense, again often restricted to a narrow subdivision of the scientific community, that an existing paradigm has ceased to function adequately in an exploration of an aspect of nature to which that paradigm itself had previously led the way. In both political and scientific development the sense of malfunction that can lead to crisis is prerequisite to revolution" (p. 92).

In reaction to the insight-oriented models, a revolution indeed took place during the 1950s and 1960s in the form of behaviorism. Such thinkers as Watson, Skinner, and Dollard and Miller postulated that environmental influences, rather than intrapsychic forces, shape behavior. On the heels of behaviorism, the family and systems paradigm of the 1960s and 1970s evolved. These thinkers—Haley, Minuchin, Bowen, Whitaker, Madanes, Nagy, Papp, and Satir, to name a few— began to view individual pathology as shaped by the systems of which individuals are a part, as well as by the interaction between the individual and those systems.

The individual paradigm had emerged in the late 1800s, when anthropologists began dating human fossils as millions of years old and when Darwin first proposed his theory of evolution. Given the intellectual climate of the time, it was natural for Freud to propose that humans were governed by drives for food and sex. During the 1960s and 1970s, with the expanding media providing Americans with a greater awareness of societal influences, such as the effects of inner-city life on those living there, it was logical that systems theory would emerge. It seemed obvious that poverty and the oppression of minorities bred hopelessness and kept families from succeeding, and that one must change the system if one is to change the person.

Now, we have more information to put into the equation. Scientists have looked into the far reaches of the universe and determined that it is about 15 billion years old. They have delved into the depths of the atom and found only photons, or light, and in the process discovered that in every atom lie the same light and energy that began in that primordial blast 15 billion years ago. We now know that, in some primal decision made soon after the big bang, the expelled particles began to work together to form hydrogen. Particles working together can evolve to a greater state of matter, and thus a greater state of consciousness, than they can separately. One molecule of carbon is just a molecule. Billions of molecules of carbon can form a human being.

According to the relatively new field of quantum physics, atomic particles act in relationship. "To tell the full story of a single particle we must tell the story of the universe, for each particle is in some way intimately present to every other particle in the universe" (Swimme & Berry, 1992). If the microcosm is a reflection of the macrocosm, then humans beings, too, are intimately interwoven with the rest of existence and with one another. We develop, we grow up, we are wounded, and we are healed in relationships with others.

FINDING SELF IN CONNECTION

The new physics is lending psychological theory a cosmology to use as a context for the evolving relational paradigm. This cosmology is based on finding the self in relationship with others. The "self-in-relation" (Jordan, Kaplan, Miller, et al., 1991) principle holds that finding a distinct yet connected sense of self is the primary drive of the growing child. This developmental impulse can be disrupted if a child's longing for validation from others remains unmet, with the child developing a coping mechanism, a defensive adaptation, to lessen the resulting pain. Pain creates self-absorption, leading the person to view the world in idiosyncratic ways and to relate to the world through the filter of his or her defensive style. Eventually, interpersonal relationships become stressed by the person's self-absorption and defensiveness, resulting in further self-protection and isolation.

We seem to have an unquenchable desire to maintain our self through what Kohut calls satisfying "self-object" experiences (Kohut, 1977, 1978). Self psychologists maintain that human psychological functioning is embedded in social interactions. Because self is found in relationship, Kohut stressed the therapist's helping the client by developing empathy through "vicarious introspection" (Kohut, 1978) into the client's experience. In other words, the therapist's job is to place himself in the client's shoes and see the world from that person's perspective. Kohut, along with Carl Rogers (1961, 1980), taught that this could be done by the therapist's mirroring the client's words and affect. Through the therapist's deep understanding of the client and the transference generated and worked through in the therapeutic relationship, the client was able to discover a sense of self.

Although their work represents a great step toward understanding the self, Kohut and Rogers were still entrenched in the individual paradigm of their era, when the client's trust of the therapist was considered more significant than the client's trust of significant others. In shifting to the relational paradigm, the therapist has to rely on the client's primary relationships to provide the mirroring and the experience of "vicarious introspection," the development of empathy, that are necessary for healing and finding a sense of self. It takes a leap of faith for a therapist to treat a relationship rather than an individual. It demands courage to trust that the relationship can heal through the dialogue process, rather than through interpretation, behavioral interventions, insight, and transference. But it can be tremendously inspiring to watch a couple giving birth to two distinct, yet connected, selves through dialogue. Although it can be painful to reveal one's "shadow side," and equally painful to see the shadow side of one's partner, partners do, in fact, become more authentic in a dialogical relationship, making genuine love, hope, and healing possible. That is the power of the relational paradigm.

WE DEVELOP WITHIN CONNECTION

Most personality theories that have emerged within the past 100 years are based on the notion that the initial task of the human being is to separate and individuate. The healthiest humans, according to such theories, are those who have a solid and distinct sense of self. That is, the self should be autonomous, self-sufficient, and separated out from the matrix of others. This is accomplished by experiencing a series of developmental crises (Erikson, 1968, 1980, 1982) that bring about a sense of individualism—a separateness of self. Only then can a human experience intimacy with another.

The relational paradigm tells another story: As the self is developing, the crisis is not as important as the connection. The self can be defined and distinguished as well in developmental connection as it can in developmental crisis, with the added benefit of the retention of empathy and intimacy. It becomes the "self-in-relation" (Jordan et al., 1991).

According to the relational paradigm, the development of self-in-relation begins in infancy with the caretaker. Babies, like seeds, have built-in developmental impulses that emerge at preordained times throughout childhood. Developmental tasks are mastered through ongoing validation of the child by childhood caretakers, who support the child's mastery of the emerging life skills that present at a given time.

Let's take a look at what happens, according to Imago theory, if all goes well in a child's early years. For the sake of illustration, we will call the child a boy, although the scenario could apply equally to a girl.

From the time a child is born until he is about 15 months old, his impulse will be to attach to his primary caretakers. He needs to be held close to the parent's chest, to be nurtured, and to be fed. Although inevitably his needs will be frustrated, it is important for him to learn, during this stage, that someone will attend to his needs in a reasonable amount of time. If his caretakers provide the right holding environment, he will master the ability to attach to people, and he will also begin to develop a basic sense of being safe in the world. He will develop a sense of security with others that will significantly lessen his fear of abandonment. As his mobility increases, and at around the age of 15 months, the next developmental impulse will emerge.

In this second stage, the child's primary urge is to explore his surroundings. He pulls things out of drawers and cabinets, breaks toys, and tests the stereo equipment. He makes elaborate crayon scribbles on freshly painted walls, and he forces his parents to chase after him whenever they visit the mall. What the child needs from his caretakers is for them to witness, mirror, and support his exploration and curiosity: "You're getting so big! Look how smart you are! You can draw such pretty pictures!" This stage lasts until around the age of three, when verbal skills and imagination have more completely developed. Then he will encounter the third developmental task—forming an identity.

At first, he has not one identity, but many. He is no longer a baby, yet is far from being big. So he sets out to discover who he is, and he finds he is many things—a dog, a cat, a cartoon character, a mommy or a daddy. His parents enjoy watching him crawl around on his hands and knees barking or pretending to fly around the house to rescue his stuffed animal. To master this stage, the child again needs his caretakers to mirror his behavior. He needs to hear things like, "Let me scratch your ears, puppy," or "Help Superman! I'm in trouble!" In other words, as he experiments with different identities, he needs those identities mirrored back to him, as though the caretakers were saying, "You are being what you think you are being." The child's search for identity will allow him to try on different aspects of himself, which will eventually allow him to respond with assuredness to the various roles that life will present to him. Through the mirroring experienced during this stage, personalities can become assured, flexible, and distinct, rather than rigid or diffuse.

Once the boy has a sense of who he is becoming, at about the age of four, he will begin to test his competence. Preschool serves as a place in which to draw, paint, and sing songs. His work comes home to Mom and Dad, to whom he will sing his songs and show his paintings with pride. The response he needs is, simply, "Great!" or "You must be proud!" This is the time for mixing cake batter on the kitchen counter with Mom or Dad, or for digging a hole in the backyard with Grandpa. No matter what the outcome of his task, the child longs to hear his work pronounced "terrific." Although he may still lack certain skills, his desire to achieve things is irresistible during the competence stage. Accolades give him the incentive he needs to continue to hone his skills; eventually, the songs sound better, the paintings are recognizable, and the cake actually rises. As a result, the child feels good about his abilities while remaining connected to the caretakers who have encouraged his competence.

By the time the boy is six years old, he has learned to attach and explore, to develop an identity, and to feel a sense of competence. It is now time for him to go to school and make friends. Because his empathic ability is still intact, he enters this fifth stage with few problems. He finds friends, choosing a special chum and flowing easily into and out of the various friendship groups that form at school. From his caretakers, he needs mirroring and encouragement, along with their modeling of positive interpersonal behavior. The child will probably spend the next five to seven years with the same peer group, learning relationship skills that will last a lifetime. This stage lays the foundation for his next developmental impulse, which is to form intimate relationships during the adolescent and young adult years.

This is an ideal senario of a young boy's growing up, but there are many factors that could alter the process, including socioeconomic deprivation, trauma, alcohol abuse, or depression in the family. Regardless of the circumstances, however, a child has the same developmental needs for connection, validation, and a safe interpersonal context.

The movement from one interpersonal developmental stage to another is not linear; rather, as in all evolutionary development, it is a "transcend and include" process (Wilber, 1996) (Figure 1.1). If children learn how to attach and feel secure, they will transcend that level and move into exploration. Still, the exploration phase demands and includes what children achieved during attachment. When the child has mastered the exploration stage and the following developmental impulse is triggered, exploration is transcended and the child enters the identity stage, while remaining able to attach and explore. Thus, a child who successfully traverses all the developmental stages is able to attach to others, explore or be curious about the world, have a strong yet flexible identity, feel competent in what he or she does, and have a sense of concern about others. Through mastering these developmental tasks within the context of relationship, and with inborn empathic ability still intact, the person finds the Self. Only then can the now young adult experience true intimacy with another.

As anyone who has worked in the mental health field long enough knows, not many people fit into this developmental scenario. The process of transcendence to the next level of anything—from atom to molecule, molecule to cell, exploration to identity—is never easy. Many don't make it: a molecule may remain separate, staying a molecule and not becoming part of something larger. A child might not leave the exploratory stage behind, even as identity issues emerge, and although he or she might pass through the later stages, a defensive adaptation becomes formed in response to developmental issues that remain unresolved. The adaptation might initially be useful for helping the child cope within the family, but it will later become a burden that affects every relationship the child enters (Figure 1.2).

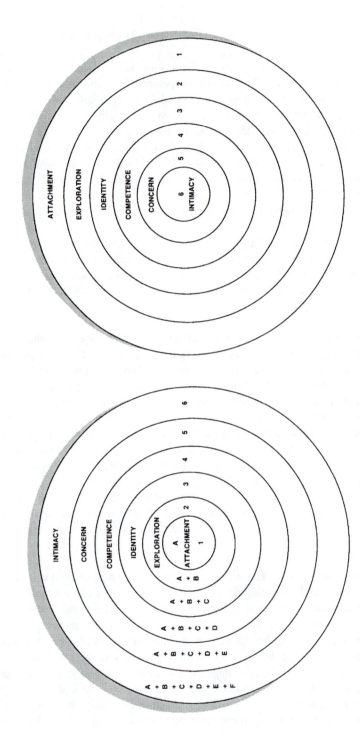

Figure 1.1. Interpersonal development stages.

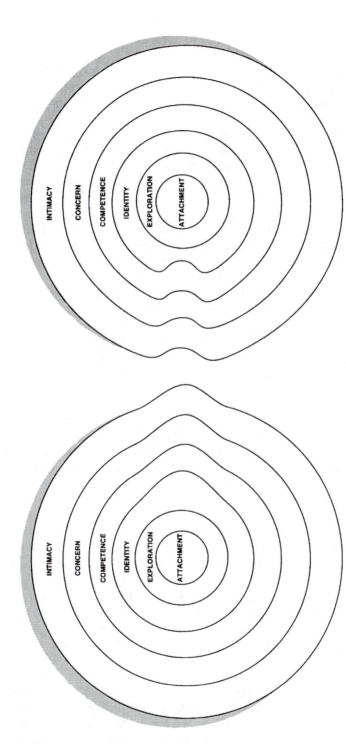

Figure 1.2. Developmental wounding of a couple: One wound fits the other.

Parents can't be perfect. Anyone who has ever raised a child will attest to the fact that you can't meet every need, nor would you want to. Without some frustration, we might not learn to walk, preferring instead that everything be brought to us. Frustrations shape personality and character, creating talents and strength and resiliency. However, if frustrations are too frequent or intense, are too opposed to the current developmental impulse, or create disconnection, children typically will generate behaviors to help them cope with their situation. Over time, the individual forgets that the adaptive behavior was self-created; it becomes a part of himself or herself.

Let's take another look at our developmental scenario, but under different circumstances. We will call this boy Chris. His father has rigid views on how he should behave at home and in public, and he controls Chris' behavior with a stern look and shaming. There are certain rules in this household, and at the age of three, Chris was expected to follow them. Chris' mother learned early on to keep the peace by giving in to her husband. She has opinions, but she gets tongue-tied when she tries to express them, so it's easier to follow her husband's lead. Because she is kind and loving, she gave Chris the holding he needed for attachment, and had few problems letting him explore. Chris' father was stricter, however, and demanded that Chris sit still more often and for longer periods than a three-year-old can.

Chris, at three, was experimenting in the identity stage. He enjoyed playing out cartoon characters and crawling around the house acting like a puppy. Mom enjoyed Chris' behavior, but her reaction toward him was often tempered by Dad's disapproval. "Quit it, Chris—act like a big boy," Chris' dad often said. This confused Chris, who thought he was indeed acting like a big boy. After all, he was not taking a bottle anymore, and he was almost potty trained. That's what three-year-olds do.

One day, Chris' dad returned from work to find Chris, dressed in an apron, stirring cookie batter with his mother. He was furious: "Get him out of that apron now! No son of mine will wear an apron. What are you trying to do? Turn him into a girl? How can I leave my son home with you if you do things like this?" Feeling overwhelmed by his anger and unable to defend herself, Chris' mother left the room. Chris now felt more confused than ever. He had been having fun with his mom, and now felt as though he had done something wrong.

Things were never quite the same after that. His dad did seem to be more involved in Chris' life: he would watch Sunday football with him, but Chris had to be quiet when they watched TV together. He waited, like a little soldier, for cues from his father about how to do things right. Chris sensed that, to avoid feeling shame, he had to become more like his father—and he did. He pretty much stopped crying, for example; boys don't cry.

When Chris turned four, he felt drawn toward building and fixing things to develop his competence. Before completing a project, however, he would always check to see if his father was pleased with what he was doing. At the age of six, Chris focused on making friends, particularly with the rough-and-tumble kind of boys. He played football and swapped tall tales with them. Chris always did his homework and was a good student; he didn't dare bring home less than an A or a B on his report card. As he got older, Chris hid his feelings more and more; he rarely cried and he usually acted as though nothing bothered him. He had maneuvered through the developmental stages with a defensive adaptation, in effect: always doing things the right way, like a man, like his father. Somewhere during his early elementary school years, this attitude became a part of Chris' personality, which might be described as rigid. He learned that to be loved, valued, and accepted, he had to be like his father. He had to deny or disown the spontaneous, creative, feminine aspects of himself that his mother had allowed but his father would not accept. Chris had been wounded in relationship.

A LID FOR EVERY POT

Meanwhile, across town, Meg, was also being raised by a strict father. Meg's parents were preoccupied with raising three other children, as well. When Meg at three years of age would beg them to watch her animal imitations, they would say that they were too busy to play with her and that she should play with her sister and brother. Meg received very little mirroring at this age, making it difficult for her to form an identity composed of the many different parts of herself. She thus learned that the best way to navigate through life was to do whatever her parents asked her to do. This won a little more attention from them, as they seemed more approving of her when she followed their lead.

As she got older and began to develop competence, at around the age of four, Meg tried to make and fix things, but usually played on her own, with little input or praise from her parents. At six, she wanted friends. Although other children liked her, she felt shy and uncertain much of the time. She avoided calling attention to herself and became a follower. Sometime during early childhood, Meg's personality traits became set, and Meg developed a "diffuse personality." She had been wounded in relationship.

Two young people from the same town, Meg and Chris, left home and went off to different colleges. After they graduated, they happened to meet at a party.

It wasn't love at first sight, but Chris was impressed enough by Meg to ask her out a few weeks later. They continued to meet, and became more and more drawn toward each other. Chris thought Meg attractive and alluring; she was quiet, but that made her a good listener. And she made Chris feel great: she seemed to adore him, to hang on to his every word. Meg found Chris smart and handsome. He seemed confident of himself and his future. He knew a lot about a lot of things, and had positive values and strong beliefs. She thought she could learn a lot from him.

A year after meeting, Meg and Chris married, and soon began their family. Two children came in rapid succession. At Chris' insistence, Meg gave up her teaching job to stay home with the children. After all, he pointed out, his mother had done so, and he was the only child, and so it was even more important to stay home to raise two kids. Chris wanted his children, above all, to learn good values and to be well-behaved. Meg didn't protest; she enjoyed homemaking and being with her children. But as the children grew older and more independent, while they were in grade school, Meg began to feel restless. When she tried to talk to Chris about her feelings, he would admonish her, "What's the problem here? You don't have to work and you have everything you need. I don't get it!" Meg would back down and push her feelings aside, figuring that things would change when the children entered adolescence.

Things did change: as the children became teenagers, they became more rebellious, and Meg became unhappier. Meg and Chris disagreed frequently over how to deal with the children, particularly their oldest son, who sassed his mother and would barely speak to his father. When Meg finally insisted that the family needed counseling, Chris became angry, announcing that he'd never bring his family to some stranger for help. For a short time, he treated Meg and the children better, but he soon fell back into his familiar ways, complaining that the house was always a mess and blaming Meg for the children's misbehavior. Meg and Chris were both, once again, being wounded in relationship.

When their youngest child was 14, Meg decided it was time to pursue her career goals, after having postponed them for over a decade to meet the needs of her family. Chris, who had just been promoted to a top position in his company, argued vehemently with her: he needed Meg to cover things at home; his new position would require a lot of travel. For the first time in her marriage, Meg refused to accede to her husband's demands, and she was accepted into the master's program at the university. Meg's courses in communication led her to become more verbal and assertive. She began to challenge Chris more and more often, causing him to feel that he was losing control. Finally, Meg delivered an ultimatum: the marriage would have to change, or it would be over.

THE PARADIGM CHOICE

Couples in therapy will learn new ways of thinking about and behaving in their relationship, depending on the orientation of the therapist. A communications therapist, for example, would teach some basic listening skills and emphasize the importance of giving and receiving clear messages. A cognitively oriented couples therapist would explore each partner's thoughts to uncover irrational or unrealistic beliefs about the partner and the relationship. Changing the partners' beliefs would be important here. A behavioral couples therapist would work with a couple to improve their problem-solving skills, underscoring the need to behave in pleasing ways toward each other. But all of these models would rest on the same assumption: each individual, married or not, needs to become autonomous, differentiated, and self-reliant. Although such characteristics can certainly contribute to healthy individual functioning, this assumption, which underlies the individual paradigm, omits other, equally compelling needs of human beings—especially our need to maintain our original state of connectedness. A broader treatment approach, one that incorporates the relational paradigm with the best of the other approaches, is called for.

IMAGO RELATIONSHIP THERAPY

Imago Relationship Therapy is a relational paradigm approach that is designed to increase couple communication, correct developmental arrests, heal wounds from childhood, and promote differentiation of the partners while restoring connection between them. Many couples who engage in Imago therapy report finding a new purpose for their relationship, as well as a renewed spiritual life.

Imago therapy's main tool is the Couples Dialogue. In dialogue, couples are trained to hear each other by using a three-part process. First, the receiving (listening) partner is asked to "mirror" back as accurately as possible what the other partner says. When the sending (speaking) partner feels that the receiving partner has understood the message, or "send," the receiver asks, "Is there more?" The receiver is asked to "contain" or hold back any response until he or she takes a turn as the sender. This is no easy task, because typically the receiving partner is feeling emotionally reactive to what the sending partner is saying. Yet, the experience of containing one's reactivity in the dialogue process teaches the partners that, if the receiving partner waits his or her turn to respond, the receiver will more accurately hear the sending partner. In turn, once they switch roles, the sending partner is more likely to hear the receiving partner. In other words, being heard makes us more willing and able to hear our partner.

When the receiving partner has mirrored back to the sender an adequate amount of information, the receiver is asked to validate what the sender has said. Validation is not agreement; it is, in essence, stating that the partner's message has logic, based on that partner's point of view. "It makes sense to me that you think what you do. I can understand how you would see it that way" exemplifies validation. When validated, the sending partner typically reports feeling calmer and more deeply understood. Partners often comment, "I don't feel crazy anymore." Each partner's world at last makes sense to the other, even if they still don't agree.

The third step of the Couples Dialogue has the receiving partner express empathy toward the sender. Judith Jordan (Jordan et al., 1991) of the Stone Center describes empathy as a two-part process: affective surrender and cognitive structure. For Jordan, empathy involves momentarily feeling the other person's feelings, and then going back into your own skin, knowing that the other's feelings are not your own, and guessing how the other might feel. "I imagine you might feel lonely, sad, and inadequate" would be an empathic statement.

The main focus of the Couples Dialogue is to help the couple create a healing connection, which is possible only when there is enough emotional safety between the partners. Some couples have spent years bruising each other emotionally, and whenever emotional safety has been ruptured, partners react toward each other as though the other were an enemy, rather than a lover.

Safety in a relationship has to become a promise, but it is a promise we all know will not be perfectly kept. In fact, safety is a promise that will be broken and must be renewed many times over the course of a relationship. Each time a couple repeats the same fight, reenacting their core scene, the primitive part of their brains take over and safety retreats. "You have not changed! All of this work is crap. You're a big fraud—how can you say you want this relationship to work?" When the fight is over, there is but one safety-producing alternative: the couple again makes a commitment to safety and begins to hear and understand one another. Such moments are opportunities for true growth for the couple. While there can be no growth or connection through fighting, growth and connection can evolve in the safety of the dialogue process.

Couples are taught to visualize a "safe place" and to practice breathing exercises to establish safety. They learn to recognize the body's response to unsafe feelings and to realize that unsafe feelings stem from the primitive part of the brain, the old brain, which keeps us physically alive and thus reacts to a lack of safety as though it were going to die. When safety has been established and the couple has some skill with the dialogue, they can use other processes to enhance the healing of the relationship. The reimaging process helps the couple reestablish empathy through understanding each other's childhood wounds and unmet longings. Restructuring frustrations has partners turn their frustrations with one another into positive desires for behavior change. To fulfill each other's desires, partners have to grow past defensive adaptations and characterological limitations, thus enhancing their own personal growth.

The need to maintain safety while communicating anger is underscored by the container process. Considered one of the most difficult forms of Imago work and usually carried out under the supervision of a therapist, the container process allows the sending partner to express anger while the receiving partner listens with as much empathy as possible. Anger that is received empathically typically softens into hurt, which the receiving partner can then begin to understand as the deeper source of the partner's rage. Containers offer partners a rare insight into one another's childhood wounds, which can enhance their motivation to engage in caring and healing behaviors that will ultimately "make history, history."

Imago therapy's last two processes are designed to restore the positive aspects of couples' relationships, overcoming the negativity that often lingers as wounds slowly heal. Gottman (1979) has shown that, in long-term stable marriages, partners exhibit five positive behaviors for every negative behavior. In reromanticizing, couples reinstate romantic behaviors that they exhibited more naturally during their early relationship. They are encouraged to flood each other with behaviors that the receiver finds pleasurable, for example, morning walks, back rubs, love notes, flowers, a hot cup of tea, frequent hugs. Surprises and belly laughs are also taught as ways of bringing romance back into the relationship.

And finally, the couple is asked to construct a positive vision for their relationship, a statement that describes "the marriage of your dreams." As in business or any other endeavor, "if you can dream it, you can build it." Couples who share a vision for their relationship are more likely to work together toward achieving it. The relationship vision serves as the road map for their journey. In Imago work, the safety and pleasure of that journey are what really matter.

A PARADIGM OF RELATIONALITY

Imago Relationship Therapy processes recreate the connection that was lost in childhood and that became severed in the couple's power struggle. The processes do not guarantee a smooth ride: couples cannot expect always to feel understood, and conflict remains inevitable. Rather, Imago therapy guides couples in using the partnership as a resource for healing, problem solving, and growth, enabling greater personal fulfillment as the partners deepen their connection.

Imago work emphasizes the crucial importance of understanding the uniqueness of one's partner, an understanding of what Buber (1958) refers to as the "otherness of the other." When we comprehend the differences, say, between our own and another culture, we become more accepting of what might have initially appeared as strange cultural practices. When we fully understand our partner's world view, we are more likely to respond with acceptance. We might not agree with our partner, but we become capable of transcending our own point of view, even if just for a moment, to understand that our partner sees the world differently. And when we are able to understand and accept our differences, we both become more clearly defined as individuals.

To apply this principle to a typical interaction, suppose a male spouse says, "Look, I plan to go fishing every Saturday morning this summer. I'm not going to stay home practically every weekend, the way I did last fishing season." His wife might then respond, "Like hell you will." In Imago work, the wife would instead encourage her partner to say more about what he needs: "What makes going fishing on Saturdays as important as it is to you?" When the woman understands more about the urgency of her husband's desires—what going fishing on weekends means to him, and why it is important to him—she becomes more likely to accept and respond to his requests. At the same time, her willingness to hear and respond to him might very well reduce his urgency to go fishing every Saturday!

Therapists trained in the individual paradigm often find relational paradigm work quite different from what they've done in the past. Perhaps the most striking difference is that the focus of intervention and transference is not the therapist, but the couple sitting in front of the therapist. It is the partners, not the therapist, who have the power to heal. The therapist is merely a coach, a midwife assisting in the birth of a conscious relationship.

RELATIONAL MYSTICISM

Becoming a distinct person and yet remaining connected with the other is the goal of therapy in the relational paradigm. In his seminal work *I and Thou*, Martin Buber (1958) discusses the necessity of understanding the other as the way of defining the self. Regarding our difficulty in dealing with, and even saying, the word *Thou*, Buber says, "This word consistently involves an affirmation of the being addressed. He is therefore compelled to reject either the other or himself. At this barrier the entering on a relation recognizes its relativity, and only simultaneously with this will the barrier be raised" (p. 16). It is only when two people intentionally make the effort to understand each other that they will both be defined. The other as mirror defines me, and I, as mirror, define the other.

A strange and powerful thing happens, something that cannot be quantified but only described, when two people fully understand each other: the space between the two people begins to feel sacred. It is the place where the creative process emerges, where self emerges, where authenticity emerges. This experience might be fleeting, but is an experience that all partners can have with each other. Helping people experience their own and their partner's authentic self may be the closest a therapist comes to heaven in his or her own office.

The jazz musician Wynton Marsalis, talking about the history of the blues, was asked why, when we listen to the blues, we don't feel sad. Here is someone singing about how life has beaten him or her down, and yet, we feel content, almost joyous, listening to the song. Marsalis explains this by saying that blues players play the blues so that the blues don't play with them. The blues players take the sadness out of their bodies and put it into words and music. Even more important, is they do it for an audience. The blues need a witness, and the audience—with their shouts of "oh yeah!" and "sing it, Sister!"—becomes a mirror for the blues player's sadness and disappointments. Our internal strife needs an external witness. When we are seen, we become real, both in our own minds and in the minds of others. In the relational paradigm, when we define the other, we emerge as a distinct Self.

Fifteen billion years ago, particles began working in relationship to form hydrogen. Hydrogen exploded to form stars, and the new particle relationships formed the elements. On our own planet, these elements joined to form living organisms, which evolved for millions of years, ultimately forming mammals. These mammals eventually gave birth to humans, who gave birth to thought, language, and the arts. As we enter a new millenium, we have the opportunity, through conscious relationships, to transcend to the next evolutionary level, one on which human beings could become consciously aware of all things around them. Through authentic relationships, we may be able to find ourselves transcending into spirit. All creativity and all transcendence occur in relationship. As Buber (1958, p. 18) put it, "In the beginning is relation." So, too, should relationship be throughout the middle and until the end.

BIBLIOGRAPHY

Buber, M. (1958). *I and thou.* New York: Scribner's.

Erikson, E. H. (1968). *Identity: Youth and crisis.* New York: Norton.

Erikson, E. H. (1980). *Identity and the life cycle.* New York: Norton.

Erikson, E. H. (1982). *The life cycle completed: A review.* New York: Norton.

Gottman, J. (1979). *Marital interaction: Experimental investigations.* New York: Academic.

Hendrix, H. (1988). *Getting the love you want: A guide for couples.* New York: Holt.

Jordan, J. V., Kaplan, A. G., Miller, J. B., Stiver, I., and Surrey, J. L. (Eds.) (1991). *Women's growth in connection.* New York: Guilford.

Kohut, H. (1977). *The restoration of the self.* New York: International Universities Press.

Kohut, H. (1978). *The search for the self: Selected writings of Heinz Kohut, 1978– 1981. Vol. I.* (P. Ornstein, Ed.). New York: International Universities Press.

Kuhn, T. S. (1970). *The structure of scientific revolutions.* Chicago: University of Chicago Press.

Rogers, C. (1961). *On becoming a person.* Boston: Houghton Mifflin.

Rogers, C. (1980). *A way of being.* Boston: Houghton Mifflin.

Swimme, B., and Berry, T. (1992). *The universe story.* New York: Harper San Francisco.

Wilber, K. (1996). *A brief history of everything.* Boston: Shambhala.

Wilber, K. (1977). *The spectrum of consciousness.* Wheaton, Ill: Quest Books.

Chapter 2

COUPLES WOUNDED AT THE ATTACHMENT PHASE

Jill M. Fein

THE DILEMMA

By the time my first daughter, Ilana, was three weeks old, I knew I was in trouble. Welling up within me was a tremendous conflict over where she should sleep: in bed with me and my husband, in a bassinet next to us, or in her own crib in another room. A part of me saw her as a helpless creature who, just a few weeks earlier, had been connected to me in the most intimate sense—although each time she'd kicked inside me, she reminded me that we were actually separate beings. I'd become convinced, in fact, that all those underwater swimming dreams I had while I was carrying Ilana came more from my baby's unconsciousness than from my own. Now that I could physically see the child who had been such an intricate part of my own being, I couldn't imagine keeping her apart from me, and from the warmth of my breasts, for more than a few minutes at a time.

Another part of me was listening to an internal chorus of warnings: "You'll spoil her. She'll never learn how to fall asleep on her own. She'll be too dependent." For months, Ilana and I struggled with my ambivalence. When she would wake up crying in the middle of the night, I would usually try everything I knew to lull her back to sleep: hold her hand through the slats of the crib, pat her back, offer a pacifier. Finally, when we were both so exhausted that neither of us could tolerate it anymore, I'd give in, take Ilana to my bed, and nurse her (and myself), back to sleep.

While Ilana was in the attachment stage, she and I were experiencing what can be termed a crisis of dependency. Imago theory offers a lens for understanding the effects of early parent–child interactions such as ours on adult romantic relationships. Although a thorough sampling of the literature on attachment is beyond the scope of this chapter, a brief overview of a sample of such orientations will provide a background for understanding the foundation and unique contributions of Imago therapy.

Beginning with the seminal work of Sigmund Freud, psychological theory viewed infants as self-absorbed, nonrelational creatures driven by intrapsychic engines. Babies' primary developmental tasks were to manage aggressive and sexual impulses while they sat at the center of their infantile world, manipulating the drama going on around them. The parents, as recipients of the edicts of this "God-King-Baby," had the task of helping children to give up narcissistic delusions and to become separate and autonomous beings. Dependence was disdained as infantile and unhealthy if it persisted beyond early childhood.

Because there is naturally some tension between the baby's dependency needs and the mother's own needs, such as the need for rest and replenishment, the parent–child relationship will be characterized by a struggle for control. Thus, along with the baby, placenta, and amniotic fluid, the power struggle is born.

Margaret Mahler and her colleagues built on Freud's work to further advance our understanding of infants' psychological development. Mahler conceptualized the psychological goal of humans as the separation–individuation process, which she defined as "the establishment of a sense of separateness from, *and relation to*, a world of reality, particularly with regard to the experiences of *one's own body* and to the principal representative of the world as the infant experiences it, *the primary love object*" (Mahler, Pine, & Bergman, 1975, p. 3). Mahler and other object-relations theorists began to acknowledge that something of significance was happening within the parent–child relationship, although they continued to emphasize the necessity of separation.

According to Mahler, achieving a sense of separateness from the mother and from others is critical to mental health. She used the term "symbiosis" to refer to "a feature of primitive cognitive-affective life wherein the differentiation between self and mother has not taken place, or where regression to that self-object undifferentiated state (which characterized the symbiotic phase) has occurred" (Mahler, Pine, & Bergman, 1975, p. 8). She stops short of claiming that there is a normal drive toward separation per se, but does maintain that humans possess an innate drive to individuate, with autonomous separation being the means to that end.

I imagine that if Margaret Mahler were coaching me while I was a new mother, she would instruct me to not interfere with my baby's growing awareness of herself as a separate being. Perhaps Mahler would have me verbally reassure my daughter of my presence and my constancy, while also encouraging her to find objects in the world with which to comfort herself. This reflects a strong value in our Western culture: encourage independence or risk spoiling the child.

A departure from this way of thinking was proposed by John Bowlby in his influential work on attachment theory. Beginning in the 1940s, Bowlby explored and wrote about the critical roles of attachment and parent–child bonding in personality development. He strongly considers "the propensity to make intimate emotional bonds to particular individuals as a basic component of human nature, already present in germinal form in the neonate and continuing through adult life into old age" (Bowlby, 1988, pp. 120–121). Bowlby asserts that attachment behavior, which he defines as attaining or maintaining closeness to someone who is seen as being better able to cope with the world, is "a fundamental form of behavior with its own internal motivation distinct from feeding and sex, and of no less importance for survival" (Bowlby, 1988, p. 27). Bowlby's research outlines many deleterious effects of inadequate attachment, which include separation anxiety, juvenile delinquent behavior, the development of a "false self," and eventually emotional or physical abuse of one's own child, which ultimately perpetuates the tragic cycle.

Bowlby views our need and capacity for attachment as organized by a control system located in the central nervous system. Like other systems, the attachment control system has an inherent tendency toward homeostasis. That is, if a parent has not experienced impairment of this system, the parent and child will together discover, through verbal and nonverbal communication, the right quantity and intensity of attachment.

Clearly, John Bowlby would advise me to pick up my crying baby immediately, encouraging us to stay close together until my daughter communicated her desire to separate and explore. The nights would have been a lot less anxious for all of us if I had been listening to Bowlby's advice.

IMAGO RELATIONSHIP THERAPY AND ATTACHMENT

The view on attachment held by Imago relationship therapy, developed by Harville Hendrix (1988, 1992), is similar to Bowlby's. Imago theory acknowledges that the first and most critical job for humans is to attach. "When the newborn utters his first cry and reaches for the mother's warmth and the nipple, the psychosocial journey is activated. The infant has a vital agenda—to close that gulf of separation that opened up so threateningly at birth, and securely reattach himself to the nurturing, protective source of his survival. He is responding to his internal mandate to exist" (Hendrix, 1992, p. 64). Thus, as long as we are alive, survival and attachment are intertwined.

During the first 18 months of life, the developmental task of attachment is paramount: it sets the stage for a person's lifelong capacity for intimate connection with other persons. In addition, attachment lays the groundwork for the developmental tasks that follow. Bowlby saw attachment as essentially complementary to exploration. "When attachment behavior is activated, often because of fear, exploratory behavior is shut down. When attachment—in the form of proximity or felt security—is achieved, attachment behaviors are shut down and exploration may begin again.. . . Thus Bowlby wrote, parents who are encouraging, supportive, and cooperative not only enable a child to feel securely attached, but also enable him to confidently explore his environment and develop a sense of competence." (Karen, 1994, p. 209).

Unfortunately, children's most profound needs must be met by parents who frequently don't really know what they are doing. Complicating matters further is the fact that very young children cannot communicate verbally, cannot move about independently, and are a bundle of nonstop demands. On reflection, we might be amazed that so many of us survive this stage with relatively minor wounding, and that we do not emerge more psychologically impaired. Or, alternatively, perhaps there is such an immense amount of "normative abuse," as Karen Walant (1995) puts it, that we've come to accept as normal the deficits from which we suffer.

A fundamental premise of Imago theory, however, is that any need that goes unmet will eventually demand its due. Just as a cut on our finger mobilizes the body's resources for healing, an unmet emotional need will press toward fulfillment. The drive for completion is omnipresent in nature: a flower matures from seed to blossom, a dog progresses from puppy to overgrown mutt, and a person develops from helpless dependency to interdependent and competent adulthood. As you think about a needy infant, picture the needy couple in your office: the distressed couple, usually unbeknown to themselves, superbly "languages" the nonverbal complaints of the infant. Like the deprived infant, the partners may be experiencing a sense of hopelessness and desperation over getting their needs met.

The First Task

A new baby makes an amazing transition upon going from the womb to the birthing room. After a nine-month-long period of instantaneous gratification, the baby confronts many frustrations: a wet diaper, a nipple that isn't immediately available or is too hard to grasp, an overstimulating environment, a gas bubble that hurts, a toy that's just out of reach. Through the first year and a half of life, the child moves through a variety of important developmental substages, each accompanied by additional opportunities for frustration and mastery. During this period, the parent's job is to be reliably available and reliably warm, that is, to "be there" for the child. The parent must also allow the child to exercise his or her natural desire to separate, if only by crawling away from the mother to pursue the family cat, while providing a safe base to which the child can then return.

As Winnicott (1965) said, many parents are "good enough." Children fortunate enough to be raised by at least one such parent will experience both merging with and separating from the parent. These children have an abundance of "immersive moments": "In an immersive moment, the individual has *gone beyond* his self to join with an other. The spirit, or breath, is taken from the self, and vice versa, the breath is taken back as it is released from the other" (Walant, 1995, p. 116). Despite my struggle with attachment issues when Ilana was an infant, the "enough" must have filtered through. I remember the time when Ilana, at about 11 months of age, was sitting on my lap facing me. She looked deeply into my eyes, then put her two little hands up and held the sides of my face. For a moment, time stopped, our physical separateness was transcended, and we experienced oneness. "Oh," I realized, "so this is love."

Barring any significant trauma, a child who has had an adequate amount of these kinds of experiences will leave the attachment stage feeling more or less securely attached. Adequately attached children are able to take life's challenges in stride. They can separate easily enough when they begin school; establish, maintain, and outgrow a number of friendships; go through adolescence's hormonal upheavals and developmental pushes and pulls; and ultimately pair with a similarly well-attached romantic partner.

As marriage partners, such individuals are unlikely to require extensive therapy. At some point in their relationship, a couple might come into the marriage counselor's office stating, "We have a basically good marriage, and we love each other tremendously, but we just seem to get stuck once in a while." An Imago therapist would teach them to use the Couples Dialogue to solve problems and to reconnect with each other when conflicts arise. Partners who have had satisfactory early-attachment experiences will be able to make good use of Imago relationship tools.

Attachment Wounds and Their Development: The Clinger

For most children, unfortunately, the outcomes of the attachment phase won't match the picture just described. Their parents were, themselves, probably wounded during childhood, leading them as children, and later as parents, to adapt a particular defensive style. This defensive adaptation, in turn, produces a corresponding coping mechanism in their offspring: either clinging or detaching.

Children tend to adapt a clinging response when a parent is inconsistently available and when available, is not reliably warm. "Such caretakers may be preoccupied, self-centered, angry, or busy; their moods and their timetables fluctuate. They are unpredictable. Perhaps they are uncomfortable with their caretaker role and try to follow some rigid formula they've read about in books, providing the necessary services, but on their own schedule or whim. They may pick the infant up and feed him regularly, but not when *he* cries or fusses for attention. Clearly the child's needs are a burden to this parent. Unable to establish a basic trust that his needs will be met, the child senses that only his incessant demands will keep him alive" (Hendrix, 1992, p. 66). These children develop a fear of abandonment because the taste of warm attachment they get from time to time often disappears just as a sense of security begins to grow. Such abandonment fears may be reinforced throughout childhood by misguided attempts to discipline or socialize the child. For example, using a "time-out" for "bad behavior" is very common today, and although some parents are vigilant about separating the deed from the doer, less secure children are likely to interpret a time-out as a rejection, not just of their behavior, but of themselves. Hence, their worst fear becomes realized: they've been abandoned.

Wounds suffered by children during the attachment stage can be reexperienced later on in childhood. Controlling an older child through threats of abandonment is common in our culture. Go to any playground, and you will eventually hear a mother coercing a child to comply with her: "If you don't come with me right now, I'm leaving without you." When encountering the threat of physical or emotional abandonment by a parent who has been inconsistently available, a child will adapt to the threat by demanding more from the parent. Crying, screaming, and throwing tantrums, after all, occasionally work. The child's reasoning becomes deeply imprinted in his or her psyche: "The more obnoxious I become, and the more pain I inflict on people around me, the more likely they are to meet my needs." Getting attention in any available form becomes paramount to survival. Eventually, the child's cries evolve into the adult's criticisms: "You're always late!" "You're completely unreliable." "I can never count on you."

In addition, the child who is wounded during the attachment period concludes that it is not acceptable for him or her to have needs. After all, if the child's needs were acceptable, then the caretakers would be meeting those needs more consistently. "You want to be picked up again?" the exhausted parent might groan. "I feel like I've been holding you all day!" Because the child identifies with the parent as a means of psychic survival, he or she will introject this prohibition against "needing too much," meanwhile accumulating a backlog of unmet needs. These children hang on to their parent's leg, afraid that letting go will lead the parent to once more become unavailable. The uninformed observer might comment that the child is spoiled, is too needy, and that the parent gives in too easily. Actually, the opposite is true—the child hasn't been allowed to be appropriately dependent. As an adult, this child becomes "the clinger" (Hendrix, 1988): in a romantic partnership, the clinger, insecure about this relationship as well, demands that the partner become more available, more gratifying, and more fulfilling of the clinging partner's needs. The future romantic partner, in attempting to meet at least some of the clinger's needs, often encounters tremendous resistance and sabotage.

Attachment Wounds and Their Development: The Avoider

The alternative adaptation to wounding at the attachment stage is detaching. Detachment is likely in children whose parents not only are inconsistently available, but also are cold and out of synch with the child. "Because contact results not in the pleasure of acceptance or satisfaction of needs but in emotional pain, the infant makes a fateful decision: avoid contact at all costs . . . . His caretaker has rejected him so he rejects the caretaker, and finally he rejects his life force" (Hendrix, 1992, p. 68). The most extreme example of this is a syndrome known as "failure to thrive," which was first documented in orphanages in England. Babies cared for by well-meaning but busy nurses were deprived of adequate human warmth and skin-to-skin contact. Although these children were provided with enough food, they were unable, or perhaps unwilling, to take in the nourishment, and they ultimately died in infancy.

Less dramatic instances of detachment in children are common. Some parents construe their children's demands as intentional and manipulative ploys. An example is the mother who scolds her three-year-old son for begging to stay up and play, telling him, "You're just trying to take advantage of me!" The child, of course, is totally unaware of his motives and is equally unable to articulate them. Although he cannot understand his mother's literal message, he does discern her negative attitude. Lacking here is the crucial capacity and willingness of this parent to transcend her own needs to meet those of her child. The likely result is a child who feels rejected by the parent and thus detaches to avoid further rejection.

Other parents more willingly interact with their children, but they overlook or ignore a child's nonverbal cues and proceed according to their own agendas. For example, their play with their child is overstimulating and insensitive to the child's need for boundaries: "Controlling and intrusive behaviors by the caregiver are among the most common causes of overstimulation. When viewed . . . most controlling behaviors involve interfering with the infant's self-regulatory behaviors" (Stern, 1977, p. 115). The child adjusts by using detachment, a survival trick that may last well into adulthood.

As opposed to the clingy child, whose behavior many find distasteful, the detached child conforms better to the norms of western culture. Such children might be described as independent and competent; he or she is a "low maintenance" kid. With each of my three daughters, in fact, people would often ask me, "Is she a good baby?" When I asked them to clarify what they meant, they would say something like, "You know, is she quiet? Does she let you get some sleep?" Thus, the adaptive behavior of the detached child is reinforced by our culture.

In reality, the detached child is no better off than the clingy one, and in some ways he or she suffers more. To survive, the detacher must, in essence, kill off the feelings, needs, and desires that invite parental rejection. Further, the child must suppress the awareness that he or she once even had such feelings. The detached child evolves into the the adult known by Hendrix (1992) as the avoider, and who, as a romantic partner, is hyperrational, avoidant, withdrawn, and passive/aggressive.

According to Imago theory, in romantic partnerships, the clinger will be attracted to the avoider, and vice versa. (For further discussion of romantic attraction and the mate-selection process, see Hendrix, 1988; Hendrix, 1992; and Luquet, 1996.)

THE COUPLE'S DYNAMICS: ATTACHMENT IN THERAPY

The extent of attachment wounding in childhood is viewed as a predictor of the capacity for adult intimacy. Some individuals with extensive wounding are incapable of a long-term intimate relationship. In those diagnosed with borderline personality disorder, for example, a striking characteristic is their ambivalence about attachment issues. These individuals appear to crave interpersonal contact, but when true empathic connection is offered, they become anxious and either withdraw from or attack the other person (see, for example, Kreisman & Straus, 1989).

In essence, every couple that comes in for couples therapy is struggling with attachment issues. Some couples might describe the problem differently, using such words as commitment, trust, intimacy, or communication, but all of these require the ability to alternate between connection and separation, which is the hallmark of healthy attachment.

My own clinical observations suggest that, in most heterosexual couples, the man is the minimizer/avoider and the woman is the maximizer/clinger. Clearly, cultural, social, child-rearing, and temperamental factors contribute to this relationship. However, the dichotomy cannot be reliably predicted by gender; in fact, the minimizing/maximizing adaptations may vary depending on the partner with whom one is coupled. In my first marriage, for example, I was consistently in the clinger role, while my husband, predictably, was the avoider. In a subsequent relationship, I had more access to the minimizer style, while my boyfriend more often presented himself as the maximizer. Because most of us are raised by parents who themselves were predominantly either minimizers or maximizers, we each adapt one of these as our dominant style while we internalize the opposite as our recessive style. Thus, beneath the armor of every minimizer lies a repressed maximizer, and vice versa. But when conflict erupts, which adaptive style does each partner fall back on? Typically, it will be that of minimizer or of maximizer.

Occasionally, a woman will tell me that she wants to get help for her marriage or relationship, but doesn't think she can get her partner to come to therapy. Can she come in by herself? Although I empathize with individuals who have this problem, I maintain a policy of seeing clients only with their partners, provided they are in a committed relationship. This position is viewed by Hendrix (1989, personal communication) as imperative to supporting the relationship context within which the partner's growth and healing will take place. The goal of Imago couples therapy (Imago work with singles is a different issue) does not include the exploration of transference/countertransference issues between client and therapist. Rather, the goal is to make conscious the unconscious issues that divide partners and to support their healthy connection. If one partner is seen individually, there is a risk of outgrowing one's partner or of developing a dependence on one's attachment to the therapist, rather than to one's partner. Indeed, some would argue that individual psychotherapy can be hazardous to the health of one's marriage.

A couple that presents with early wounding (i.e., in the attachment stage) presents an immediate and important challenge to the therapist: to create safe contact and connection with both partners. Although safety might mean something different to each partner, there are some universal behaviors that, I believe, contribute to creating safety, particularly for attachment-wounded couples. I make sure to greet them at the appointed time and to avoid rescheduling their appointment. I provide nurturing by, for example, offering them coffee or tea. I make eye contact, smile, introduce myself, and shake their hands. The therapist working with these couples invariably confronts his or her own attachment issues. This might present as sympathy toward one partner accompanied by negative countertransferential feelings toward the other partner. Such internal reactions might provide diagnostic information, but it is imperative that the therapist be aware of the nature of his or her feelings and keep them from having an undesired impact on the couple's therapeutic process.

The first visit might be particularly difficult for these couples, with the clinger typically being the "dragger" and the avoider the "draggee." Often, an overt or covert ultimatum—get into therapy or else—has been issued. Surprisingly, when invited to say what brings them in at this time, the minimizer/avoider often speaks first and the maximizer/clinger seems content with this. It's as though, in the initial moments of safe contact, each partner "forgets" to use the usual adaptive armor.

Greg and Terri: An Attachment-Wounded Couple

During the first session, I tell the couple a little about myself and about how I became involved in this work, and then ask them how they came to seek out a therapist at this time. Instead of taking a traditional history, I allow the details of the couple's life together to unfold through the dialogical process. I next invite them to step into each other's shoes for a moment and to state what they imagine might cause *their partner* to become frustrated in the relationship. By mirroring back each partner's statements, I teach and model for them the Imago processes of mirroring and containment. This provides them with their first glimpse of a new way of seeing their relationship, a perspective that moves them out of their symbiotic point of view. I began this way with Greg and Terri.

> **Therapist:** *Terri, I'd like you to step out of your world for just a moment and tell me what you imagine are Greg's frustrations with the relationship now. Greg, I'd like you to just listen, and when Terri is done, I'll check in with you, so that you can tell us if what she said is accurate for you, or if you want to add or delete anything from her list. Of course, once we've done that, we'll reverse your roles.*
> **Terri:** *Hmm. Well, I think he's frustrated that I'm so frustrated about wanting us to settle on setting a wedding date. I mean, I told all our*

friends and family that Greg and I are getting married, but now that he's gotten fired and everything . . .

Therapist: *O.K., let me see if I've got this. You imagine Greg is frustrated with your being frustrated. Did I get that? Then it sounds like you started going into what your frustrations are, which is, of course, much easier to focus on. Let's go back to imagining what it's like for Greg in this relationship.*

Terri: *Oh, well, I know I'm probably not too nice to be around sometimes. I can be bossy. But I just see Greg having so much potential and it gets to me that he doesn't go back to school and finish his B.A., because then he'd be so much more marketable! I don't know why he doesn't talk to me more about all this. Plus, he gives me such a hard time whenever I offer some suggestions about what might be useful. I only want to help! Is that so bad?*

This is a typical communication from a maximizer before he or she has been taught to dialogue. Emotions run high and boundaries are blurry. Terri floats freely between Greg's frustrations and her own, his responsibilities in life and what she's compelled to take over. Her questions appear engaging but are actually received as intrusive and controlling. Terri needed gentle but consistent reminders to speak in terms of "I" and to talk about her experience instead of complaining about Greg. With my mirroring and coaching, Terri was able to acknowledge her feelings of anxiety about their future and her sense of powerlessness in making any impact on their lives together. This reminded her of her childhood when she, the eldest child of four, grew up with a depressed mother and an alcoholic father.

Therapist: *O.K., Terri, one thing you're aware of is that Greg may experience you as bossy. Is there more?*

Terri: *Our sexual appetites seem to be going in opposite directions. At first, Greg was always interested. Now I seem to be the one initiating all the time. He probably feels like I'm pressuring him, but once or twice a month just doesn't do it for me.*

Therapist: *So another frustration of Greg's is your pressuring him sexually, is that right? Is there more?*

Terri: *Well, there probably is, but that's all I can think of right now.*

Therapist: *Greg, how accurate are Terri's perceptions? Anything you want to add or subtract?*

Greg: *She's right, she can be kind of bossy. I mean, I want to get a good job even more than she wants me to. But her breathing down my back, asking me a million questions—that doesn't help. With sex, none of the excitement is there anymore. But she's the one who's changed. She nags me like she's my mother, then expects me to perform in bed.*

> **Therapist:**   *So Terri's perceptions are quite accurate. If I've got it right, you see her as having changed, having become more nagging and demanding. Did I get that? Is there anything else she forgot to mention?*
> **Greg:**   *No, I don't think so.*

Greg's failing to mention additional frustrations does not necessarily reflect contentment on his part. Minimizing defenses keeps one's needs hidden from one's partner and outside of the awareness of the minimizer. In later dialogues, Greg revealed that his parents had been infertile, and that he had been adopted by them at the age of three months. Predictably, he denied having any feelings about being adopted. His adoptive mother, although not an affectionate woman, doted on him, treating him like her little showpiece. His adoptive father was a rageaholic who physically abused Greg, but not his younger sister, who was also adopted. Nothing was known about Greg's birth parents other than that they were teenagers when Greg was born.

> **Therapist:**   *O.K., Greg, what do you imagine are Terri's frustrations with this relationship?*
> **Greg:**   *She's mad because we haven't set a wedding date yet. She's mad because we don't have sex more often. She thinks I'm lazy. Oh, yeah, and she doesn't like it that I have a few beers to unwind.*
> **Therapist:**   *So Terri is mad at you for not setting a wedding date, for not having sex more often, and she thinks you're lazy and doesn't like it when you drink a few beers. Is that right? Is there more?*
> **Greg:**   *No, you've got it all.*
> **Therapist:**   *Let's check that out with Terri.*
> **Terri:**   *Well, it's not really that I think he's lazy. Or maybe I do, I don't know. But the beer drinking is really becoming a problem. And that affects our sex life, too.*

Listening for Attachment Wounds

Both Greg and Terri show direct and indirect evidence of attachment wounding. Although Greg's first three months of life remain a mystery, we can safely assume that the teenage mother who put him up for adoption did not allow Greg to adequately attach to her. His adoptive mother's love for Greg seemed superficial, and his adoptive father was a traveling salesperson who was emotionally unavailable and physically abusive.

Terri grew up with a mother who, although basically warm and affectionate, withdrew into depression to cope with her husband's alcoholism. To compensate for her parents' ongoing emotional abandonment of her, Terri took on the role of the competent child, the one person in the house who faithfully cared for others and put others' needs before her own.

Although Terri and Greg, like all couples I see, presented unique challenges, they are like virtually all other couples in their having complementary character structures with opposite defensive styles: clinging for Terri, distancing for Greg. Like most other couples, too, neither is fully aware that his or her defensive behaviors are what elicits and reinforces the pain-inducing behavior of the partner. The more the clinger pursues, the more stubbornly the avoider withdraws. The more the avoider withdraws, the more doggedly will the clinger pursue.

The good news is that within this comedy of errors lies the greatest opportunity for growth. Growth occurs when partners make that empathic leap into understanding the experience of the other and validating the other's pain. When partners are able to own their part of the problem, acknowledging that they are not merely victims of the partner's misbehavior but also perpetuate their own misery, then profound changes can occur in the couple system.

The Couples Dialogue is the structure that Imago therapy uses to help couples make that leap. Dialogue about sensitive topics, the Parent–Child Dialogue, the Behavior Change Request—all facilitate the partners' movement out of symbiotic self-absorption into an acknowledgment of the otherness of the other. Once such validation occurs, empathy has an opportunity to flow. Safe contact is thus restored through this reciprocal process, rebalancing the minimizer/maximizer split: the minimizer stretches by verbally expressing what he or she normally keeps hidden, while the maximizer stretches by containing his or her reactivity. Through the dialogue, both partners can have their valid need for attachment finally met.

Engaging in the Process

Terri and Greg's first therapy session focused on the use of mirroring. This was followed by a homework assignment to mirror back and forth for 20 minutes a day on nonconflictual topics. To ensure safety and success, the therapist should give an assignment that the couple is capable of completing without the therapist's being there to coach them. The second session was used to teach validation and empathy (see Luquet, 1996, for details) and to practice a complete three-step dialogue. As a tool for teaching dialogue, I'll ask one partner to relate a memory of some negative message from childhood. Greg did this:

> **Greg:** *In my family, strong feelings were not O.K. If we cried, we were told we had to stop. No one could really get angry, except my dad.*

> **Terri:**   *So, Greg, if I'm getting it, in your family expressing feelings was really discouraged; you even had to stop crying. The only one who could get angry was your dad. Is that right? Is there more?*
> **Greg:**   *Well, I'm sure it's not that big a deal. That's just how it was.*

Minimizers will frequently refute their own statements after they've heard them mirrored back by a maximizing partner. It's as though, through the mirroring process, the statements become uncomfortably intensified. This demonstrates how this process can be growth producing for both parties: it stretches the affective experiencing of the minimizer and contains the reactive intensity of the maximizer.

> **Therapist:**   *So, Greg, the rule in your family was that you couldn't have feelings, is that right? How do you see that rule getting played out in your relationship with Terri?*
> **Greg:**   *In our relationship, I can't stand it when you cry, and I feel guilty for feeling angry about it.*
> **Terri:**   *If I've got it, you're saying that when I cry, you can't stand it and it makes you angry. Then you feel guilty for even feeling angry. Is that right? Is there more?*
> **Greg:**   *No, that's it.*

I then asked Terri if what Greg had said to her made sense. Terri could easily validate what Greg had said: after all, she'd been the recipient of these unconscious messages for a long time.

> **Terri:**   *Yes, it makes perfect sense that my crying triggers those feelings in you. I understand that you get angry because you've been taught that crying is bad, and you also feel bad because you're not supposed to be angry.*

I asked Terri to imagine how Greg might feel, given all of that.

> **Terri:**   *I imagine that, when I cry, it makes you feel angry and guilty and upset about both of us. Wow! I had no idea. I thought you were just being a jerk.*

The therapist can also help the partners make a conscious connection between adult relationship conflicts and childhood wounds by having them voice a current frustration, and then explore how the frustration reminds them of feelings they had during childhood.

Attachment Restored

During the third session, I led Terri and Greg through a guided imagery to help them get in touch with their major childhood frustrations. This was followed by the Parent–Child Dialogue and the holding exercise, which they used for sharing their childhood memories. These processes can be powerfully healing, particularly for attachment-wounded couples. However, as with all couples, the therapist must be careful to assess the clients' readiness to engage in this type of regressive work.

My work with Terri and Greg was not brief, especially according to managed-care standards. We worked together weekly for almost eight months, during which they attended a "Getting the Love You Want" weekend workshop; then I saw them once a month for an additional three months. After the first four months of therapy, they set their wedding date—it was the second marriage for both of them. Six weeks later, they got married. Certainly, all their issues hadn't been resolved, and their relationship wasn't free of conflict, although there had been a dramatic shift in how they managed conflict. What they were beginning to experience, however, was profound: they felt the warm and consistent connection they had always wanted.

I often end each couples session with a joke or amusing story, much as the nightly news anchor does. I do this consciously and intentionally to provoke laughter and provide another opportunity for the couple to experience their therapy session as a safe place where they can feel their full aliveness and original state of relaxed joyfulness. And most importantly, when a couple can laugh in each other's presence, they share an immersive moment, a moment of trancendent attachment where all is right with the world.

BIBLIOGRAPHY

Bowlby, J. (1988). *A secure base: Parent–child attachment and healthy human development*. New York: Basic Books.

Freud, S. (1914/1967). On narcissism: An introduction. In J. Strachey (Ed.), *Standard edition*, Vol. 14 (pp. 67–102). London: Hogarth Press.

Hendrix, H. (1988). *Getting the love you want: A guide for couples*. New York: Holt.

Hendrix, H. (1992). *Keeping the love you find: A guide for singles*. New York: Pocket Books.

Karen, R. (1994). *Becoming attached: Unfolding the mystery of the infant–mother bond and its impact on later life*. New York: Warner Books.

Kreisman, J., & Straus, H. (1989). *I hate you—don't leave me: Understanding the borderline personality*. New York: Avon Books.

Luquet, W. (1996). *Short-term couples therapy: The Imago model in action*. New York: Brunner/Mazel.

Mahler, M., Pine, F., & Bergman, A. (1975). *The psychological birth of the human infant: Symbiosis and individuation*. New York: Basic Books.

Stern, D. (1977). *The first relationship: infant and mother*. Cambridge, Mass.: Harvard University Press.

Walant, K. (1995). *Creating the capacity for attachment: Treating addictions and the alienated self*. Northvale, N.J.: Jason Aronson.

Winnicott, D. W. (1965). *The maturational processes and the facilitating environment*. New York: International Universities Press.

EDITORS' COMMENTARY

This description of the attachment-wounded couple acts as a springboard for all the chapters that follow. In a sense, all childhood wounds are wounds of attachment. Whether the question partners ask is "Am I loved even when you are away from me?" or "Can I be myself and still be loved by you?" or "Am I loved by you whether I succeed or whether I fail?"—questions associated with the exploration, identity, and competence stages, respectively—the partners are, in essence, asking, "Is our connection safe enough to ensure that I will stay alive?"

Fein's case is a good demonstration of how complementary defensive adaptations operate in couples. We see the maximizing partner and the minimizing partner as triggering each other's primitive defensive maneuvers—the desperate clinging of the maximizer met by the phobiclike avoidance of the minimizer. The faster one runs, the faster the other follows: each partner treats the other in ways that perpetuate their inability to create, as a couple, the safe attachment they so desperately need.

As we'll observe in the upcoming cases, maximizing and minimizing behaviors show up in virtually all couples. But the hair-trigger reactivity, the extreme exaggeration and denial of feelings we see in Greg and Terri's interactions, are typical of so-called early-wounded couples. Imago theory holds that the earlier the wounding, the greater will be its effects on later interpersonal functioning. Attachment-wounded partners, unschooled in the basics of interpersonal relating, enter adulthood with a vast handicapping collection of relationship deficits— momentos of their caretakers' inability to relate to them as children. It is the attachment-wounded partner who has the greatest difficulty seeing the other as a person longing for connectedness, rather than as an echo of his or her own disconnection with early-life caretakers.

Fein points out another sobering repercussion of childhood wounding: parenting deficits affect not only our adult romantic relationships, but also the quality of our parenting. The author's agonizing over where her infant should sleep is less about parenting skills than about her fear of replicating her own childhood wounding. In the absence of conscious awareness, we tend to deprive our children during the same developmental periods our parents deprived us (Hendrix & Hunt, 1997)—following the notion that "you can't give what you haven't gotten." Here, as Fein implies, Imago work aims not merely to heal the wounds of childhood, and not only the pain of romantic relationships gone awry, but is designed to break the chain of intergenerational wounding, with the ultimate goal of healing our species.

Greg and Terri might seem a particularly difficult couple, whose problems with the rudimentaries of relationships—allowing ourselves to need relationships, acknowledging our need, trusting others to meet that need—prohibit effective relating. However, Greg and Terri's fear is the fear of every couple, reflected in the question, "How can you and I be attached to one another and yet remain free to be our distinct selves?" Imago therapy can make it possible for couples to accomplish that very thing—connection in tandem with separation—which is the inherent dilemma in romantic relationships.

REFERENCE

Hendrix, H. and Hunt, H. (1997). *Giving the love that heals.* New York: Pocket Books.

Chapter 3

THE EXPLORATORY-WOUNDED COUPLE

Wade Luquet and Betsy Chadwick

Bill and Alice had been fighting. Alice did most of the yelling; Bill clammed up, telling Alice she needed to get her head examined. When she cried, he told her she was too emotional and asked too much of him. Then he left and went to work in his large corner CEO office, where he spent most of his time. Alice cried for hours, wondering if she should go into the kitchen, pull out a knife, and end her misery. That would teach him! Finally, after many phone calls to friends, family, and pastors, she calmed down, made Bill's dinner, and apologized to him when he returned home. This same scene has been replayed between Bill and Alice about once a month throughout the 20 years of their marriage.

Bill, the "logical" one, assumed he was always right, since Alice was so "hysterical." The more cool and rational Bill became, the louder and more emotional Alice would become, lending more credence to Bill's belief that Alice was, quite simply, crazy, and so should have her head examined.

Alice did have her head examined; in fact, she was in therapy for two years with a psychoanalyst who quickly labeled her a borderline personality. During her sessions, Alice's therapist would not say much. This infuriated Alice, who would scream that she needed some advice from him. He would simply respond, "You're angry," and write in his notebook. Bill, on the other hand, was a successful person who would never consider going into therapy. There wasn't a thing wrong with him. After all, he remained very calm with Alice even when she acted so crazily.

SHE'S A BORDERLINE; HE'S A NARCISSIST

It would be tempting for most clinicians to label Alice a borderline personality. She does, in fact, yell at the top of her lungs; she never seems satisfied, and she resorts to flamboyant behavior to make a point. Bill seems the classic narcissist. He is self-centered, perfectionistic, and emotionally immovable. Together, the two look like a classic narcissistic/borderline couple (Lachkar, 1992). But to merely classify the couple this way precludes the richness of their dynamics, the purpose behind their behaviors, and the potential even such a disturbed relationship has to bring healing to the partners.

The personality disorders are thought to have their genesis during the second year of life (Kernberg, 1980; Masterson, 1981). The child who experiences engulfment or abandonment by the caretaker fails to develop a sense of object constancy. In reaction, the child attempts to define himself or herself by hanging onto the coattails of others, that is, by relying on other persons and things external to the self. This child may become clingy and overly reactive. On the other hand, the child may shut others out, deciding that no one else will define him or her. The eventual outcome for such a child is an untouchable, nonempathic self. Should the person enter therapy, the objective would be to use the therapeutic relationship to help develop object constancy, which, in turn, would allow the client to develop an autonomous self.

Clinicians following this model view child development through the lens of the individual paradigm, which espouses the ideals of autonomy, self-sufficiency, and an internalized definition of self. Such goals seem plausible. We would argue, however, that such perspectives overlook the crucial context within which development, as well as emotional wounding and healing, takes place.

According to the relational paradigm, development occurs against the backdrop of a child's relationship with the caretakers, who support the child's emerging developmental impulses. For example, during the first phase, attachment, the child's task is to achieve a sense of secure connection to the caretakers who, by responding reliably and appropriately to the infant's needs, teach the child to trust in the reliability and availability of others. With trust in place, the child is ready to transcend attachment concerns and to begin focusing on the next developmental impulse, the need to explore. Now the child relies on the caretakers to support his or her curiosity in exploring the world, which allows the child to become differentiated—to experience the world with curiosity, through eyes that are separate from those of the caretakers, with whom the child remains connected. In this manner, the self begins to form.

Kohut (1971, 1977, 1984) echoed relational thinking with his concept of selfobject experiences.

> Throughout his life a person will experience himself as a cohesive harmonious firm unit in time and space, connected with his past and pointing meaningfully into a creative-productive future, [but] only as long as, at each stage in his life, he experiences certain representatives of his human surroundings as joyfully responding to him, as available to him as sources of idealized strength and calmness, as being silently present but in essence like him, and, at any rate, able to grasp his inner life more or less accurately so that their responses are attuned to his needs and allow him to grasp their inner life when his is in need of assistance. (1984, p. 52).

The diffusion of infancy yields to the distinctness of the self through the inculcation of selfobjects. Actually, the selfobject is not an object per se, but rather another person who, through repeated empathic mirroring of the child's experiences in the world, contributes to the child's sense of self.

Think of the child's mind as an empty photo album. Each time a parent mirrors the child's experience, a new photo is placed in the album. According to traditional analytic/object relations thinking, the child needs pictures of his or her caretakers to develop object constancy. Once the album contains enough pictures of the parents, the child is able to separate and individuate, because he or she is able to hold onto the picture of the parents. That is, the parents have become constant objects.

According to relational paradigm thinking, when the parent mirrors the child, two pictures are placed in the child's photo album—one of the caretakers and the other of the child's self. So when a parent says, "Look how big you are," the child receives a snapshot of the mother, as well as a picture of the self as "big." Likewise, when the parent mirrors the child's feelings by saying, "You seem sad," one picture shows an empathic parent while the other depicts the child's having feelings. By the time the photo album is full, it includes pictures of the child's self along with those of the caretakers and significant others, and of a myriad of painful and pleasurable experiences. The self is thus made up of this diverse array of pictures that represent the sum total of the child's selfobject experiences. Given an adequate photo collection, the child develops not only a cohesive self, but also the capacity to picture things outside of the self; that is, he or she attains empathic capacity.

EXPLORATORY-STAGE WOUNDS

Wounding during the exploratory stage can yield a very different-looking photo album, one with blank spaces or one that is overcrowded or even has missing pages. Some caretakers, for example, to keep the child from harm, smother his or her natural curiosity by restricting the child to a small physical area. Similarly, some well-intended parents try to shape the child's feelings and interests to match those of the parents, to ensure that the child will turn out like "one of us." Likewise, the exploratory-aged child might be neglected or experience inadequate mirroring. Wounding during the exploration phase, as in all developmental stages, elicits defensive behaviors or adaptations that the child adopts to defend against further wounding. For example, some children adapt by anxiously conforming to parental expectations, fearfully disowning any desire to separate from the caretaker. Whatever the nature of the wounding, the child will adopt one of two primary adaptive styles to cope with it: he or she denies needing parental validation or screams bloody murder, as loud and as often as necessary, to ensure that he or she will get it. Once in place, these defensive adaptations, although of some usefulness during childhood, impair the adult's empathic capacity, leading to disturbed interpersonal relating, particularly in romantic relationships. Depending on the defensive style and the extent and severity of impairment, some individuals wounded during exploration meet the diagnostic criteria for borderline or narcissistic personality disorder.

Bill and Alice

Exploratory-wounded couples are among the most difficult of couples to work with. Bill and Alice were no exception, having come to therapy after Bill had announced that he had had enough and wanted out. At the first visit, Bill explained, "It's never going to change. She's been to therapy but nothing is different. She can't do life on her own at all, and she expects me to be there for her all the time. I have other things to do besides take care of her. So I've decided it would be best to just get out now." Alice was already in tears. "You can't just cast me out without giving me a chance. I'm doing better. You know things are not as bad as they used to be. Just give me one more chance!" Bill looked away from her, staring ahead coldly.

It was the classic borderline–narcissistic dance: one partner desperate for contact with the other partner, who has little desire or capacity for contact. One has insatiable needs; the other feels smothered by the partner's neediness. As Solomon (1989) put it, "The conflict later can manifest as a need to fuse with an idealized other who can read one's mind and respond immediately in a perfect caretaking function" (p. 69).

Neither Bill nor Alice had wanted it to turn out this way. When they first met, over 25 years earlier, like all couples, they wanted things to work, and were determined to accomplish that end. They just never expected committed relationship to be so hard. Their relational development provides clues to the source of their difficulties.

Bill was the prototypical pampered child, the center of his parents' universe. His parents' job was to get the best for their son; Bill's was to make his parents proud. Bill did his job well: he was a high-achieving student, captain of the high school football team, and popular with everyone, especially the girls. Bill's parents were always there, cheering from the sidelines. They considered all the hard work they had invested in raising him—teaching him how to think, how to act, how to achieve goals—as well worth it. Like his father, Bill became wealthy, fulfilling the American dream, which was the dream his parents had had for him.

Alice's story was entirely different. Her parents were alcoholics who had little time for her, leaving her to, in effect, raise herself. Their house was always a mess, and she was embarrassed to have friends visit. Her parents hardly ever spoke to each other; when they did, it was usually by yelling.

When Alice was about five years old, an uncle who visited frequently began fondling her. This continued sporadically until Alice was 13. Although she hated it, it also made her feel special; she got more attention from the uncle than from anyone else.

As she moved into adolescence, Alice desperately wanted to separate herself from her family, but she didn't know how. She had at least one thing going for her: she was beautiful. She decided that being popular would be her way of being different from her family, her ticket out. She started to dress provocatively and developed a reputation as "easy to get." Boys began to fall at her feet. It was at a party following a football game in her senior year that she met Bill. He went to college the following year, and she rearranged her life to follow him there. They married after graduation.

Alice had found just the man she was looking for. Bill was confident and smart, and he knew what he wanted to do with his life. To Bill, on the other hand, Alice was someone who would always love and adore him, as his parents believed a woman should. He knew that wherever he led, she would follow. Sexually, she was incredible, willing to try almost anything.

Their relationship worked fairly well until they had their first child. Around that time, Bill started a business that often required him to work long hours and to travel overseas. Burdened with the brunt of the child care, Alice complained bitterly about Bill's time away from home, but she had to admit that she enjoyed the perks of Bill's business: a bigger house, a new car every year, an expensive piece of jewelry on her birthday, a full-time housekeeper. Their friends were wealthy, they went to nice parties, and Alice experienced the popularity she'd sought so desperately as a teenager. She had come a long way from her childhood home. Yet Bill wasn't there to enjoy it all with her; he was out gathering accolades while she remained at home, feeling lonely and unfulfilled without him. She had everything she always wanted—except Bill.

Echo and Narcissus

The ancient Greeks knew about this couple pairing. The exploratory-wounded couple is nicely illustrated, including a treatment plan, in the mythological tale of Echo and Narcissus. Most of us are familiar with the tale of the young Narcissus, who looked into a reflecting pool and fell in love with his own image—hence the term "narcissist." But the whole story as described in Bullfinch's *Mythology* (1959), includes the story of Echo.

> Echo, a beautiful wood nymph who was a favorite of the Goddess Diana, had one failing: she was "fond of talking, and whether in chat or argument, would have the last word" (p. 88). One day, while the Goddess Juno was looking for her husband, who was amusing himself among the nymphs, Echo detained her with her gift for talk so that the others could escape. Juno realizing what had happened, became angry and passed a sentence upon Echo: "You shall forfeit the use of that tongue with which you have cheated me, except for that one purpose for which you are so fond of—reply. You shall have the last word, but no power to speak the first" (p. 88).
>
> When Echo saw Narcissus in the woods, she immediately fell in love with him and began to follow him. She wanted to talk to him, but did not have the power to do so. She could only wait for him to speak and then answer. One day, Narcissus losing his way in the woods, shouted: "Who's here?" and Echo replied, "Here." Narcissus did not see anyone and shouted "Come!" and Echo replied, "Come," but she stayed hidden. "Why do you shun me?" asked Narcissus and Echo answered, "Why do you shun me?" "Let us join one another." said Narcissus. Echo replied, "Let us join one another," and ran to where Narcissus stood, ready to embrace him. Stepping back, he

shouted, "I would rather die than you should have me," to which Echo whimpered, "Have me."

But her was plea in vain. Soon, Echo's form faded with grief and her bones turned to stone and there was nothing left, but her voice. "With that she is still ready to reply to any one who calls her, and keeps up her old habit of having the last word" (p. 88).

Narcissus often was cruel to the nymphs. When a maiden he had spurned prayed that someday he might feel what it was to love and meet no return of affection, an avenging goddess heard her and granted her wish.

Another time, while walking in the woods, Narcissus came across a clear fountain with water like silver that had not been disturbed by man, animal, or fallen leaves. When he bent to take a drink, he saw his own image and thought it a water spirit. It was the most beautiful image he had ever seen, and he fell in love with himself. He brought his lips near and plunged his arms in to touch, but the spirit disappeared, only to return a few moments later. The image fled every time he tried to grasp it, and yet he was so fascinated, that he began to lose all interest in food and drink. He talked to the supposed spirit: "Why, beautiful spirit, do you shun me?" Echo, hiding nearby repeated, "Why, beautiful spirit do you shun me?" And each time Narcissus spoke to the spirit, Echo repeated his words. Soon, Narcissus pined away and died. The nymphs, mourning for him, prepared a funeral pyre but could not find his body. In its place was a flower, "purple within, and surrounded with white leaves, which bears the name and preserves the memory of Narcissus" (p. 89).

A MYTH SO VALID: THE BORDERLINE– NARCISSISTIC RELATIONSHIP

The exploratory-wounded couple generally consists of one partner with an overly strong sense of self (narcissistic) and one with a weak sense of self (borderline) (Figure 3.1). The borderline partner can identify with the narcissist's self-aggrandizement and convictions of superiority, and uses them as a source of self-identity. In the borderline partner, the narcissist has an unending source of admiration and loyalty. This type of relationship is an exceptionally reactive one, with the narcissist complaining about the borderline's constant smothering and the borderline complaining of the narcissist's threats of abandonment.

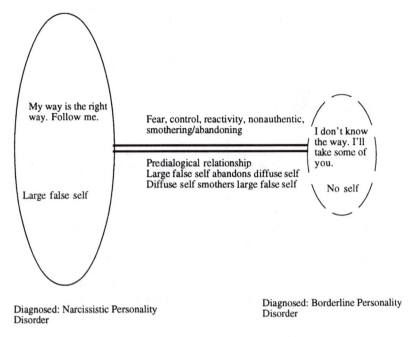

Figure 3.1.   Exploratory-wounded couple, predialogical.

Such partners, like Bill and Alice, need to embrace the notion that both of them are right. This means they must become able to relate empathically instead of reactively. In other words, they must transcend themselves and experience their partner in a new and authentic way. They must step out of the false selves they've created for a moment to recognize the falsity of those selves. This is an especially difficult step for these couples owing to the nature of the partners' adaptations. Both struggle to hold on to what they have, fearing that giving up any part of the territory of the self means losing the self forever.

For this couple, like all couples, the struggle can become the birthplace of true love. This can occur, however, only if one partner is willing to risk bringing down the defenses, exposing his or her vulnerability, and relating authentically to the other, thus empowering the other to respond in the same manner (Figure 3.2).

To accomplish this, the therapist needs to establish a safe holding environment in which vulnerability eventually becomes the norm. Initially, the safe moments may be fleeting, quickly giving way to angry accusations, some directed at the therapist. Exploratory-wounded partners are famous for engaging in the well-documented phenomenon of splitting—the black/white, all-or-nothing thinking

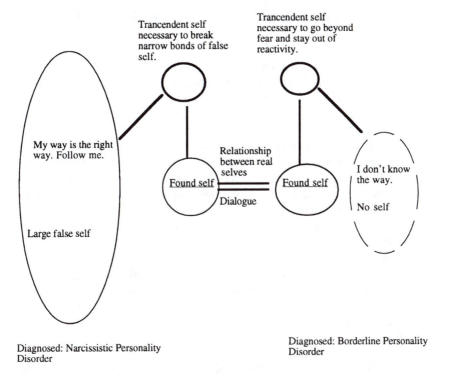

Figure 3.2.   Exploratory-wounded couple, dialogical.

they exhibit when they blame the therapist for the problems they continue to experience. The therapist needs to respond to this just like the partners are advised to respond to each other: through fully hearing and mirroring the partners' frustrations. When the couple feels heard by the therapist, they will back away from their stance and return to cooperating with the process.

In conducting Imago therapy with exploratory-wounded couples, one of two scenarios eventually plays out. The couple clings to the defensive structure, accuses the therapist of not knowing what he or she is doing, and leaves therapy, either to work with another therapist or to resume life as usual. Or, in a more hopeful scenario, the couple experiences enough insight to recognize, at last, that the defensive behavior has kept both of them from getting what they want from the relationship. This is obviously the harder, although the wiser, road for a couple to travel. To learn how to relate to one another as separate yet connected beings, they will need as much structure, support, mirroring, and coaching as would an exploring two-year-old. The therapy becomes a process of mirroring and validating their emerging true selves.

BILL AND ALICE ON THE LESS-TRAVELED ROAD

Bill and Alice decided to take an Imago couples weekend workshop, where they learned to use the Couples Dialogue and other Imago processes. Although skeptical at first, Bill was able to relax his logical exterior long enough to hear Alice's pain and to confront some of the pain of his own childhood.

Bill realized that, although his parents had good intentions, they did not allow him to emerge as a distinct person. He had been living almost his entire life with a false self that had been designed for him by his parents. He recalled having given up certain interests, such as a fascination with nature, because he feared disappointing his parents, who considered aimless activities a waste of time. Alice spoke to Bill, feeling heard this time, about growing up in a family devoid of connection and validation.

It was important to facilitate Bill and Alice's use of the dialogue through regularly scheduled therapy appointments. Couples wounded at the exploration stage can easily slip back into their reactive and hurtful styles of relating. Bill and Alice were seen biweekly for several months, during which they entered into some fruitful dialogues.

> **Bill:**   *I don't remember my mom or dad playing with me much. They might have been there, but it was always business with them. I could not be myself—only what they wanted me to be.*
>
> **Alice:**   *So if I am getting it, you don't remember your mom and dad playing with you much. They were always there, but it was all business. You could not be yourself, but only what they wanted you to be. Did I get that?*
>
> **Bill:**   *Yes. It seemed that, if I wanted to do something they didn't like, I would get shamed. I mean, if I wanted to wear jeans to go out on a Saturday night, you would have thought I committed a mortal sin!*
>
> **Alice:**   *So if you did something your parents did not like, they would shame you. Things like wearing a pair of jeans on a Saturday night were a mortal sin to them. Did I get that?*
>
> **Bill:**   *Yeah. So I just followed the straight and narrow. I figured they knew best, so I gave them everything they could possibly want in a son. I would not let anything stand in the way of my making them proud of me. Not even you. The problem is, I forgot about me and about you in the process. I thought I knew who I was. Now I don't know who I am, or who you are, either.*

Alice: *So you followed the straight and narrow. You gave your parents everything they wanted in a son, you wouldn't let anything, including me, stand in the way of their being proud of you. But in the process, you left out both of us, and now you don't know who I am or who you are anymore. All of this makes a lot of sense to me. Your parents told you who to become. Who you wanted to become was not part of the equation. I imagine you must now feel lost, confused, and a little scared.*

Alice saw that, Bill's emerging sense of self was now at a most vulnerable stage. She discovered the power of empathic understanding in supporting him as he reconfigured his sense of self to include both greater connection and individuation. Through the structure of the dialogue, Alice was able to supply what Bill needed without triggering his fear of being smothered. The dialogue also gave Alice the feeling of connection with Bill for which she'd been hungering. Alice learned that, when she feels connected with Bill, she is far less prone to engaging in the reactive behavior that alienates him.

Bill's task also was to step out of his typical defensive posture to listen to Alice empathically, without imposing his own point of view on her, to support her in forming a distinct self. In attempting to do this, Bill began to glimpse how difficult a task this was for Alice.

Alice: *I was not allowed to have a self. My parents hardly noticed me, but when they did, and whenever I would try to tell them what I was thinking or feeling about what was happening in our home, they'd quickly squash me down: "How dare you talk that way to us! We don't want to hear it." I was always second-guessing them, trying to think of the right thing to say to keep out of trouble. I guess I ended up being afraid to have any opinions of my own. I was afraid of losing the little bit of love I somehow managed to get.*

Bill: *So you are saying that you could not have a sense of who you are because they would always cut you down. They would tell you, "How dare you think or feel that way." So you were always second-guessing them, and finally ended up without any opinions of your own. Did I get that? Is there more?*

Alice: *Yes, you did. So that is why I have always looked to you to guide me. You always seemed to know exactly what you wanted, and I just wanted to grab onto that. But when I started feeling that you were leaving me out, ignoring me like my parents did, I got scared. I would scream to get your attention. I don't feel I can exist on my own without you.*

Bill: *So since you were not allowed to make a decision as a child, you always counted on me to guide you. When I started leaving you out, you got scared and would scream to get my attention. You don't feel that you can be on your own without me. Did I get that?*

Alice: *You did get it. I am realizing lately that I cannot stay totally dependent on you, but I'm still too scared to do a lot of things on my own right now. I need your support to get myself together. I also need to know that you won't rush me or try to get me to hurry up and get fixed.*

Bill: *So you are realizing that you can't totally depend on me, but you are too scared to be totally on your own right now. You need my support to help you get your life together, and you don't want me to rush you or tell you to hurry up and get fixed. Did I get it?*

Alice: *Yes.*

Bill: *Well, it is making sense to me that, given your family background, you would have trouble making decisions and would need someone else to depend on, since you were forbidden to think for yourself. It also makes sense that you would need my support and not want me to rush you to be independent. I imagine you must feel scared and vulnerable, and you are hoping that I will be there to support you.*

Alice: *Yes.*

Therapist: *Alice, would you be willing to make a Behavior Change Request of Bill, three different requests stated in positive terms, that would help you work toward making your own decisions, but without losing connection with Bill? Remember to tell Bill specifically what you would like him to do, how often you want him to do it, and for how long.*

Alice: *Well, let's see if I can do this. O.K., I would like you to ask my opinion on a business decision you have to make. I would like you to give me enough time to formulate my own ideas and express them to you from beginning to end without any interruptions. And then I would like you to mirror them back to me, without commenting on them. Save that for another day. I'd like you to do this once a week for the next couple of weeks.*

Bill: *So, you would like me to request your opinion on a business decision I have to make, once a week, for the next two weeks. You would like me to give you the time you need to gather your ideas and then to present them to me. Then you would like me to mirror you back and save any comments for another day. Did I get that?*

Alice: *Yes, you did.*

Bill: *Is there more?*

Alice: *Yes. One time this month, the day before you leave on a trip, I would like you to spend 20 minutes dialoguing with me about how scared I am that you are leaving. I really get scared when you leave.*

Bill: *So, once this month, the day before I leave for a trip, you would like me to have a dialogue with you about how scary it is for you when I leave. It sounds like you would really like me to listen to how really scary it is for you when I leave. Did I get that? Is there more?*

Alice: *Yes, one more. I know that you are well versed in foreign affairs because of your business. Well, I read news magazines to keep up with the world news. Three times during the next month, I would like us to spend 20 minutes discussing world events and have you take my opinions seriously.*

Therapist: *Alice, how would you know whether or not Bill is taking you seriously?*

Alice: *I would know if you would mirror me and, when you are ready, say something like you understand how I could come to such a conclusion. After that, I would like to hear your opinion on the subject and then mirror and validate you.*

Bill: *Wow! So you are saying that three times this month, for 20 minutes at a time, you would like us to discuss world events. You would like me to mirror and then, when I get a picture of what you are saying, validate your opinion. You would also like to hear my opinion, and then mirror and validate it. Did I get that?*

Alice: *Yes.*

Therapist: *So, Alice, please tell Bill how, if he did any of these three things, it would help to heal the childhood wounds you've dialogued about today.*

Alice: *If you did those things, it would begin to heal my childhood wound of feeling invisible and unimportant, and my fear of being abandoned if I expressed an opinion in the family.*

Bill: *So, if I did any of these three requests, it would begin to heal your childhood wound of feeling invisible and unimportant, and help you overcome the fear that you would be abandoned if you expressed an opinion of your own. That makes a lot of sense to me, because I had a similar experience in my own childhood. I can also see how this whole thing gets played out in our relationship.*

At first, like many couples, Bill and Alice had more success with the dialogue in the therapist's office than they did at home. However, they eventually began to report having had major blow-ups at home that they'd manage to stop by dialoguing instead of fighting. As time went on, their fights became fewer and farther between, with the duration of the fights, along with the cold war that followed, becoming shorter. Given where Bill and Alice were when they started, this was clearly progress.

TWO STEPS FORWARD; ONE STEP BACK

There is much ground to cover with exploratory-wounded couples. There has been profound wounding, not only during their childhoods, but also during the marriage; emotional abuse by one or both partners has likely been present. All the pain of their relationship history needs to be discussed, validated, and eventually forgiven. Agreements must be made to avoid rewounding behaviors, to take time-outs, and to take other precautions to lessen the chance of returning to abusive behaviors.

Progress is always tenuous: with just a little extra stress, the couple might revert to their argumentative ways, with one partner seeking contact while the other becomes impenetrable. Should they explode during a session, the therapist should intercede by using positive triangulation; that is, the therapist should begin mirroring for each of them until they are capable of mirroring one another.

> **Alice:**   *I really need you to understand that when you go away on trips, I feel all alone. I don't think I can tolerate more than two days a month.*
> **Bill:**   *Well, other wives can manage it. When I'm gone, just go do some things with them.*
> **Alice:**   *You don't get it, do you? Every time I think we are making headway, you say something stupid like that. You'll never understand how I feel. We might as well split up now, because I know you'll be up to your old ways again in no time. I might as well call the lawyer now.*
> **Bill:**   *If that's how you feel, then call the lawyer.*
> **Alice:**   *You bastard. You're such a self-righteous ass.*
> **Therapist:**   *O.K., just a minute here. Sit back and breathe. Alice, let me take a minute to mirror you, if I may. I think I am hearing you say that Bill is not getting how you feel about being left alone when he goes away. His last comment about your not being like the other wives has triggered you. You are feeling disconnected from him and misunderstood. Am I getting that right?*
> **Alice:**   *Yes, and I am not sure that he will ever understand me.*
> **Therapist:**   *And you are not sure whether he will ever understand you. That makes a lot of sense to me, because it seems like he is not understanding you right now. I imagine you must be feeling misunderstood, rejected, incompetent, and lonely. Did I get that?*
> **Alice:**   *You did.*

Therapist: *Alice, please take a moment to think about how you would like Bill to understand your need for his presence with you. I want to mirror Bill for a moment. Bill, I'm hearing you say that you don't understand why Alice has such a hard time being alone when you are on trips. You said that the other wives seem to do just fine, and you wondered why she doesn't just go do something with them. Did I get that?*
Bill: *You did. And then she crapped all over me with her stuff about calling the lawyer.*
Therapist: *And you felt crapped on when she talked about calling the lawyer. It makes sense to me that you would feel crapped on when she brought up the lawyer. Lawyers can be a frightening subject. I imagine that you felt startled, angry, and maybe inadequate.*
Bill: *Yeah, I don't think she needed to jump to that so quickly.*
Therapist: *So you don't think she needed to jump so quickly to the idea of calling a lawyer. Bill, I'm wondering if I can respond to this. Would you be willing to take a moment to put yourself in a safe place to hear me for a few minutes.*
Bill: *I'll try.*
Therapist: *Thanks, Bill. I'm wondering if you could try to hear all of what Alice has to say before responding. I notice that the two of you get into your arguments when you are not fully hearing each other. So I'm wondering if you could get yourself safe enough to hear Alice fully and then mirror her back. You do not have to agree with her that you should be home more, nor do you have to agree to traveling no more than two days a week. But you do have to hear her, if you want to be able to understand what she is trying to say to you. Would you be willing to give that a try?*
Bill: *I'll try. Give me a minute to get focused.*

Bill then listened to Alice. He did not agree to stay home more, but he understood the points she made about feeling lonely and abandoned. He expressed empathy toward her when she talked about being a child and feeling no sense of connection with her family. He felt moved when she cried over not being held as a child and not being told she was beautiful or smart. Alice explained that, when Bill goes away, she feels the same void she felt when she was a child. She knows that Bill cannot fix the void for her, but she wants him to understand that she feels stronger and more connected when he acknowledges her feelings. Bill was finally able to reinterpret what he referred to as Alice's neediness as her way of trying to make contact with him. As long as he was willing to hear and acknowledge Alice's needs, she was able to tolerate his inability to meet all her needs all of the time. Bill and Alice were discovering the self-in-relationship.

BILL AND ALICE REVISITED

There is no such thing as short-term therapy for a couple like Bill and Alice. This does not imply that such couples must be in therapy for the rest of their lives, but they will have to use the processes they learned in therapy for many years to come. There is hope but no guarantee of marital bliss for exploratory-wounded couples. Many times these couples can easily grasp the processes and will initially use them, but later return to the old familiar and hurtful ways of relating to each other.

A year after treatment, Bill and Alice were contacted for a routine follow-up. Alice said that, although she was doing better, Bill seemed to have pulled back into his work. However, an interesting switch had taken place: Alice was now the more confident partner. She said that the Imago work had helped her come to believe in herself. "Bill's got to relate to me as the person I am now. This is now the way I see myself, and I can't go back. I feel good about myself. I've told Bill that if he wants a relationship with me, he will have to talk to me as an equal. I think he heard me."

Progress in couples work, particularly with early-wounded couples like Bill and Alice, can often be measured only in tiny increments—fewer explosions, longer periods without threats to leave the relationship, and greater optimism about the future. Bill and Alice were happier together, although still far from wedded bliss. Yet we believe that their work had highly positive outcomes: Alice now feels good about herself and Bill seems to be hearing her. Best of all, they are "keeping their paddle in the water": they are willing to continue the struggle, which, as difficult as it sometimes gets, serves as their passage to growth.

BIBLIOGRAPHY

Kernberg, O. (1980). Developmental theory, structural organization and psycho-analytic technique. In Ruth Lax et. al., *Rapprochement*. New York: Jason Aronson.

Kohut, H. (1971). *The analysis of the self*. New York: International Universities Press.

Kohut, H. (1977). *The restoration of the self*. New York: International Universities Press.

Kohut, H. (1984). *How does psychoanalysis cure?* Chicago: University of Chicago Press.

Lachkar, J. (1992). *The narcissistic/borderline couple.* New York: Brunner/Mazel.

Masterson, J. F. (1981). *The narcissistic and borderline disorders.* New York: Brunner/Mazel.

Solomon, M. F. (1989). *Narcissism and intimacy.* New York: Norton.

Solomon, M. F. (1959). Echo and Narcissus. In T. Bullfinch, *Mythology* (pp. 87–89). New York: Dell.

EDITORS' COMMENTARY

This chapter underscores the unique perspective that Imago theory takes on behavior that emerges in the context of a relationship. Although some clinical approaches label problematic interpersonal styles as pathological—for example, the "borderline" or "narcissistic" partner—Imago views such characteristics as behavioral adaptations that have become necessary for survival in relationship.

This relational viewpoint is reflected in the authors' description of Bill and Alice. The louder Alice yelled, the quieter Bill became. The harder Alice pushed, the harder Bill pulled. Their behaviors might look dysfunctional, but they are, quite simply, the manifestation of tbe couplehood of two wounded people. In situations unrelated to their marriage, Bill and Alice behave as healthy, productive individuals. In their romantic relationship, the match is set to the fuel, the lid is off the id, and their defenses emerge with a vengeance.

Just as attachment lays the groundwork for exploration, so does the exploratory phase lay the foundation for the development of an identity. During the exploration stage, children feel courageous enough to explore the external world only if they receive enough parental encouragement and validation for their exploratory behaviors. Such support for exploration impulses soothes the child as he or she suffers the inevitable bumps and knocks and injuries that come from his or her encounters with the world. Given an adequate grasp of what the outer world is all about, a child is prepared to explore the unique inner world of the self. Absent such preparation, defensive behavioral adaptations take over, forcing the work of identity formation to go on hiatus.

Bill and Alice's relationship epitomizes the effects of exploration wounds. Bill denies the need for any validation of his thoughts and feelings, as though insisting, "I know what I think and feel and believe. I know what I've experienced. So why should I listen to what you think and feel and believe?" In contrast, Bonnie needs constant validation of her inner world, as if to plea, "Tell me that what I see is accurate. In fact, I don't even know what I should be experiencing. Tell me what to experience."

Clearly illustrated in this chapter is a common feature of distressed couples: the minimizing partner, in this case, Bill, looks healthier than the maximizing partner. In our society, at least, minimizing behaviors are more socially acceptable than are maximizing behaviors. The guy who stays cool, calm, and collected during a fight with his partner has it all together; the woman who loses it and becomes hysterical is just plain crazy. What remains invisible is the internalized pain of the minimizer, which drives Bill's defensiveness as strongly as the externalized pain of the maximizer compels Alice to behave as she does. By revealing the equal depth of his wounding to Alice, Bill frees her from the role of the sick one. Bill and Alice, like all partners, hold the key to their own healing. They also hold the key to their partner's healing—a key available only if they have the courage to use it on themselves first.

Chapter **4**

THE RIGID/DIFFUSE COUPLE

Gary Brainerd and Wade Luquet

"We've been going together for two years and he will not commit to marrying me." Bonnie was frustrated because she felt she had been jumping through hoops for two years to give Don whatever he wanted. Now Don was voicing greater expectations, ones she simply could not meet.

Don, a 53-year-old manufacturing executive, had been, as he put it, burned before. Five years earlier, he and his wife of 20 years had gone through a less than amicable divorce. Don and his ex-wife had disagreed on almost everything— property, pension plans, the rearing of their two children. Don blames his ex-wife, "the stupid bitch," for most of his present misery. He is adamant about not making the same mistake again.

Bonnie, a tall and elegant 47-year-old former model, owns a successful interior design business. Married and divorced twice, she has no children. She views herself as masterful in business but at a loss when it comes to relationships. She was physically abused by her first husband, and in all of her romantic relationships, she takes a passive and subservient role that sharply contrasts with her competent leadership style at work.

Don was raised by strict parents who ran their home like a military academy. There was little tolerance for anything less than perfection. Clean rooms, beds perfectly made, homework done accurately, and unquestioning obedience were expected of the children. In Don's words, "I was raised to be successful at whatever I did." Bonnie, on the other hand, came from a chaotic family. Preoccupied with their careers, her parents were seldom available to her. It was a high school art teacher who took an interest in Bonnie's artistic talents and persuaded Bonnie to pursue an art degree.

PARENTING THAT WOUNDS: TWO TYPES OF WOUNDING

There are two types of wounds that parents, wittingly or unwittingly, can inflict on their children: wounds that tend to produce the minimizer style of self-protection and wounds that tend to produce the maximizer style of self-protection.

Wounds that Create Minimizers

Wounds that tend to create a minimizing protection result from "too much" parenting: too much control or otherwise painful interactions, including rejecting, smothering, dominating, or shaming the child. During the identity stage, in particular, the child's developing sense of self is so dependent on the responses of the environment that any disapproval or put-downs by his or her caretakers forces the child to use defensive adaptations. Unless some intervention occurs, these adaptations eventually solidify and become part of the child's personality.

Selective Mirroring A parent who selectively mirrors a child will recognize, respond to, and mirror only those traits that the parent condones. Disapproved traits are ignored in an attempt to shape the child's behavior and sense of self. For example, if the child pretends to be a soldier at war, and the parents believe that being a soldier is not acceptable, they might ignore the child's pretending, hoping it will go away. If a boy says, "I'm a great dancer," or a girl says, "I'm a great football player," some parents, fearing the child will be confused about his or her gender, ignore or discourage such expressions. Unfortunately, parents' attempts to mold the child's developing self can damage it.

Shaming Responses Communicating disapproval through shaming remarks is even more wounding than simply ignoring the child's identifications. To the boy playing soldier, such comments as, "In this family, we don't believe in killing people," or "How can you play at killing people?" will cause the child to hesitate to be fully himself in his play. He may learn to dislike, disown, or repress the "soldier-like" part of himself he was trying to express, which could later produce self-rejection and the creation of rigid self-boundaries.

Similarly, the girl who plays soldier may be teased for choosing a typical male role. "You can be a nurse or a hairdresser. Don't be silly; you're not a boy!" Ignoring or shaming will cause a child to avoid incorporating the ignored or shamed parts into his or her identity. The immediate effects might seem minimal, with the child merely narrowing the range of his or her play activities. When the child grows into adulthood, however, and especially in romantic relationships, the effects on the personality and selfhood become obvious.

Shaming is an effective attempt to control the person being shamed, but it has a major side effect: lowered self-esteem combined with denial of the shamed parts of the self.

Dominating Responses Not suprisingly, persons who have been shamed or dominated during childhood will come to shame and dominate others. They will also hold rigid opinions, have difficulty dealing with the ambiguous or "gray areas" of life, and avoid disclosing any personal weaknesses or flaws.

Don joked about having the meanest mother in the northern hemisphere and then proceeded to argue that he had not been wounded by this: rather, he said, he was tempered by it, as steel is tempered by fire. He appreciated his childhood experiences because they made him successful. The suggestion that his mother's behavior could have wounded him triggered a strong and intense reaction in Don, who responded with a lecture on how we are becoming a nation of victims.

For Don, any acknowledgment of having been shamed would itself be shameful. Don is what we call the "shame denial" wounded person—a very difficult client to work with.

Wounds that Create Maximizers

Wounds that create maximizing protections result from some form of neglect by caretakers, such as abandonment, "benign" neglect, or the child's feeling lost or invisible in the family. The identity-wounded person with a maximizing adaptation has a wound of invisibility, that is, of not mattering, not having an impact on others. Persons with maximizing wounds adapted by exaggerating their emotional expression. There is a simple logic to this. If a child is neglected, he or she will discover that one way of getting attention is to make a lot of noise when upset. Maximizing spouses do likewise.

IDENTIFYING THE IDENTITY-WOUNDED COUPLE

Shame-wounded persons have a highly defined sense of who they are. They hold strong opinions, have a high need for control, and are very sensitive to criticism. They minimize or constrict their feelings to reduce the risk of being shamed for having them.

Invisibility-wounded persons, on the other hand, find it difficult to define themselves. Generally compliant and cooperative with others, they may lapse into blaming and criticizing when they feel threatened. They are emotionally reactive and, fearing being unimportant to their partner, they express their feelings dramatically, to make a maximum impact.

Don and Bonnie

Don and Bonnie describe their relationship as "80 percent great." They are financially secure and have the income and free time to take trips and enjoy a variety of leisure-time activities together. Their trouble emerges when Bonnie does not meet Don's expectations and he reacts with some type of shaming behavior, for example, by angrily criticizing her. Bonnie then feels stupid, and when she tries to explain her position to Don, he does not listen.

Don's wound came from a rigid upbringing in which work was valued more than pleasure. Imaginative play, in particular, was discouraged; expectations of productive behavior were high. Whenever Don violated a rule, his parents quickly shamed him, leading Don to avoid such behavior. He became the good boy, "a chip off the old block who made his old man proud."

Bonnie's upbringing was a lonely one: She usually played by herself. She started drawing at a young age and showed considerable talent, but her artwork was seldom praised or even noticed by her family. She felt chronically unsure of herself and her abilities, and was always what she termed "a follower."

In couples therapy, as the Couples Dialogue was explained to them, Don looked dumbstruck. "You want me to repeat back what she said? What good will that do?" He stated that he always felt safe. Why should he have to go to a safe place to listen to Bonnie?

Don struggled with the Imago processes each weekly session. He complained that they were going too slowly. He wanted to "cut to the chase. I never have to do this in business. I just make a decision and do it." Nevertheless, he would return every week, although reluctantly. "I can see where this is helping Bonnie," he observed.

Bonnie liked the therapy processes because they slowed Don down, which helped her to get her points across. Dialogue gave her the chance to formulate her opinions, present them, change them if she needed to, and have Don validate them in a nonthreatening and nonshaming manner. She said that the dialogue made her feel valid, heard, and important as a human being.

In the fifth session, Don and Bonnie were introduced to the Parent–Child Dialogue. In this process, one partner takes the role of a parent of the sending partner. The receiving partner is instructed to ask questions, including, "I am your mother/father. What was it like to live with me?" The receiver then listens with empathy. Bonnie chose to talk to her father.

> **Bonnie:** *It was difficult living with you. You were home, but you never seemed there for me. You always seemed more interested in your trains, TV, or the newspaper. I felt invisible around you.*
> **Don:** *So you felt invisible. Tell me more about that.*
> **Bonnie (tearful):** *It was like nothing I did mattered. I would show you my drawings, and it was like you were staring into nothing. I'd tell you my ideas and it was like you did not hear me. I needed you to tell me I was talented, or if my ideas made any sense at all. I still don't know if I make sense. I still doubt my talents. But I deserved to be noticed.*
> **Don:** *You never felt noticed and you deserved to be noticed.*
> **Bonnie:** *Yes.*

After this dialogue, Don shared his reaction to what Bonnie had revealed.

> **Don:** *I was really touched by what you said. I did not know it was that bad for you. You are talented and that should have been noticed by your father. I can see how this would affect you now. I just hope my listening to you will help you get over this.*
> **Therapist:** *Don, I can really see that you are touched by what Bonnie has told you. But I'd like to add that the goal is not for Bonnie to get over the problem, but to have you understand her experience. This could*

also help you understand how some of your behavior can be rewounding her.

In the following session, it was Don's turn to talk to one of his parents. Don chose his father.

Don: *I don't remember anything bad about you. I think you did the best you could with me. You wanted the best for me and you made sure I stayed on the straight and narrow. I want to thank you for raising me to be successful and giving me the skills to make it in the world. I mean, you yelled and stuff sometime. You used your belt on me sometimes. But I deserved it and I can't see that it did me any harm. It made me respect you, and I think respect is important.*

As the therapist prodded him to express some less positive feelings, Don started to become more and more annoyed. This is a common phenomenon with rigid/diffuse couples. As in Don's case, rigid partners often have a difficult time remembering problems in their family, stating that their parents did the best they could and only wanted what was best for their children. A continuation of that position is reflected in their adult romantic partnerships, such as when the rigid partner criticizes the other partner's behavior because "I only want what's best for him/her." The diffuse partner is seeking understanding from the rigid partner; the rigid partner just wants things fixed, and fixed right.

Although the Couples Dialogue and other Imago processes could have helped this couple, Don and Bonnie did not seem fully satisfied. Don's lack of emotional connection to Bonnie left her thirsty for his understanding. Don continued to wonder why Bonnie had to hang on to her feelings, why she could not just get over them quickly. After all, he pointed out, he was listening to her more when they dialogued. Because of all this, he could not commit to marrying her. He wondered, as before, that although things were better, if they were having problems before getting married, what would happen afterward?

DETERMINING IDENTITY WOUNDS

The Identity Test

To help couples decide whether or not they have identity wounds, ask them to write at the top of a sheet of paper the following sentence stem: "I am a person who . . ." Have them number blank lines from 1 to 10, using the blanks to complete the sentence stem with 10 different sentence endings. Let them know first that they will be sharing their list with people who are important to them, such as family members and friends. When they have completed this task, ask them to respond to the following questions:

- Was this was a very difficult task for you? If so, you might have an identity wound.
- Did you think this task was stupid and therefore refused to do it? You might have a wound of shame.
- Did you edit out items that might not be acceptable, or did you worry about what others might think about your list? If so, you might have a shame wound.
- Did you have a difficult time thinking of items that would define yourself? If so, you might have an invisibility wound.
- Did you think no one would be interested in reading your list, or were you overly eager to have someone read your list? If so, you might have an invisibility wound.
- Were you afraid that others would criticize your list? If so, you might have a wound of either shame or invisibility.

It is not the answers themselves but the experiences a person had while responding to this identity test—his or her expectations, anxieties, or struggles—that provide evidence of identity wounds.

The Identity Checklist

Another way for partners to determine whether they have an identity wound is to use the following checklist.

Minimizer—wound of shame

- (a) ____ Fears being shamed, criticized, or dominated
- (b) ____ Tends to be controlling of self and others
- (c) ____ Can be shaming and blaming when feeling distressed
- (d) ____ Tends to be at least a little rigid about things
- (e) ____ Has strong feelings about how things should be

Maximizer—wound of invisibility

- (a) ____ Fears not mattering, not counting
- (b) ____ Wound of invisibility
- (c) ____ Tends at first to be compliant and cooperative

(d) _____ Periodically tends to blame, accuse, criticize
(e) _____ Struggles with self-definition

WOUNDS OF SHAME AND CONTROL—MINIMIZER TYPE

The shame-based person's behaviors are used to reduce fear or to meet unmet needs.

The Fears

The shame-based person is afraid of being wrong. Any suggestion that he or she might be wrong is interpreted as meaning, "If you are wrong, then you are also bad, and if bad, you will be humiliated." Because feeling humiliated is intolerable, to defend against such experiences, the shame-based person will develop rigid boundaries, including an inflexible sense of "rightness."

Likewise, if one is misunderstood, then shame and humiliation can result. The shamed/dominated person often responds angrily to misunderstandings, and in turn, will start shaming and dominating his or her partner.

The shamed/dominated individual may also be very sensitive to control issues in relationships. In this way, he or she is similar to the isolator; therefore, this particular characteristic on its own doesn't necessarily signify an identity wound.

The Desires

For the shamed/dominated person, respect is more important than love. Being respected means that you will not be shamed or controlled. Conversely, if you are not respected, shame and control are constant threats. Consequently, being honest and open about one's own weaknesses or mistakes is very difficult for the shamed/dominated person.

All of this leaves the shamed/dominated person with a deep, although often unarticulated, longing for a fully understanding and accepting partner.

Unconditional acceptance, understanding, and respect are like ointment on the shamed/dominated person's wounds. Unfortunately, this person typically cannot admit to having such needs, because the acknowledgment elicits feelings of vulnerability and unsafety.

What Makes Them Reactive?

It is important to recognize the unconscious triggers that drive the identity-wounded person, minimizer type, into reactivity.

As just discussed, being misunderstood is triggering to the shame-wounded person, because the next step is to be unfairly judged, criticized, and humiliated for being wrong. Imprecise mirroring is also upsetting; it means that the partner does not understand the person or has a false view that is hurtful and shameful. And mirroring imprecisely is exactly what the compliant/diffuse partner will do when in dialogue.

Even friendly teasing can trigger reactivity in the old brain of the shame-wounded partner. When an identity-wounded couple is working on healing their marriage, teasing should be shelved, perhaps forever. The risk of rewounding the shame-wounded partner is just too high.

The fear of the shamed/dominated wounded person is to be blamed, shamed, or controlled. This is part of the reason for his or her attraction to the compliant/diffuse person. When the shamed/dominated partner is able to lead, thus defining what is "true," the risk of being wrong, and thus shamed, is lower. Unfortunately, even their compliant/diffuse partner will periodically lapse into blaming, shaming, and accusing.

After a number of sessions, Don was able to admit that he was "a bit controlling." He went on to say, half facetiously, "But hey, I'm right most of the time. I'm the one with common sense." He arrived at one session with a grin, announcing that he had developed the "Rigid/Diffuse Couples Dialogue." He explained, "Now, when Bonnie says something to me, I mirror her back by saying, 'So what you meant to say was ...' "

Although said in humor, Don's joke gives a good description of the impasse and power struggle of the identity-wounded couple. One thinks for the other. One has a rigid, impermeable self, and the other a vague and uncertain one. One is "always right," whereas the other wonders if he or she will ever be right.

Growth Requirement

There are five basic growth requirements for the identity-wounded person.

Many shamed/dominated partners have a profound self-hatred, one that remains unacknowledged until the couple has been in therapy for a while. Self-acceptance is, therefore, a primary requirement. In the early phases of therapy, psychoeducation, modeling, and some self-disclosure by the therapist are helpful in engendering such self-acceptance.

The shame-wounded person must also eventually begin to work on control issues, learning especially to distinguish between personal power and control power. When partners fear being controlled, they might, ironically, use control as self-protection. They first control themselves by denying any weaknesses and suppressing unacceptable thoughts and impulses. Later they will extend this by controlling others, believing that a compliant world is a safe world. Letting go of control and acknowledging the validity of another's position activates deep anxiety, which can be reduced if the rigid partner refuses to give up control. The therapeutic goal is to understand that not allowing oneself to be defined by another is quite different from needing to control and define others.

The rigid partner must learn that validating the other means seeing the gray areas in thinking and feeling—a necessary step toward self-acceptance and wholeness. Being married to a diffuse person provides ample opportunities to practice seeing the gray areas. It also presents a major growth challenge to the rigid partner.

In the dialogue process, mirroring will be fairly easy, but validation and empathy are much more challenging for shamed/dominated partners. Validation demands letting go of a rigid self-defined belief system and acknowledging the legitimacy of what the partner thinks, believes, and feels. Another major stretch is the development of empathy. The self-absorption required to maintain a rigid world view is challenged by the practice of empathy. It is particularly difficult for rigid partners to express empathy, given that they have little tolerance for the feelings with which they are being asked to empathize. However, at the very least, the dialogue should appeal to the shamed/dominated person, as it offers a structure for handling and controlling the complexities of communication.

Being a minimizer, the shame-wounded person will resist expressing his or her needs. Initially, such persons will focus on complaining about the imperfections of their partners; this is acceptable as long as they stay within the dialogue structure. However, the therapist should begin to move them toward talking about their own personal concerns, particularly about what they need from their partners—no matter how small or insignificant such things might seem.

DON SWEATS OVER CHANGE

Dialogue can be very difficult for the shame-wounded rigid partner, for whom listening to the partner's frustration is akin to walking through fire. Shame can be reignited if the person is not adequately prepared for the dialogue.

Don and Bonnie brought up an incident in which the two had been socializing with some of Don's business friends; Don huddled with his business buddies, and Bonnie felt abandoned. Don could clearly see that Bonnie was hurt about this, but he could not feel much empathy. "It's business. It's what guys do," he stated. They were asked to dialogue about this.

> **Therapist:** *Don, would you be willing to listen to Bonnie's frustration about this?*
> **Don:** *I'll try, but this is really hard for me. Give me a minute to get myself together. (He was quiet for a minute.) You may not believe this, but I'm so nervous that my hands are sweating.*
> **Therapist:** *Don, you know, I can understand that, for you, this must be like stepping into hell. I can imagine that you are very nervous about this. Who would willingly do what you are about to do? My bet is that it taps into some sort of shameful feelings for you.*
> **Don:** *I think you hit the nail right on the head. That's exactly it: it feels like shame. You know, I had this dad who was really tough on me and expected me to be right all the time. Talking about this stuff with Bonnie and hearing her complain about me makes me feel like I'm the wrong one, and it makes me feel the same way I felt with my dad.*
> **Therapist:** *That makes sense. And as you go to your safe place, remind yourself that Bonnie is not your father and that you are not going to die as a result of her words. What she is going to say is not about shame, but about something that she needs from you. Can you settle for that?*
> **Don:** *Yeah, I'll give it my best. I'm ready.*
> **Bonnie:** *I get really upset when we are with your business friends for a social evening, and the men separate to one area of the room. It feels like you don't even know I'm there, and I'm more of a burden to you than someone you want to be with.*

Don (mirrors):   *Did I get that? Is there more?*

Bonnie: *Yeah, I know it does not bother the other women as much, but I feel very much alone when that happens. It's like no one sees me, and I wonder why I am there.*

Don (mirrors):   *Did I get that? Is there more?*

Therapist: *And what that reminds me of when I was a kid . . .*

Bonnie (tearfully):   *We would go to my aunt's house and my mom and dad would start talking to the adults and my sisters and cousins would start playing together, and I would be by myself. No one would notice me. It was like I wasn't there. No one bothered to make contact with me. It was like I was paralyzed. Also, at home, when my mother was having her fits and being verbally abusive, my father did not do a thing. He just sat there, drunk. It was like we didn't matter. (Crying) He could have done something. We were just kids and we felt so alone.*

Don (mirrors):   *So it felt like your father could have done something. You were kids and you felt so alone.*

Therapist: *Don, can you validate what Bonnie just said?*

Don: *Yeah, it makes sense to me that . . . (Don starts to cry) It makes sense to me that you would feel all alone and like no one saw you. (Crying) It makes sense that you would have wanted your father to protect you from the abuse you were receiving.*

Therapist: *And I imagine that would make you feel . . .*

Don: *I would imagine that would make you feel vulnerable, invisible, and scared.*

Bonnie: *I really feel like you got the empathy part just right this time.*

Therapist: *Great. Don, I was wondering if your tears were about your shame, or about how you were feeling about what Bonnie was saying?*

Don: *It was about what she was saying. It hit me that I've never waited long enough to hear her. I don't know if I have ever really gotten to validation. I can see how important it is, but I've never felt safe enough to do it. And when I did it just now, I could feel her pain.*

Bonnie: *Thank you, Don. That felt good. I'm really proud of you.*

For a few moments, Don experienced empathy for Bonnie. He was very touched by her story and could see how his behavior triggered her old wounds. Even though it was not his intention to abandon her at parties, his action reactivated the emotional baggage Bonnie has been carrying with her since childhood.

Bonnie made several Behavior Change Requests involving Don's showing her more attention. His experience of empathy gave him the fuel he needed to work on granting her requests.

WOUNDS OF INVISIBILITY AND INVASION—MAXIMIZER TYPE

The partner of the shamed/dominated person is typically a person who has experienced significant neglect during childhood. This is particularly damaging to a child who is going through the identity phase. We will see, once again, that the reduction of anxiety and the meeting of unmet needs are major motivations for this person, just as they are for the shamed/dominated partner.

One of the basic unmet needs for the invisibility-wounded person is being important, making an impact, and mattering to others. Such persons especially long to be important to their partners. Unfortunately, they have learned to be important by adapting, cooperating, and being compliant. This makes them feel accepted, but at a high cost: giving up a large part of their own identity.

Related to the need for importance is a deep longing to be given special attention and consideration. Diffuse partners' complaints often focus on times that the other partner did not look at them, never directed his or her attention to them, or never asked their opinion. Being noticed, included, and considered, even in minor ways, is tremendously healing to the invisibility-wounded person.

Rigid/diffuse partners are similar in their overwhelming need for respect—having their ideas, opinions, and thoughts seen as legitimate and of importance. This is where the validation step in the dialogue process becomes essential. The first time Don said to Bonnie, "That makes sense," Bonnie replied, "Really? Do you mean that?" Tears welled up in her eyes. Don was greatly surprised by this.

What Makes Them Reactive?

Feeling ignored is a chronic trigger for the invisibility-wounded partner. The rigid partner is highly self-absorbed and thus often oblivious to the nuances of paying attention to the diffuse partner. When the rigid partner focuses on other people or things, such as work or hobbies, the invisibility-wounded partner feels diminished and unimportant—regardless of the rigid partner's benign intentions. For example, one day, after arriving at the airport following a business trip, Don called his office before calling Bonnie. Bonnie was devastated, interpreting this as solid proof that work was more important to Don than she was.

If the opinions of the diffuse partner are not solicited and honored, he or she will feel dismissed. But because the rigid partner doesn't naturally seek input from the diffuse partner, the invisibility-wounded partner will frequently have feelings of being overlooked, invalidated, and dismissed.

Growth Requirements

Because their selves have not fully developed, invisibility-wounded persons have difficulty defining who they are, what they think, and what they want. They tend to use global and tentative language, and their diffuseness becomes manifest in their difficulty with separating their own opinions from those of others. For example, Bonnie would use the word "we" when talking about her own beliefs: "We believe it is important to be involved in church." To mirror this type of communication can be difficult for the rigid partner.

Likewise, the diffuse partner can have tremendous difficulty mirroring the more precise and powerfully stated opinions of the rigid partner, as the following exchange demonstrates.

> **Don:** *I'm concerned about your going to school, because then you'd be working less, and we need the money right now to stay on track for retirement.*
> **Bonnie (mirroring):** *We don't have the money for me to go to school.*
> **Don:** *No, I didn't say that. We have the money, but it would be a major setback, as far as reaching our retirement goals is concerned.*
> **Bonnie:** *Let me see if I'm getting it. We have the money, but you don't want to spend it on my going to school.*
> **Don:** *I didn't say that. I wouldn't mind spending it on school, but it just isn't a wise thing for us right now.*

The dialogue ended with Bonnie's using "convex mirroring," that is, adding her own meaning to what Don was saying. This illustrates both the difficulty with containment and the diffuse partner's tendency to blame and accuse when frustrated. Invisibility-wounded partners, as maximizers, have to channel their impulses to deflect or subtract from their partners' messages.

Because his or her psychological boundaries were neither clearly developed nor respected in childhood, the invisibility-wounded person often has difficulty seeing and respecting another's boundaries or limits. For example, such a person might resist staying on an agreed-upon budget, staying in the receiver role in the dialogue process, or following through on plans.

THE POWER STRUGGLE

Initially, the shamed/dominated and invisibility-wounded partners work together fairly well. The partner with the invisibility wound complies with the rigid partner's controlling behavior. But eventually, the balance breaks down, and the maximizing partner explodes with blaming and accusing, rage and resistance. This, in turn, activates the minimizer's shame, leading to a horrendous playing out of the couple's core scene, or a "relationship nightmare." The crisis is typically resolved when the maximizer apologizes and once again complies. The equilibrium is temporarily restored, and the relationship continues until the minimizer has another eruption of blaming and shaming.

DON AND BONNIE'S BIG MOVE

Although Don still hesitated to make a commitment, he now wanted nothing more than to have Bonnie move in with him. He had it all figured out. "You can sell your house and most of your furniture. If you have things you really want to keep, I'll rent you a storage area, and maybe, when my furniture gets old, we can use your stuff. This would save you $1,000 a month on your mortgage, and we'd save money on furniture later on. Makes perfect sense to me! What do you say?"

Bonnie was confused and angry. Although it made sense, it did not feel right. She felt a surge of rebellion. "I'd need to think about it," she replied. Don looked stunned. "What is there to think about?" he shot back. " I did all the math, and this makes the most sense for us." They proceeded to have a fight, which they brought with them into the next session.

After the couple related the triggering event, the therapist turned to Don.

> **Therapist:** *In a few minutes, I'm going to ask you to listen to Bonnie in dialogue. But first I want to tell you that I can see how Bonnie's reaction triggered you. You know that we have discussed your rigidity and need to control. Here is a good example of how that comes through: how difficult it is for you to have your ideas questioned and to not be in control. You know that your idea makes sense logically. But I would like to see you make some room for Bonnie's feelings about the idea. Feelings are not always logical, but they are important. Would you be willing to listen to Bonnie's feelings for a few minutes?*

Don: *This seems stupid to me because I know my idea makes the most sense. But I'll give it a try, anyway. (Don takes a minute to center himself.) Okay, I'm ready to hear you now.*

Bonnie: *I get really anxious when you throw ideas at me so fast and then expect me to agree with you.*

Don (mirrors):   *Did I get that? Is there more?*

Bonnie: *Yes. I have a feeling that something isn't right about this idea, but I can't come up with the words to describe it. I get scared and tongue-tied around you. I know I am going to set you off, and I'm afraid you'll say that my feelings aren't legitimate.*

Don (mirrors):   *Did I get that? Is there more?*

Bonnie: *It reminds me of when I was a child. I was an artist, and I would draw the way I felt. But that did not matter in my family. They did not see me or my artwork as important.*

Don (mirrors):   *Did I get that? Is there more?*

Bonnie: *My home now is like my pictures; it's a reflection of me. I know that you have a bigger house and that it would make sense for me to move there, but I need to know that I will be able to express who I am in my home. I cannot be invisible. I need to have a presence.*

Don (mirrors):   *It makes sense to me that you need to have a presence in your home, because you did not have one in your family. I imagine you felt invisible then, and that my trying to rush you into this decision makes you feel like you don't have any voice or any importance in it.*

Bonnie: *Yes.*

Therapist: *Great, Don. I can see how you really stretched to see this the way Bonnie sees it. Would you be willing to stretch a little more and let Bonnie come up with a few Behavior Change Requests?*

Don: *I think so.*

Bonnie: *Well, my desire is to have my thoughts and feelings taken seriously in this relationship. So my first request would be that, twice this month, when you plan on making a decision that will affect both of us, you say to me something like, "I want to get your input about something that we need to make a decision on."*

Don (mirrors):   *Did I get that?*

Bonnie: *Yes. My second request would be that we talk about my selling my house. I'd like to talk about this for maybe an hour each week, over the next month. I want to use the dialogue process and have you give me the time I need to come up with my own ideas and tell you them. I want to be sure you hear my ideas and that you validate them, no matter how stupid you think they are.*

Don (laughing):   *So for one hour each week, you want me to listen to you while you talk about selling your house. And you want me to mirror*

and validate your thoughts and feelings about this, no matter how stupid
I might think the ideas are. Did I get that?
Bonnie (laughing): *You actually did!*
Therapist (to Bonnie): *And if you did that, Don, it would begin to heal*
my wound of . . .
Bonnie: *Don, if you did that, it would begin to heal my wound of feeling*
invisible and not having my opinions count. And I would feel better about
doing things my own way, like the artist that I am.
Don (mirrors): *You know, that makes sense. After all, you are an artist.*

THE RIGID/DIFFUSE COUPLE'S HEALING PROCESS

Generally, healing of childhood wounds occurs in two ways: (1) getting needs
that were not met in childhood met now, and (2) when reexperiencing the pain of
childhood wounds, getting now what you didn't get then. The latter calls for an
empathic person who mirrors, validates, comforts, and loves us as we go through
the painful reexperiencing.

Healing Shame Wounds

Accurate, Precise Mirroring. Because the rigid partner usually marries a
person with unclear boundaries, when learning the dialogue, the person will often
get overly global or abstract mirroring. This triggers fear that the diffuse partner is
becoming critical, which makes the rigid partner feel anxious, rather than safe. The
rigid partner will then grow impatient with the inaccuracy of the diffuse partner,
which shifts the anticipated criticism from oneself to the partner. Therefore, it
is crucial that these couples learn to mirror accurately and precisely. When rigid
partners receive such mirroring, their fear of being wrongly perceived and shamed
or put down or made wrong is relieved.

Validation. Validation is especially important to the shame-wounded person, especially as he or she begins to express more vulnerability and to reveal
weaknesses. The wise partner will carefully validate the shame-wounded person's
thoughts and feelings, taking particular care to avoid triggering further feelings of
shame.

Deep Appreciation of the Breadth of Human Experience. Shame-based
persons often feel that their personal thoughts, needs, desires, fantasies, and

impulses are unacceptable to others. Therefore, they need to get the message that their ideas are not warped, unusual, or shameful in any way.

Respect at the Moment of Vulnerability. Particularly at moments of great vulnerability, such as when their anger turns to sadness and grief, shame-wounded persons need gentle mirroring of their feelings.

Appreciation. Everyone needs appreciation for what they do. Because shame-wounded persons feel they have received more than their fair share of criticism, they need to be flooded with appreciation. Criticism might have caused the shamed person to deny his or her need for such appreciation. Even if the partner responds with a shrug or a complaint of feeling patronized, appreciation should be expressed anyway. The rigid partner will, sooner or later, learn to enjoy it.

Avoiding Blaming, Accusing, Criticizing. Even constructive criticism can elicit reactivity in the shamed-based person. The best way to approach a rigid partner is to make requests that are positive, specific, measurable, and achievable.

Healing Invisibility

During childhood, people with an invisibility wound were deprived of (1) an interested person who paid close attention to them, (2) respect for their emerging self, and (3) understanding of their pain. In romantic relationships, then, invisibility-wounded partners need to receive all of the above reliably, consistently, and over an extended time.

Attending Behavior. Attending behavior means paying deliberate and thoughtful attention to another, for example, asking how the day went, if the partner would like a drink, or simply, "How are you doing?" These are the kinds of behaviors that help to heal the wound of invisibility.

Validation. When the compliant diffuser starts expressing opinions, feelings, desires, and so forth, it is vital that his or her partner mirror and, especially, validate those expressions. Although one might disagree with what the diffuse partner is stating, it is extremely important to recognize and validate his or her internal logic. This gives the message, "Your ideas are important. You count. You matter to me."

Remembering. The act of simply remembering and acting on something that the diffuse partner has expressed—such as something needed, desired, wished for, or enjoyed—is healing to the person with an invisibility wound. For example, his or her partner might come home with a loaf of freshly baked bread and say, "I knew you liked that rye bread from the corner deli, because you always order it when we have lunch there."

Valuing. The invisibility-wounded person feels devalued; to that person, his or her ideas, opinions, and needs seem either not seen or not valued by others. Such persons need their partners to acknowledge the value of their contributions to the partnership and to the world.

Asking Opinions and Validating Ideas. "What do you think about this?" "I'd like your input on this." "I started to buy a new suit, but I wanted your opinion before I did." These are statements that will deeply please the person with an invisibility wound, as they acknowledge the importance of the person's thoughts and opinions.

Questions That Show Conscious Attending. These include such questions as: "What can I do to make you feel loved and cared about?" "Where would you like us to go to dinner tonight?" "What would you like to do on your birthday?" "What's the first thing you'd like to have happen when you come home from work?" These show an attitude of special consideration and caring.

DON AND BONNIE: THE BURIED TREASURE

Although Don and Bonnie have worked hard on their relationship using the Imago processes, like many couples, they often revert to their old ways. Sometimes Bonnie allows Don to make decisions in which she doesn't have a voice. She sometimes still feels invisible to him. However, she now lets him know her feelings, and she often interjects her opinions, whether Don likes it or not. Once Bonnie got a taste of what it was like to have a strong but flexible sense of self, she rarely looked back. As she became more confident, her business flourished even more.

For his part, Don learned to dialogue with Bonnie and began to understand that Bonnie and others often see things differently than he does. He still becomes anxious when he hears Bonnie saying something he doesn't like or agree with, but he tries to avoid reacting out of his anxiety. He is working on seeing her differentness not as a threat, but as an adventure.

Don and Bonnie are finding their authentic selves through their relationship. Once they began to let go of who they had become in childhood, each discovered a self that was more clearly identified than the one he or she had created. They now like themselves, and their relationship, much better.

EDITORS' COMMENTARY

As children build an identity, they struggle to strike a balance between closeness and distance with their caretakers. Moving from infancy to early childhood, a child's need for physical holding subsides, but something equally crucial must replace it to facilitate the child's self-development. Brainert and Luquet propose mirroring as that next developmental prerequisite.

Because language skills are now in place, the identity stage is the first point in the developmental process at which the child understands verbal mirroring. During the attachment and exploratory stages, the child's connection with caretakers is built on the touch, voice tone, and other nonverbal behaviors of the parent. In the identity stage, that connection is based on spoken language. If, through mirroring, children are encouraged to explore all aspects of their identity, they will eventually feel courageous enough to accept all of the complementary aspects of their being—their "acceptable" and "unacceptable" parts, their real and imagined selves, their masculine and feminine sides—and to integrate these parts into the developing self. If they hear shaming messages, they develop a rigid and limited self, acknowledging certain aspects of identity and rejecting the others. If messages are absent altogether, children develop a diffuse self, resigning themselves to having no identity at all.

When identity-wounded children become romantic partners, their defensive adaptations actually mesh very well, as evidenced by the prevalence of role-based marriages in our culture. If the diffuse partner can tolerate living with a diminished sense of self, the couple might never develop a level of conflict that would lead them to a therapist's office. But often a diffuse partner will grow dissatisfied with living in the shadow of a rigid partner, and eventually, will begin to demand a say and a place in the relationship. Likewise, sooner or later, many rigid partners grow bored with a relationship in which they feel no impact, touch, or connection coming from their appeasing partner.

Rigid partners like Don have to learn to tolerate the anxiety of not always being in control. What better teacher than a partner who has lived with a chronic feeling of being out of control! Rigid partners also must accept the possibility of being "wrong." Again, a humble and sensitive partner, with an abundance of experience in being "wrong," is just the type of person with whom the rigid person can open up and become vulnerable.

Bonnie, as are other diffuse partners, is on a quest to find a self. Who would be a better companion for this journey than a partner like Don, with his definite opinions and strong sense of selfhood? Like all Imago matches, Don and Bonnie fit together perfectly, each filling in the developmental gaps of the other. They are each other's lost self, and so are a major source of the other's healing and wholeness.

Chapter 5

THERAPIST, HEAL THYSELF: A PASSIVE/COMPETITIVE COUPLE

Mo Therese Hannah

Whenever I begin couples therapy with a couple in which one or both partners are psychotherapists, I get ready to stretch, both professionally and personally. Contrary to what might seem like common sense, therapists are not the easiest clients to work with; most of us are, as Mom used to say, too smart for our own good. What I hear from the therapists with whom I work is similar, I suppose, to what medical doctors hear from the physicians they treat: "Yes, Doctor; I already know that, Doctor." I myself am in a romantic partnership with another therapist; I'm well aware of the demands we place on the therapists who are foolish enough to work with us on our marital dilemmas. I know Imago work is supposed to awaken empathy for my partner, but during most therapy sessions in which my partner and I are the clients, the person I feel the deepest empathy for is not my partner, but our therapist. I'd hate to work with us. Further, my therapist-clients, having read many of the same books and taken the same therapy training that I have, know the same therapeutic maneuvers I do. Some are better at using their clinical savvy to thwart the therapy process than I am at helping their relationship. Complicating matters is the well-known fact that therapists are high in reactance, in resisting external influence or direction from others, including other therapists. Finally, in my experience, couples containing at least one therapist or other helping professional often present as a passive/competitive partnership. In this duo, both partners have unresolved conflicts lingering from the fourth childhood developmental stage of competence. And each adapted to his or her wounding at this stage in opposite ways.

SAM AND JESSICA'S EARLY HISTORY

I wasn't thrilled, therefore, to discover that Sam and Jessica were both therapists; in fact, Jessica was a couples therapist. Hearing this, I vowed fervently to take the therapeutic stance that moves couples the fastest and the furthest, whatever their idiosyncrasies. This involves showing unremitting empathy, keeping the process simple, and trusting in the power of dialogue. I reminded myself of what I tell couples who've become lost in a maze of mutual negative projection: when you fall out of dialogue, return to the dialogue. I hadn't yet found a relationship knot that couldn't be loosened as long as the couple remained in dialogue, and I mean not merely the technique of dialogue, but also its essential attitude, a "willingness to be touched by being in contact with the other."

After my first couple of sessions with Sam and Jessica, my therapeutic hubris ebbing away, I was convinced that, before we got started, the two must have made an exhaustive list of all the possible strategies a therapist might use to help them change their relationship—and then had written "No, we won't" across each item.

I soon became aware that Sam and Jessica's partnership was a complex pattern of similarities and polarities. They were in their 20th year of marriage; both were now in their early 40s. Their two children, a boy and a girl, were young, the older in second grade and the younger still a preschooler. The two of them radiated intelligence—the down-to-earth savvy of people who understand other people. Jessica had a Ph.D. degree from a well-known research university; Sam had two masters' degrees, one in counseling and the other in acting and directing. Jessica was a psychologist with a successful therapy practice, which included a substantial number of couples. Although she hadn't been trained in Imago therapy, she'd read *Getting the Love You Want* (1988) by Harville Hendrix and had been struck by the similarities between its description of the "power struggle" and her relationship with Sam.

Some would call Sam a renaissance man: he was a trained actor, a trained counselor, a partially trained salesperson, and an untrained composer and musician. When I asked him how he made a living, Jessica immediately interjected, "He doesn't." I let the comment go, promising myself that we'd work on this sort of thing later. Sam also ignored her comment, stating, "I do a little of a lot of different things."

Jessica had been one of eight children, with both older and younger siblings. When I asked which parent had made the greatest impact on her, she didn't hesitate: "My father. He was a genius." "Any more about that?" I asked. "Well, he was a very complex person. Critical, demanding, unreasonable, passionate. He drove me nuts, but he was my model." She paused, then continued. "He was a therapist, as well. A marriage counselor. How Freudian, huh?" Jessica's mother stayed at home to raise the children. She never drove, never worked outside the home, and never demanded much from Jessica's father or, in fact, from anybody. She was even-tempered, serene—the opposite of Jessica's father. Jessica described her mom this way: "Remember Edith Bunker, Archie's wife in *All in the Family*? That's my mother." Sam added, "We nicknamed her 'pillow.' Soft and warm. She's a saint." What was Jessica's strongest memory of growing up? "I remember my mom's sleeping a lot. When I'd look for her, I'd find her in bed. She always seemed to be exhausted. Probably from dealing with my dad and us kids!" I asked her to describe her family of origin. "Well . . . loud, Catholic, and chaotic. Everyone competing with everyone else—whoever screamed the loudest got their fair share."

Sam, was a year younger than his sister, his only sibling. His father, a CPA, worked as a college comptroller; his mother stayed at home. Which parent had made the greatest impact on Sam? "Neither," Sam responded. "My dad was a great guy," he added. "Still is. Perfect gentleman. But I can't say my dad and I interacted very much. He played with me some, but mainly he just sort of let me be. I don't remember his doing much with me. I don't even remember his ever yelling at me. In fact, I think I saw him mad maybe once the entire time I was growing up. He was very mellow." His mom? "Oh, that's different. She was intense, emotional, moody . . . critical, sometimes." Sam added, "She was totally into me, till I was a teenager and started sleeping with girls." How would Sam describe his family? "Sort of like Ozzie and Harriet. Dad went to work; Mom stayed home. My mom would get mad, and my dad would just ignore her. Typical gender-role stuff, I guess."

During the couple's first years together, as Jessica put it, she and Sam were "post-hippie flower children" who'd always been more interested in helping humanity than in making a fortune. They were the "spiritual type." After their youthful meandering through a smorgasbord of "lunatic fringe" religious alternatives, they'd settled on the Catholicism with which Jessica had grown up. "Catholicism was one of the saner religions we'd come across," Sam commented.

Jessica's next comment followed on the heels of Sam's. "The problem is, now we have two kids, two college tuitions coming up, two retirements to save for, two car payments, one mortgage, and loads of other bills," "I've changed my life," she said, more loudly, "because of what all that means. It means you have to grow up. Sam hasn't. That's our biggest problem. That's our only problem." Sam muttered a comment; I didn't catch it.

Work, money, and responsibilities—the issues I'd been expecting to emerge. I hypothesized that Jessica was projecting her lost childlike self onto Sam, who'd still maintained his own childlike characteristics. Maybe Sam had been wounded during the identity or competence stage by parents who paid too little or too much attention to his emerging sense of self. Maybe Jessica now acts *in loco parentis* to Sam. This is not an uncommon pattern among couples. It's also not an easy one to work with.

For the first few years that they were married, Sam and Jessica had "no kids and lots of fun. We lived simply; what was really important to us was to change our corner of the world." Sam agreed that during the early years of their relationship, "neither of us gave a damn about money, owning things, status, any of that stuff. We just lived off our love."

Their mutual interest in working with disadvantaged groups eventually led to full-time jobs in group homes for children with emotional and behavioral problems. Sam recalled, "At the time, I don't think I knew what I was doing. I wasn't even sure I'd survive the experience." "But," Jessica pointed out to him, "We stuck it out longer than any other couple there. I was better at all the paperwork; you were really good with the kids. I was stricter; you were the more lenient one. I thought we balanced each other perfectly." "Yeah, but believe me, I'd never do that again," Sam said.

Both Sam and Jessica demonstrated positive features of personal development: interpersonal attachment, personal autonomy, a sense of identity, and competence. They had been able to work together cooperatively, despite the difference in their approaches. They had shown respect for each other's strengths. At such an early point in their relationship, however, it's possible that romance was overruling reality. The couple's complementarities, their polar opposite characteristics, were as real then as they were at present. But back then, the couple was still in the grip of mutual positive projection.

Both partners had finished their bachelors' degrees after they'd met and about a year before they were married. Sam's was in theatre, Jessica's in psychology. Sam had won accolades for his undergraduate stage work, although his grades in all other subjects were less noteworthy (" 'gentlemen's Bs and Cs,' " Jessica scoffed). But Sam's interest in the stage soon faded. "There was too much competition in the acting world; I didn't want to get caught up in that scene. It was one thing to act in college, but another to compete for roles with hundreds of other people. Plus, at the time, I wanted to help people, not spend all my time memorizing lines. I didn't have any need to prove myself. That's not what I was into."

Jessica had earned her bachelor's degree summa cum laude. "I couldn't stand getting anything less than an A, and I almost never did," she related. "But it's not like my grades came automatically. It's not like I'm all that smart. I killed myself to get straight As. I just can't settle for anything less than best, and not just in school—in anything I do." "Or in anything I do, either," Sam added, then directed his next comment to me. "Now, there's one of our problems."

By the time our first session ended, I'd honed in on a theme: both partners are invested in what they do; it's how they invest in what they do that's different. Jessica's self-esteem hinges on meeting academic and career goals; she needs tangible accomplishments to feel she matters to the world. While she was growing up, her self-worth came from pleasing her parents, by getting good grades and doing other things of which adults approve. I concluded that Jessica had always been at the top of the heap and gained her sense of competence by doing what others expected of her, and doing it well.

Sam, on the other hand, does his own thing—a dated phrase, but one that fits him. While Jessica was walking at full speed down the straight and narrow road to success, Sam was strolling down a less-traveled path, a scenic route. While other men his age were going to the office, Sam was working on becoming a better person, developing his spirituality and serving humanity. He had no need to prove anything or to be anybody; he was content with who he was.

This type of difference between partners' goal orientations might not matter much when they're young, but as they grow older, especially as they move past the intimacy stage of early adulthood and into generativity, where they focus on creating careers and a family, how partners express generativity can lead to major conflict. Sam and Jessica's power struggle emerged, therefore, pretty much on schedule.

ENTER THE POWER STRUGGLE

Despite their solid school records, neither had made plans to pursue an advanced degree. "Actually," Jessica reflected, "I did consider going to graduate school right after I'd finished my bachelor's. It hit me how much I'd be limiting myself with just a B.A. in psychology. But I wasn't ready to jump back into school. I was in love, and all I wanted was to spend time with Sam." Since both partners liked working with children, but didn't like the poor pay, they agreed to look for better opportunities. Jessica discovered that a master's-level counseling degree would open the door to more lucrative positions in the mental health field. "Money wasn't that important to us, but I figured, why not do some good and make better money at the same time?" Sam had no objections, so they moved east to begin graduate studies.

While they were working on their masters' degrees, Sam and Jessica bought a house in the East Coast town where they were studying and building their private counseling practice. Later, they would agree that this was one of the happiest phases of their marriage: "For a while there, we operated like two sides of the same brain," Jessica observed. "We studied together, worked together, played music together, traveled together—we did everything together." She looked pensive. "We really enjoyed being together back then." "Boy," Sam said, "how did we manage to get along so well, when life was so demanding—getting our masters' degrees, working all week, building a private practice ... how did we do it?" "Are you kidding?" Jessica answered. "Life was easy back then, a piece of cake. We had only one job each and no kids."

Here was a glimpse of Sam and Jessica's tendency to polarize each other, a tendency that emerged before the overt fighting began. We see this, for example, in the push-and-pull nature of how they handled their work imbalance in their private practices. The more clients Jessica accepted, the fewer Sam did. Evidently, Jessica was too much in love and too busy seeing clients to notice.

The couple did have a relatively long romantic phase, which was helped by their remaining childless for the first 10 years of their marriage. Jessica recalled thinking of Sam as "my other half, the male version of me, incredibly gentle and artistic." Sam's feelings were similarly rosy: "She was the ideal woman; she was both soft and strong. I'd never met a woman with such power and energy."

In the early phases of their relationship, they managed to cooperate, instead of compete, in making major decisions, such as where to live and work and how to progress along their career paths. This collaborative spirit helped them build the trust they needed to work together during those early years. The couple was able to stay out of the power struggle both because they had no children and because they were still "playing at" their work. Money and career weren't yet primary issues; the couple was still focused on developing intimacy. It's when building a career and raising children became important concerns that the passive/competitive tug-of-war is likely to be activated.

Another manifestation of cooperation was their mutual decision to postpone having children. "Our attitude was, let's have kids later, if we feel like it; there's plenty of time for that," Sam said. Jessica agreed: "We were happy with our life the way it was. At that point, we weren't even sure we wanted kids. Every time my mother or my sisters asked me when Sam and I were going to 'get started,' I'd say, 'Don't worry, we will.' It got pretty annoying, with everyone dropping hints about how we were getting older. It was no one else's business but ours. But, thinking back on it, even though we'd decided together to put off having kids, I think I was scared of the idea. I wasn't sure I'd make a good mother. I wasn't too crazy about how I'd been raised. My parents did their best, but I was still carrying a lot of pain from my childhood. I got completely lost in my family when I was growing up. My parents just didn't have the time or energy or patience for all of us kids. Would I have time for my kids? I didn't want to repeat history."

Jessica's family, dominated by a distancing and high-achieving father, lived by the philosophy that all that counts in life is what you do. No one deserves validation merely because of who they are; what matters is what you accomplish. As a child, Jessica concluded that the only way to get noticed in her family, to emotionally survive being a member of that family, was to do more than the others and to do it better. This adaptation worked well for her; it won Jessica, first, her father's acclamations, and later, the world's validation. She evolved into a prototypical doer, a Type A personality who does many things at once, does them well, and, when they're done, looks for something else to do. Should Jessica not find something more—should she be called on simply to be in the world instead of doing something in it—she would become anxious. And it would be Sam, her nonambitious Imago match, who would come to exemplify and mirror that anxiety.

Sam's reasons for remaining childless were more pragmatic. "I wasn't worried about making a good parent, like Jessica was. I'd always loved kids and got along great with them. But I liked the way our life was going, with just the two of us. And, well, maybe I wasn't looking all that forward to the responsibility of having a family, either."

"Sam," Jessica observed, "I think our problems started back then. You remember, when we were in practice, I was always the one to take on more clients. Because you didn't think we needed more money, because you wouldn't take on any more work than you wanted to, I would have to do more. Before then, I think we used to see eye-to-eye about your work and my work." "I don't remember us ever seeing eye-to-eye on that," Sam replied.

I'd come to realize that, for Sam, life is like a table spread with the fruits of one's labors. As the younger child in a two-child family and as heir to his father's, grandfather's, great-grandfather's, and great-great grandfather's name, Sam was honored and cherished for no other reason than the fact that he existed. His upbringing was of the hands-off variety; little was expected of him, there was little pressure on him to produce and, consequently, he didn't need to do much to earn the adoration of his caretakers. Whatever his achievement, whether it was great or small, he was greeted with the same muted enthusiasm. Intelligent, charming, and artistically inclined, Sam had little difficulty earning good grades in school, winning leading roles in school plays, even getting Jessica to fall in love with him. It was only when he was confronted by the adult world, a world that evaluates a person not on the basis of who he or she is, but on the basis of what he or she produces, that Sam's easygoing adaptation stopped working so well. Jessica came to symbolize, to Sam, a world that tested him, criticized him, and found him wanting. As an adult, Sam would deal with his terror of being proved incompetent—the same fear that Jessica had—by avoiding the competence endeavor altogether.

Meanwhile, Jessica was geared up for her next challenge, a doctorate, and not just any doctorate, but one in the fiercely competitive area of clinical psychology, which would give her the most career options. Since there were no doctoral programs within driving distance, the couple would have to move elsewhere. Sam, clearly a "go with the flow" kind of guy, was atypically and adamantly opposed to moving anywhere. He liked their home, their work, and their lifestyle just the way they were. Sam described his reactions to Jessica's plans: "I said, you know, 'Why screw up a good thing? Look at what you've accomplished. Look at what we've accomplished. What's wrong with that? Why does there always have to be more?'" Jessica's response was easy to predict: "Instead of looking at what you've already accomplished, Sam, why don't you look at what you *could* accomplish, with a little more effort?"

This would become a familiar theme in the couple's lives. It was one of those recurring conflicts that Imago therapists refer to as "core scenes." Couples entrenched in the power struggle repeat these arguments, with slight modifications, throughout their relationship and in diverse situations. The metaphor I use is that of a feature film that's just been released. If you go to Boston, that film will be showing in at least one theatre. Go to Cincinnati and you'll find the same movie. Go to Chicago, Minneapolis, or Miami, and you'll find the same picture playing. Different city, different theatre, same film. That's what the core-scene is like. As Imago therapists point out, the content of the core-scene argument is not what the couple is "really" fighting about; they're fighting over the emotional essentials they've felt deprived of by their partner, their caretakers, and other important people in their lives. In the heat of battle, when emotions are high, partners are fighting not just with each other, but with an amalgam of the partner, previous partners, and their parents.

Sam and Jessica's core-scene argument encompassed a lot of unfinished business from their childhoods: Sam's resentment toward his father, who hadn't taught Sam enough about "what men do," like paying bills and balancing checkbooks, and Jessica's fear of being invisible, which made her need to stand out in every crowd; Sam's passive surrender to his competent wife, who, like Sam's mother, communicated silent disapproval when Sam failed a competence test; and Jessica's having received too little nurturing from a loving but emotionally absent, as well as absentminded, mother. Sam and Jessica's core-scene arguments would unfold all these issues before me, in amazing detail.

THE PASSIVE/COMPETITIVE DANCE

I was slowly getting a picture of this couple's passive/competitive dance. Jessica's adaptation to her wounding during the competence stage was that of the maximizer, who thrusts her energy out into the world to convince others, as well as herself, that she is capable. In comparison, Sam's response to his wounding at that stage was the choice of the minimizer: Sam conserved his energy, focusing it internally, and meanwhile resisted the pursuit of the type of competence that the world—and Jessica—recognizes. Similar wounding, complementary adaptations, as Imago therapists say. However, as Imago theory also states, "Both partners are both." In Sam and Jessica's case, this means that the supercompetent Jessica carries within her, although rarely expresses, the passive end of the pole. Likewise, the passively resistant Sam, who always seems to be running many miles behind Jessica, keeps an upper hand by frustrating his partner's attempts to mold him in her image. As I'd see later on, each partner would take a turn or two trying out the defensive behaviors typically used by the other partner.

Characteristically, Sam folded and Jessica proceeded with her plans. The couple moved across the country and settled into the one-bedroom apartment in the building to which Jessica was assigned as a dorm director, a position that would pay the rent plus a small salary. In addition to coursework, she did statistical consulting and taught undergraduate courses. Meanwhile, the only job Sam was able to land was a part-time position in a group home for developmentally disabled adults. It was during that period that Sam had the abundance of free time that would come, in Jessica's mind, to characterize his lifestyle. Sam would wander over to the theatre department's main stage to watch rehearsals. Convinced that he could do the roles better than the actors, his interest in the theatre was reignited. "I thought I'd gotten acting completely out of my system, but once I started to get back into it, all the old feelings came back," Sam reported. "On top of it, I was getting pretty damn tired of doing counseling."

Although he had sworn off returning to school, Sam announced his plans to get an M.F.A. degree in acting/directing. He was surprised when Jessica readily agreed. "I was working my head off at school and work, but at least I was enjoying what I was doing," Jessica said. "I felt guilty that Sam wasn't able to do what he liked, and I was beginning to worry that his career wouldn't amount to much. I was glad he became interested in acting again. I figured that maybe an M.F.A. would open some doors for him, too."

Later, Sam would admit that getting the degree wasn't so much about opening doors as it was about closing the door on a career that he'd begun to see as Jessica's choice, not his. Sam explained, "It's not that I minded counseling. I used to figure that counseling was helping others, and that's what I'd always thought was important. But to be honest, I never thought I was a very good counselor. Jessica was always the one who knew what she was doing; I always felt like I was faking it. But when I was acting, I felt like I knew what I was doing. I felt like myself." "Oh, bull," Jessica countered. "You mean that the only time you feel like yourself is when you're acting? That doesn't make sense." "That's not what I mean," Sam shot back.

Sam was accepted into the M.F.A. program, and while working on this second master's degree, he began to earn local fame for his stage performances. Eventually, a talent agent spotted Sam and helped him land a role in a film being shot in the area. Although he had just one sentence—Sam played a firefighter who ran out of a burning building and proclaimed, "It's an inferno in there"—his first words on film earned him the right to a Screen Actors' Guild (SAG) card, the key to future film acting. Dazzled by the ease of the work and the chance to mingle with the famous (he did movies with Elizabeth Taylor and Val Kilmer), Sam's interest in doing anything else slipped away.

Acting was Sam's chance at a double dose of competence and identity. He could identify himself with well-known people, have his work watched by millions, and have the satisfaction of getting a big paycheck for what was, to Sam, just a little bit of work and a lot of fun.

At that point, Sam was jamming in graduate coursework during the day, stage work at night, and film work in between. Jessica was in her third year of juggling graduate work and various part-time jobs. Then, to their astonishment, they encountered the unthinkable: Jessica was pregnant. Shaken at first, the couple eventually grew excited by the prospect of parenthood. "Sure, it wasn't a good time for us to have a kid. But, hell, no time is a good time to have a kid," Sam pointed out.

Their daughter, Layla, was born inconveniently during the middle of a semester. Jessica delivered the baby at home one afternoon and went grocery shopping the same evening. She took a few weeks off from her classes and jobs, then went back to business as usual. Sam changed a lot of diapers and rocked Layla to sleep every night while Jessica worked on her dissertation proposal. He brought the baby to wherever Mommy's breasts happened to be; Jessica nursed Layla between classes and on her work breaks. Far from being disenchanted with fatherhood, Sam was euphoric. Although not the most organized of parents—the couple sometimes found themselves ready to head out the door, mistakenly assuming that the other had hired a sitter—they managed to parent and finish graduate school at the same time.

They did this so well, in fact, that they planned to have their next child before Jessica would be finished with graduate school, so that the siblings wouldn't be too far apart in age. Their son, Sammy, arrived a few days after Jessica's successful dissertation defense. "Exquisite timing," she related. "I was hugely pregnant, and I used that to milk my dissertation committee for all the sympathy I could get. They couldn't wait to get me out of there. They must've been afraid I'd start labor any minute."

As the couple entered a new phase, parenthood, they enjoyed what seemed to be a brief return to the romantic phase. It was actually a short-lived truce in the power struggle. The birth of their first child engendered hints of the blissful fusion that they'd enjoyed during their romantic phase. But Layla's birth would also trigger the reemergence of the competence issues that had gone underground temporarily, issues that would come back to stay for a long, long time.

Once Sam finished his M.F.A. later that year, he engaged Jessica in the first of a series of hot debates, this one over their next move. Sam felt it was now his turn to steer the family ship and to aim it in the direction he wanted to go. Given that he'd landed some of the juiciest roles on the university stage and, more important, had already broken into the world of film, he was convinced he could make a living as a working actor. The most logical place to go for that was Hollywood. "I wanted nothing else out of life," Sam confessed. "I felt like, finally, here's my chance to be somebody; here's work that I love and that I can do well."

Jessica described her reaction to Sam's "delusion" of Hollywood success: "Do you know what it's like trying to make a living as a film actor? Here's how one of Sam's acting books put it. Imagine you're on a ship with 200 other people; there's only one lifeboat, and it holds four people. The ship is sinking, so 200 people need that one lifeboat. That's how hard it is to get a film role in Hollywood. I was just starting out as a psychologist; I knew I wouldn't be making that great an income for a while. We had two children by the time Sam came up with the idea of trying to support a family by making it in Hollywood!"

I asked Jessica what living in Los Angeles had been like for her. "I hated L.A.," she responded. "To me, the place was nothing but gangs, crime, earthquakes, mudslides, graffiti, traffic jams, crowds, riots, filth, and poverty. And Sam never got an acting job!" "No film acting jobs," Sam corrected her. "That's not unusual for the short time we were there. If we'd have stayed longer, I would have gotten film work."

"So you left," I commented. "Where did you go next?"

Jessica answered, "I wanted to go back to our hometown, like we'd agreed. But Sam wouldn't even consider it. He wanted to leave his acting options open." Sam had said he'd be reasonable; if they weren't going to live in Los Angeles, the premium locale for aspiring actors, he'd be willing to settle for the next best place, New York City. He'd find there more stage work than film work, but at least he'd still be "in the loop."

This battle ended with an additional compromise: they would live close enough to New York City that Sam could get to auditions, but far enough away that they wouldn't be raising their children in another inner-city war zone. Long Island fit the criteria, and they had friends there, so that's where they ended up.

And so it was that, as Jessica was trodding with a vengeance down the road to certain success, Sam persisted in his journey along one of the least likely roads to prosperity, a film-acting career. Meanwhile, the power struggle would heighten and expand with Jessica complaining that she was overworked and unappreciated for all that she did and Sam feeling criticized for what he didn't do and unappreciated for what he did do. The more bitterly Jessica complained, the less attention Sam paid to her complaints.

Sam said, "I thought we had a great setup on Long Island. I could go to auditions in the city; it was only an hour's train ride away. Jessica had a good job." Jessica stared at Sam as though he'd suddenly started speaking Chinese. "I hated that job. A 9-to-5 at a hospital. I only did it so that we could afford to live there." Sam looked abashed and said, "Oh, O.K." Jessica turned to me. "This was getting to be a pattern. It had started in L.A. Sam had to keep his days free, just in case he got an audition. He taught a few acting classes in the evenings, maybe 10 hours a week, tops. Meanwhile, I worked at a full-time day job and did some private practice at night. I was working about 50 hours a week; he was working 10. You see?" she said.

"So," I asked gingerly, "You obviously left Long Island to settle here. How did that happen? Sam?"

Sam looked uneasy. "That was Jessica's call. I would have been happy to stay near New York City. If I'd hung in long enough. . ."

Jessica interrupted him. "Yeah, right. Here I am, with two kids, working 50 hours a week, living on Long Island, one of the most expensive places in the country, trying to keep up with the bills so that Sam could go to auditions. You know, just in case he gets an acting job." Jessica's fury was building fast. "That was when I really began to go over the edge. I wasn't doing what I wanted to do; he was doing what he wanted, and I was paying for it!"

Sam responded, "Well, we moved again, didn't we?" He sounded peeved. "I gave up my hopes and dreams when we moved to where we are now. It's not a bad place to live, but I'm never going to have an acting career here."

"So, leaving L.A. and Long Island must have been hard for you, Sam. It was the end of a dream. What led you to agree to these moves?"

Leaning back in his chair, Sam stared up at the ceiling for a moment. Then he said, "There were a lot of reasons. Jessica was unhappy all the time and blamed me because she was unhappy. I mean, I loved acting, I knew I could make it as an actor, but I'd started to wonder if it was worth it. I heard this report on what air pollution in cities does to little kids' lungs. We had our two kids by then. That finally convinced me: I couldn't do this to my kids."

It was a risky question, but I had to ask it: "Sam, given how Jessica felt about living in these places, how unhappy she was … might you have moved even if you hadn't had kids—just because of Jessica's feelings?"

Sam stared at me for a moment, then shook his head. "That's too hypothetical. I can't answer that."

As though on cue, Jessica exploded. "You see?" She pointed at Sam. "That's the problem! It doesn't matter how I feel about anything. He goes his merry way, living his life in ways that drive me crazy. He acts as though nothing he does affects me. But it does affect me!" I'd seen Jessica angry before, but this was the first time I'd seen her enraged.

THE FIRST DIALOGUE

It was clearly time to move the couple into dialogue. After explaining the three steps of the Couples Dialogue, I asked Sam to mirror back what Jessica said. I asked Jessica to repeat what she'd just said, but to "soften" it by lowering her voice and beginning her statement with "I feel…"

"I feel like I've been living with a stupid idiot for the last 18 years," Jessica sputtered. "Try it this way, Jessica," I coaxed her. "Sam, I feel tremendous frustration when you. . ."

Jessica said nothing. She was seething, looking at the wall. "Would you be willing to make eye contact with one another?" I asked. Sam looked at Jessica; Jessica looked away from Sam. I prompted her, " 'Sam, I feel very frustrated when you. . .'."

"I cannot stand you," Jessica screamed at Sam. "I don't want to live with you anymore! I am tired of living like this!"

There wasn't much else to do than to ask Sam to mirror her back. I reminded him, almost in a whisper, to remain nonreactive. I was relieved when he contained his feelings. "So, you don't want to live with me anymore. You can't stand me, and you're tired of living like this." He spoke calmly. I asked him to say, " 'Is there more?' "

There was more: more words at the same volume. "I have been killing myself to keep you afloat. I worked in L.A. while you were busy not getting acting jobs. I've put up with your irresponsibility for years. I've had it!"

Sam was handling this well. "Is there more?"

"I've had to be the grown-up in this relationship," Jessica immediately shot back. "I've supported this family while you've slept late and taken naps. And then you criticize me for being a 'workaholic.' You force me into being some sort of superwoman, and then make it impossible for me to work less and relax. You take me for granted. I am so tired of it!"

Jessica had begun to cry. Sam again asked, more quietly, "Is there more?"

Jessica was now sobbing. This was the emotional breakthrough, the transition from anger to sadness that Imago therapists wait for. It signals the potential for connection between the partners.

No one said anything for several moments. As Jessica quieted, I cued Sam to ask her again, "Is there more?"

Jessica heaved a sigh. Her voice was much quieter now. She finally looked at Sam. "I'm so tired of being the strong one in this relationship. I'm so tired of feeling unappreciated. I'm tired of your having an easy life while I work my butt off." Sam mirrored this back. He was getting good at this. Jessica continued, "I've been feeling tremendously frustrated by this arrangement of ours. I do the work, and you reap the benefits."

I offered Jessica this sentence stem: "And all of this reminds me of. . ." Jessica looked at me; I asked her to keep her eyes on Sam's. "My father and my mother, of course," she said. "My dad was always working, always complaining about how my mother didn't keep up with the housework, how he had to do everything—go out and earn a living, then come home and do the things she never got done because she was sleeping." Jessica paused. "Now I know how my father felt!" She glared at Sam. "I 've turned into him. And I don't like being him. You've made me become like him." Again Sam mirrored her, and then I offered Jessica another sentence stem: "And what I do to contribute to all of this is. . ." A long silence. Jessica finally said to Sam, "I've turned you into my mother." I gave Jessica one more sentence stem: "And what I'm needing now from you, to help me with all of that, is. . ." Jessica's answer came quickly: "Stop turning me into my father."

Now it was Sam's turn to be the sender. "Sam," I suggested, "Why don't you start with 'what I'm feeling now, listening to you talk about this, is. . .'"

Sam had a bemused smile on his face. "What's the difference what I feel?" he said. "She blames me for all the problems in this relationship. There's nothing I can say to change that." The dynamic had a familiar feel to it: the outspoken maximizer who flings globalizing accusations at the quiet minimizer, who retaliates by refusing to share his feelings with his partner. This time, I did the mirroring. "So you aren't sure, Sam, if there's any point in sharing your feelings with Jessica. You believe she sees you as responsible for everything wrong with your relationship." "That's right," Sam replied. I continued, "And that makes you feel. . ."

I expected Sam's answer to this. "Hopeless," he said. "Like giving up."

"So, Sam," I said gently, "would you be willing to say more about that to Jessica?"

Sam stared impassively at his partner. A long silence. Finally, he started to talk. "For years, I have felt blamed by you just for being who I am." I asked Jessica to begin mirroring him now, hoping to make it safe enough for Sam to continue sharing his feelings. Then Jessica did what maximizers have a tendency to do: she used mirroring as a weapon. Jessica rolled her eyes, turned away from Sam, and said icily, "You think I blame you for being who you are?" I interrupted her. "Jessica, see if you can mirror him with your tone of voice and your body, too." She glumly turned toward Sam. I asked him to go on. He sounded defensive, but the words came more easily. "No matter what I do for you, it's never enough. All you notice is what I don't do, what I haven't done, what I forgot to do. Never what I do!" Jessica stared at Sam silently; I prompted her to mirror him. She did, and asked him if there was more. "I do a lot for this family," Sam continued. "I'm the one who tries to make the house more comfortable for you. I put the pictures up and rearrange the furniture. I keep the kids quiet while you're working. I gave up an acting career so that you could have a more stable life. Can't you see how hard that was for me? I could have made it; I know I could have. But I knew I was asking you for too much." Jessica was mirroring him well now. "I've wanted so much to be someone, to be the person I was meant to be. I have a lot to give. But the world's not set up for me to make a living the way I want to." Sam's voice was pleading now. "Do you know what it's like to live with someone who so easily does the things that are so hard for me? Who I want to please so badly, but can't, because I'm not you. I can't be you!" Jessica's voice was gentle as she mirrored him back. Sam's voice was shaky. "I've given up. Either I become the person you want me to be and deny who I am, or I give up trying to be what you want me to be and get rejected by you. There's no winning with you!" Jessica was right on target: "Is there more about that, Sam?" Sam looked down at the floor. I noticed tears in his eyes. He was quiet for a while. Again Jessica asked him, her tone tender now, "Is there more?" Sam began to cry. "My life is such a mess. . ."

I asked Sam and Jessica if they would be willing to hold each other. Neither resisted; they embraced silently while I savored the last few moments of the session.

A GLIMPSE AHEAD: SESSION EIGHT

The first dialogue had taken place during our third session. We spent several more sessions using the dialogue process to work through the anger, hurt, and frustration that had built up over the couple's years of passive-competitive pushing and pulling. I had to be especially fastidious about adhering to the dialogue structure; Jessica's volatility and Sam's seething resistance seemed about to erupt whenever one partner didn't mirror the other. Over the course of several sessions, however, the emergence of relaxation and trust between the two slowly became palpable. By session eight, the two were regularly making eye contact; both tears and laughter came more easily, and when I'd ask them to engage in high-energy fun after intense dialogues, they no longer responded as though I were asking them to sacrifice their first-born child.

Some Behavior Change Requests (BCRs) were warranted, and we were ready to begin working on these during the eighth session, as well. In this process, the "sender" first gives a brief, one- or two-sentence description of a frustration with the other partner. The description is followed by a statement of how the sender feels about and reacts to the partner's frustrating behavior. Finally, the sender suggests three possible behavior changes and requests that the partner commit to fulfilling one of the three.

The gist of BCRs is to help partners turn negatives into positives, the impossible into the possible. They're designed to contain or structure the frustration one partner feels with the other, offer insight into the childhood precursors of the frustration, and enable the partner to "gift" the other with the changed behavior.

The BCR structure was torturous for Jessica, who never used one or two sentences when 10 or 12 would do, and who found it very difficult to make specific and doable requests of Sam.

An example of Jessica's initial requests was: "I want you, next month, to work as hard as I do and make as much money as I do."

I wouldn't let Sam mirror that one. "Make it more specific, Jessica," I said.

Jessica looked nonplussed, then continued. "Well, O.K. I want you to work a solid eight hours a day, and earn a minimum of $200 a day, every day, for the next month."

Sam looked as though Jessica were requesting that he undergo a sex-change operation. I suggested, "That's better, Jessica, but make it smaller."

She remained somber. "Well, how about working eight-hour days and making $150 a day?" I laughed. "You're getting closer."

Finally, Jessica asked Sam to commit to keeping track of his work hours every day for two weeks, as well as to dialogue with Jessica twice a week during that time about his work and financial progress. Sam was willing to do this.

SAM AND JESSICA: AN IMAGO FORMULATION

As Imago theory holds, the roots of this couple's impasse were entrenched well before they ever met. We can see the early glimmers of the impasse in Jessica's complaints about the difference in the workloads they were carrying. But the impasse is not about apparent issues; it's about the fundamental differences in the ways in which each partner deals with life's pain and struggles. Like all good Imago matches, the two were "incompatible"—a normal and desirable condition between partners. Like everyone else's, Sam and Jessica's character structures were set well before they met, by the time they had finished adolescence, in fact. Their incompatability arose from the deficiencies of those character structures, the "holes" that needed filling in through conscious partnership and that, without it, brought the couple to the height of their power struggle.

Jessica is a woman in competition not just with her spouse, but with life itself. For her, living is jumping through a series of hoops. Jessica can always work more, make more, and achieve more, no matter how far she's already come. She applies a leave-no-stones-unturned approach to virtually all her interactions, especially those with her partner. When she tries to get Sam to do things her way, for example, she uses the same maneuvers that have worked for her in other realms of her life. And like any partner who views his spouse as a Sherman tank headed toward him, Sam responds to Jessica's maneuvers by resisting with all his might.

Sam is the actor who has the gift of being the character he's portraying, feeling the character's feelings, thinking his thoughts, and acting from the motives of the moment. Sam figures that "someone's got to swallow the wine," a line from a song he wrote, and that, in his marriage, given whom he was married to, that someone might as well be him. To Sam, life is about enjoying the journey; accomplishments "happen" along the way. He was genuinely puzzled by Jessica's rush to excellence. Didn't she realize that "all good things come to those who wait"? If only Sam could get Jessica to slow down, she could enjoy the feast of life with him. But the slower Sam went, the harder Jessica pushed him to hurry up and make something of himself. The more Jessica hurried Sam, the more Sam would slow down—to mediocrity, Jessica believed. We see this passive/competitive teeter-totter effect at many points in their relationship: in Sam's opposition to Jessica's jumping yet another hurdle by earning her doctorate, and in Jessica's pushing Sam out of a slowly moving artistic career. Of course, this tug-of-war failed to get the partners what they wanted, which was for the partner to be more like oneself. The only outcome thus far had been mutual rewounding and alienation.

We see in Sam and Jessica's partnership two incomplete people walking together toward maturity, and who, in the midst of their power struggle, view the other as the person least capable of helping them get what they want out of life. In fighting with one another, Sam and Jessica were really fighting against regaining, through their partnership, the parts of themselves they'd lost long before they'd started their journey together.

As I say to the couples with whom I work, each partner has some stretching to do; each contributes to the nightmare and each can cocreate a new relationship. Sam needed to do, for Jessica, exactly what he'd been secretly dreaming, for years, of doing for himself: he had to find a way to make an impact on the world. Jessica's ambitious and successful father had formed an integral part of her Imago, the image of what a "lover" looks like. Sam needed to surrender to the reality that he'd married a woman who not only embodied what he, Sam, didn't believe he possessed, but who would also demand that he grow in the ways he most needed to grow. In sum, Sam needed to become more like Jessica, more focused, achievement oriented, and self-disciplined. Similarly, Jessica's distaste for Sam's laid-back style reflected the tendencies that she most feared, yet needed to reclaim in herself. Jessica never relaxed; she never gave herself permission to be average— to be incompetent in some ways—while maintaining her self-esteem. Her need for consistent self-reassurance was like a junkie's need for the next fix; but the next one's never enough. Jessica had to learn that she was enough. And the best teacher she could find for this lesson, of course, was Sam, the consummate expert on being. Jessica needed to incorporate more of Sam's ways—his tolerance of others, his acceptance of himself, his equanimity toward life—to become more like the person she really longed to be. Sam was the image of the fulfillment of her longing.

SAM AND JESSICA: AN EPILOGUE

Sam and Jessica weren't the sort of couple that could be transformed in 12 easy sessions. But as they continued to dialogue, they laid down the first thin layers of the foundation on which they began to build a safer relationship. Through connecting their childhood wounding—Jessica's terror of incompetence, Sam's conviction that he was incompetent—with the frustrations of their relationship, they began to understand the roots of their emotional reactions toward one another. Sam realized that, in depriving Jessica of what she most needed from him—greater occupational success and a goal-oriented attitude toward life—he was robbing himself of the very characteristics he'd long regretted not having. Jessica recognized how her condemnation of Sam's *joie de vivre* was keeping her from accessing and accepting the part of her that longed to relax and enjoy life. As Sam began expressing the empathy he'd been holding back from Jessica, in reaction to her rage toward him, Jessica's anger softened, yielding eventually to the underlying sadness and hurt she'd been carrying with her throughout her life. Having Sam hear and validate her pain helped her to reenvision him as someone who had what she wanted, and as a partner who had made many positive contributions to her life. Sensing Sam's commitment to take on more, as his gift to her, of the hard work of life freed Jessica to take on, in turn, some of Sam's carefree and easy-living spirit.

A cautionary comment on Sam and Jessica's dynamics, one that applies to many minimizer–maximizer combinations, should be made here. It is tempting to view Jessica, with her ambition, incisive logic, and string of successes, as the "healthy" partner in this relationship. Sam, conversely, might be considered the immature goof-off. The individual paradigm might label Sam a "dependent" personality; viewed from systems perspective, Jessica is the "overfunctioning" partner while Sam "underfunctions." From Imago's relational viewpoint, however, both Sam and Jessica have been practicing, in their marriage, the long-established defensive maneuvers that made them feel emotionally safe during childhood, but that now keep them in disconnection from each other and from their own essential wholeness.

As their connection grew stronger, their dialogue deepened, later moving into discussions of each partner's personal pain. Sam revealed to Jessica how he mourned the opportunities he'd passed up to accomplish things that would have made an impact on the world, the impact he had dreamed of since his youth. Jessica acknowledged to Sam how her obsession with such accomplishments had made it virtually impossible for her to allow herself to be ordinary, to be imperfect, to simply be.

The transformation had begun. To Sam, Jessica was no longer the mirror image of his failures, of the missing parts of himself; he was coming to see her as a woman he could admire and use as a model for his own growth. And Jessica came to appreciate Sam's potential to become a stronger and more available "pillow" than her mom had ever been.

BIBLIOGRAPHY

Hendrix, H. (1988). *Getting the love you want: A guide for couples.* New York Holt.

EDITORS' COMMENTARY

If this couple seems familiar, maybe it's because you are in a romantic partnership that looks like theirs! Passive/competitive couples are the ones who show up most frequently in therapy offices and at couples workshops. Their pressure to "do things right" makes them want to "do the marriage right" as well. Therapy works with these couples because they work at therapy. Furthermore, because they didn't experience early wounding, as did the couples we read about in the first few chapters, passive/competitive couples are free of personality disturbances, which impair one's basic ability to relate to another as "the other."

That's the good news. The bad news is that when passive/competitive partners enter couples therapy, the same dynamics that dominate their relationship will begin to dominate the therapy process—sometimes even before the therapist has had time to say "Hello."

Although these partners seem strikingly different in their behavior, their personality style, and even their physical appearance—the sharp contrasts are almost comical, in some cases—their underlying fear is the same; it is the fear of being proved incompetent. As Dr. Hannah points out, passive-competitive wounds stem from children's experiences between the ages of four and six years, when being noticed and praised for accomplishments matters the most. Sam and Jessica had caretakers who either overvalued or downplayed their accomplishments. Just as identity-wounded children somehow missed hearing, "You are somebody," Sam and Jessica didn't hear, loudly and strongly enough, the message, "You are competent and capable." And like all wounded partners, these two are on a search mission, seeking out now what they didn't get back then. Unfortunately, the one person who they hoped would give it to them wasn't competent to do so!

Just as earlier-wounded partners need unconditional love from one another, Sam and Jessica need unconditional praise—to hear that, whatever they're doing, what they're doing is great. Sounds simple, but it's not easy. Deep down, Sam is afraid that praising Jessica would unleash a supercompetent monster who would crush his own meager—in Sam's view—attempts to make a mark in the world. Sam would then be left in the dust and seen as a failure, particularly in comparison with his partner.

There's no question that, unlike Jessica, Sam leaves the occasional string untied. But people with a relaxed and contented outlook on life aren't disturbed by untied strings or, for that matter, by a lot of the things that their competent partners can't stand. Jessica focuses primarily on Sam's untied strings. Her criticisms help keep Sam in the same wounded condition he was in throughout much of his childhood. Back then, Sam would ask, "Why do something if it doesn't matter whether or not I get it right?" When Sam asks that same question now, in his relationship with Jessica, she's apt to respond, "Forget it. I'll do it myself." As a result, Jessica, too, stays stuck in her wounded frame of mind, the one that forces her to do everything, and to do everything right, so that she can feel she is loved and valued. And so the dance goes on: she overfunctions, he underfunctions. The harder she works, the harder he plays.

With couples like Sam and Jessica, the most crucial task of the therapist is to equalize the partners' contribution to the passive-competitive dance. Because the competitive partner appears to be functioning very well while the the passive partner seems to be functioning poorly, a fast logical leap ends with the conclusion that the passive partner owns the problem. True, the passive partner needs to stretch to get things done and to do things right. But the competitive partner also has a lot of stretching to do. Jessica had considerable difficulty with appreciating the simple things in life—walks in the park, sleeping in on weekends, enjoying her children, and getting in touch with the childlike part of herself. The competitive partner needs to say, more frequently, No to work and Yes to life. This is not, of course, a popular statement in our culture, which applauds the competitive partner for being competitive. But the road to healing is seldom a popular route. How ironic—and how consistent with Imago theory—that Sam and Jessica each married the perfect partner, the one from whom they could learn what competence really is.

Chapter 6

IS IMAGO THERAPY CULTURALLY RELEVANT? CASE STUDIES WITH AFRICAN-AMERICAN COUPLES

Helen Weiser and Cora Thompson

This chapter demonstrates the application of Imago therapy in working with African-American couples. We utilize Hendrix's (1988) concept of the "journeys of the self" to provide an empathic overview of the unique conflicts, courage, and spirituality of African Americans as they integrate psychological services into their culture. We are convinced that the phenomenal growth we have seen in these couples would not have been possible without the use of Imago therapeutic tools.

THE HISTORICAL JOURNEY

European-Americans tend to oversimplify the impact that enslavement has had on African Americans, whose struggle is sometimes compared to that of other immigrant groups who have had to adjust to the American environment. Unlike these voluntary immigrants, however, Africans were not seeking to escape their homelands. For them, America offered persecution rather than refuge; freedom meant escape to a "free state" rather than acculturation. The women were often held as sexual hostages, and an African-American male would be murdered, beaten, or sold if he interfered with the master's having sex, and even children, with the enslaved wife. Even after slavery was officially abolished, African-American men were castrated, hanged, or beaten for merely looking at white women, whether the gaze had been actual or in someone's imagination. Children with "non-African" features were taken from their black parents and raised as white. Thus, the African-American male was disempowered to protect his family. The current phenomenon of violence among African-American men may have its roots in this lack of power.

When slavery ended, black economic power flourished in many places. In the early to mid 1900s black sports were as lively and lucrative as those of whites, and black businesses began to grow at the same rapid pace. Then came integration in the 1950s and 1960s, with the assumption that merging black with white institutions was desirable. As a result, the black economy and its institutions soon died. The community, connectedness, and oneness that had been established among African Americans was once again destroyed.

Now, over 100 years later, African-American males are attempting to take control and show presence in their homes. Without spiritual connection and a sense of unity within the family, violence often becomes the only means by which they can assert their power.

THE SPIRITUAL JOURNEY

To be of African ancestry implies an integration of earthly systems with one's lifestyle. For centuries, the African's lifestyle relied on the daily maintenance of harmony with nature, which necessitated the avoidance of conflict in personal interactions. Actions that promoted the good of the group were of top priority. For thousands of years, Africans promulgated this spiritual heritage, with spirituality being reflected in all human behavior, including sexual conduct. Sexual intercourse was viewed as the connection that made two people one and linked human existence with the spiritual dimension. For African Americans, connectedness and reconnecting, which are similar to the Imago concept of rediscovering empathy through relationship, play a central role in their spirituality, their relationships, and their lives.

Their religion today is a manifestation of the ongoing attempts by African Americans to come to terms with the conflict between their spirituality, as experienced throughout their history, and the forces of the white world in which they were enslaved. Enslaved men were appointed preachers and were instructed to use the Bible and God to keep the slaves indoctrinated with the idea that they should be "less than" the white man. But regardless of its dubious origins, the evolution of the African-American church into what it is now—an active force for personal, spiritual, economic, and political development—reflects how African Americans weave spirituality into all human endeavors.

THE PSYCHOLOGICAL JOURNEY

African Americans are slowly working toward making peace with the mental health services system. Because their history in this country has been traumatic and brutal, they view with suspicion and distrust much of what European-Americans have to offer. For years, African Americans were accepted into the white culture solely on the basis of their status as slaves, persons whose bodies and minds were under the control of others. Thus, the wariness with which African Americans view the psychological services offered by whites, and their fear that, through the use of such services, others might try to control their minds, is understandable.

Historically, the African-American church has denounced psychological theories and practices. However, one way in which psychological theories have made inroads into the African-American culture is through the integration of psychology and African rituals, such as mating, healing, and seasonal harvest rituals. Although such rituals are also used as means of controlling others, they are familiar and congruent with the belief systems of African peoples.

AFRICAN/EUROPEAN-AMERICAN HEALING: WHERE DO WE GO FROM HERE?

Imago therapy can play a significant role in the emotional, spiritual, and psychological growth of the African-American couple. But to work effectively with African Americans, it is essential for the therapist also to recognize and appreciate African-American history, the uniqueness of their struggle, and their contribution to the American culture.

Imago methods encourage open communication and empathy and integrate ways to communicate about and resolve conflict. Practicing empathy strengthens emotional connection, and emotional connection is an avenue along which African Americans can regain spiritual worth. In addition, Imago's commitment to maintaining relationships mirrors the essential notion of the ancient African spiritual heritage that was shattered by enslavement.

Case Study 1: The Henrys*

William Henry wielded control through battering and intimidation. Although he was successful as an ordained preacher, spirituality was lacking in his relationship with his wife. She sought control through manipulation and victimization. Their emotional bonding was limited to sexual interactions. Both felt helpless and frustrated.

Mr. Henry spent the first three sessions asking questions, demanding proof, rigidly resisting explanations, and, at all times, working hard to take control. His only recourse, it seemed, was to accuse and blame his wife for whatever problem was being discussed. Mr. Henry perceived the therapist's interventions as attempts to control him while offering sympathy and support to his wife. The dialogue process, however, gave him the sense of regaining control that he needed. His attitude began to shift during the third session, when he realized that dialogue was a symmetrical process; both he and his wife were asked to mirror, validate, and empathize. Fairness, respect, and the restoration of equity were the building blocks for safety with this couple, and they finally began to dialogue constructively.

Mr. Henry shared how, as an added bonus to the community, as well as for his own spiritual healing, the tone of his sermons had changed. He still used biblical references for current issues, but his tone had become softer and nonabusive. The damnation, fire, and brimstone were no longer present.

As a therapist, I was able to give up much of my own emotional tension as I saw them embrace these tools. It was gratifying to see such a transformation in the couple's dynamics; I felt released from watching for dangerous exchanges and was able to work freely with them. Safety, I came to realize, is important for the therapist, as well as for the clients.

Stages

Following this first case, we hypothesized four stages that African Americans progress through as they embrace the tools of Imago therapy and begin to engage in the dialogue process.

Stage 1: Suspicion (Internal and External). Movement through this stage will depend on the therapist's ability to respect the client's suspiciousness while

---

*Presented by Dr. Thompson.

avoiding taking personal responsibility for the client's cultural and intrapsychic issues.

Stage 2: Creation of Safety. This is, of course, a challenge for all Imago therapists, but when working with African Americans, it is of even greater importance. Imago therapy has great appeal to African Americans because of the fact that they, rather than the therapist, control the sessions. This increases safety for the couple, who can learn the Imago tools to help them grow even while they retain some degree of suspicion. The nonsexist nature of Imago therapy promotes safety, particularly for African-American males, who are less responsive to the European-American culture than are African-American females.

One knows safety has been established when all participants in the therapeutic process are able to express their true feelings and let go of defensiveness, which they have used to shield themselves both from each other and from a hostile society.

Stage 3: Empowerment. In the next stage, the couple will let go of control and claim their own power. This is the next movement toward trust for the African-American couple—trust in their own feelings, trust in their ability to relate authentically within the mainstream culture. Power replaces control, leading to the potential for true dialogue.

Stage 4: Sprituality. Imago Relationship Therapy offers African Americans an opportunity to reexperience their ancient spiritual connectedness by trusting that inner voice that for so long has been silenced by internal fears and doubt.

For healing to occur, often it is necessary to engage not only the couple but the extended family, acknowledging the communal aspect of the African-American culture. We will see this need as particularly evident in the following case study, that of the Johnson/Burt family. The couple was attempting to regain custody of their young children, who were in the care of the maternal grandparents.

Case Study 2: Danielle and Steven Johnson*

Stage 1: Suspicion. This couple, desperate with pain and confusion, entered therapy as a last resort. They lost custody of their children when Steven became angry, hit his son, and was reported for child abuse. Had they not been court ordered to therapy (a recent phenomenon that has forced many African Americans into a process they fear and resent), they would never have contacted us. Could we build

*Presented by Dr. Thompson and Helen Weiser.

a therapeutic rapport, we wondered, given this situation? However, we found that by validating their complaints about their treatment by a hostile legal system, we were able to join with them, and they began to believe that we actually wanted to help.

Stage 2: Safety. After a few sessions, our office became a refuge where they could express their buried feelings without judgment or recrimination. Nobody wanted this couple to stay together, yet they were not willing to separate. As Danielle put it, "Everyone talks about family values. What about staying married? These children need both of us. There has to be a way."

The dialogue process solidified their bond and provided them with the support they so desperately needed from each other. During the holding exercise, they poured out to each other their mutual grief about the loss of their children. They took turns comforting and holding each other as they described their deepest pain and fears. We let our own tears flow along with theirs.

Stage 3: Empowerment. Danielle and Steven learned, through their dialogue, how their own wounding had led them, in turn, to oppress their children. They were replacing control, which had been their previous version of safety, with support and trust.

A test of trust arose when they came to our office in crisis. Their baby had been injured at her day care center and was rushed to the hospital. Danielle and Steven were not permitted to be with the baby. As Danielle began to panic, we encouraged them to dialogue, with Danielle as the sender:

> **Danielle:**   *When Ronnie fell and had to go to the hospital, I couldn't be there, so there was no one to help her and treat her special.*
> **Steven:**   *You're saying that when Ronnie got hurt, and you couldn't be there, nobody was there to treat her special. Did I get it?*
> **Danielle:**   *Yes, you got it.*
> **Steven:**   *Is there more?*
> **Danielle:**   *That's it (crying softly).*
> **Therapist:**   *Steven, do you have a reaction to what Danielle is saying about Ronnie?*
> **Steven:**   *I feel the same way.*
> **Therapist:**   *I was wondering if you had a response to the level of pain that Danielle is in.*
> **Steven:**   *I believe that Ronnie is going to be all right. Jimmy will give her special attention.*

Although this statement was intended to comfort Danielle, it had the opposite effect.

> **Danielle:** *I don't think that's right. Jimmy shouldn't have to do that. Jimmy is just a baby himself.*
> **Steven:** *You don't think Jimmy should have to do that because he is just a baby himself. Did I get it?*
> **Danielle:** *Yes (crying, looking lost and hopeless).*

There was a long pause, broken only by Danielle's quiet sobbing. It was suggested that perhaps they both needed a deeper level of support, and that we do the holding exercise. The presence of two therapists was very helpful, because the partners needed to be held. We physically held them. Steven held Danielle first; her crying deepened as she allowed herself to accept his comfort.

> **Danielle:** *Ronnie is just another body to those people at the hospital. She needs me.*
> **Steven:** *Ronnie needs you and you can't be there.*
> **Therapist:** *And what that reminds you of from your childhood is . . .*
> **Danielle:** *I was alone so much. When I was little, I felt special to my dad. When he left, it was like I became nothing.*
> **Steven:** *When you were little, you were so special to your dad. Then after he left, you were very lonely.*
> **Danielle:** *And now Ronnie's all alone (crying as she held Steven tightly).*

When Danielle stopped crying, she agreed to hold Steven, who became the sender.

> **Steven:** *How can you love me? It's all my fault. I caused all this pain.*
> **Danielle:** *You believe you caused all this pain, and you don't know how I can love you.*
> **Steven:** *I would do anything to take it away.*
> **Danielle:** *You really want to take the pain away.*
> **Steven:** *I wish I'd never hurt Jimmy. (Steven began to cry as Danielle continued to hold him.)*
> **Danielle:** *You wish you'd never hurt Jimmy.*

As Steven's crying subsided, Danielle asked if she could send to him.

> **Danielle:** *This wasn't all your fault. I gave to you my role of disciplining the kids. I needed to be there when Jimmy was misbehaving. I shouldn't have had you do it all.*

> **Steven:**   *You think you should have been there to discipline the kids.*
> **Danielle:**   *Yes. I saw how frustrated you were becoming. I could have helped. I couldn't discipline them. Now that I understand more about my own childhood, I can meet those needs for the kids.*

This couple was releasing a great deal of anger and resentment, toward society, themselves, each other, and their parents, and replacing it with forgiveness.

Stage 4: Spirituality. Steven and Danielle had been able to trust us in learning the Imago process, but more important, they had made it their own. Steven described an internal message to approach his father-in-law at the courthouse as a prompt from God. It was not a suggestion from us or anyone else, so we could not offer any other explanation.

The couple had planned to leave town as soon as they got their children back, so great was their resentment toward Mr. Burt, Danielle's father. But Danielle had undergone a spiritual transformation, which was evident in the final session with the extended family, when she made this statement: "I want to thank my dad for not giving in to us at a time when we were very mixed up. He did what was right, and I hope he will be around as grandfather to our children for many years to come." Her father beamed with the pride and pleasure of a parent who feels successful in the most important role he or she will ever undertake.

Case Study 3: Grandfather Burt*

Stage 1: Suspicion. Grandfather Burt was determined to avoid giving in to his daughter and son-in-law. He had convinced himself that his grandson was in danger at home, so he used the social services system to gain custody of the child. In doing so, he appeared to have made peace with the European-American culture, but at a high price: sacrificing what he really believed. Unable to trust his daughter, whom he loved, he was put in the untenable position of relying on a system he suspected and hated.

He therefore agreed to talk with a psychologist (me). Our first meeting had a rocky start. He said, "You're helping my daughter get her son back. Why would you want this child to go back to live with a known abuser?" I tried my best professional stance. "Counseling," I told him, as calmly as I could, "has been known to help people learn new skills and become better parents." "Right," he replied. "It doesn't

*Presented by Helen Weiser.

always work, does it?" He then recited statistics, summaries of legal cases, and his own anecdotal evidence, using all my weapons against me before I could use them to argue with him. "We are at war here," he said. "I hope you realize that, if you win, and anything happens to my grandson, it will be your fault. But don't worry, you are not going to win." Something shifted inside of me: my defenses moved out of the way, and at that moment, I felt great respect and empathy for this man. Sometimes, when we are working with very wounded people, we need to trust them even though they cannot trust us. We need to demonstrate faith when they have none. And we need to acknowledge our powerlessness over outcomes, even as they are demanding that we make guarantees.

"Mr. Burt," I said, "you are absolutely right. I don't know what will happen in the final analysis, nor can I guarantee that your son-in-law will never harm your grandson. I can offer you only what I have, and I ask only that you reserve judgment until the counseling process is over." This helped Mr. Burt shift out of his attack mode. I was able to join him in his concern about his grandson, sharing his feelings about his responsibilities as a grandparent. Having his concerns mirrored brought us to the beginning of a new relationship. By the end of the session, Mr. Burt's suspiciousness had lessened. He allowed me a glimpse of a very important part of himself: he asked, with obvious frustration in his voice, "Can you tell me why our kids can't learn from us? Why do they have to make the same mistakes?" I mirrored him, then added, "You really want your children to listen to you, so that you can help guide them in their life choices." By the time the session ended, Mr. Burt's tone was gentler, and I could hear hope in his voice. This man wanted to believe in his children; he simply did not know how to do it. We made a contract: he would come to the sessions and use the tools we taught him. I told him that, when he had finished with the sessions, he would know the answer to his question. His answer would come not from research or statistics, but from a place inside himself. With, of course, some skepticism he agreed.

Stage 2: Safety. Mr. Burt needed to feel heard by me before he was able to feel safe enough to learn something from me in our sessions. Likewise, his safety level increased when he saw that his daughter and son-in-law also were able to hear him. The couple had been using the Intentional Dialogue for at least three months before Mr. Burt was brought into the picture.

Danielle, Mr. Burt's daughter, did a good job teaching him to mirror. At one point, she told him, "I am angry that you treat everyone in the family as special but me; now I want you to mirror that." Mr. Burt had difficulty mirroring her, because he had always believed that his children got into trouble because they did not listen to him. She said she would not listen to him unless he mirrored her. Finally he conceded, and we were able to use these sessions as opportunities to teach him Imago skills.

Following a particularly difficult session, during which Mr. Burt demanded proof that his son-in-law, Steven, would never again harm his grandson, I reminded Mr. Burt that he needed to get to know his son-in-law. Mr. Burt would then know whether or not Steven could be trusted with the grandson. I encouraged Mr. Burt and Steven to dialogue. Steven agreed to send first.

> **Steven:** *I was real new at the job of parenting, and sometimes I just did not know what to do.*
> **Mr. Burt:** *You say you were new at parenting and didn't know what to do. Is there more?*
> **Steven:** *Yes. I believed you knew this about me and held it against me.*
> **Mr. Burt:** *You thought I held this against you.*

At this point, Mr. Burt had difficulty containing his need to respond, so they agreed to switch, with Mr. Burt sending and Steven receiving.

> **Mr. Burt:** *Why didn't you call me? I wanted to be helpful. I've had years of experience. My problem with you is that you were so proud; you never wanted to hear from me.*
> **Steven:** *You are wondering why I never called on you to help. You think I am too proud to ask for help.*

At this point, Steven began to cry softly. They again shifted roles, with Steven being the sender.

> **Steven:** *You never liked me. How could I call you?*
> **Mr. Burt (covering his face and beginning to cry):** *You thought I didn't like you, and that's why you never asked for my help.*
> **Steven:** *You saw how frustrated I was, but you couldn't help me. Now you think you can.*

We suggested that the two men spend some time in dialogue the following week. As their relationship improved and deepened, Danielle complained facetiously that her dad was paying more attention to Steven than he was to her. (Danielle had been wounded by not getting enough of her father's attention. She had worked on this issue in previous sessions with Steven, and so was able to share her feelings with her father, even with some humor.)

Stage 3: Empowerment. Mr. Burt learned powerful truths from the dialogue: Rather than wanting to reject him, his daughter loved him and longed for his attention. His son-in-law wanted and valued his counsel. Consequently, Mr. Burt was able to respond to them more genuinely than before. He no longer needed to control and manipulate. In our final session, he communicated love and respect for both his daughter and his son-in-law.

Stage 4: Spirituality. In the unlikely setting of a courthouse, a turning point occurred. The tension was profound as parents and children girded themselves to battle over their children and grandchildren. When Steven walked up to his father-in-law, we were worried that he was about to start a fight. Instead, Steven embraced his father-in-law and whispered something to him. We all stared in fascination. Later, we asked Steven what had happened. He responded, "Well, all of a sudden, I let go of all the anger and bitterness, and I felt the strongest impulse to go up to him and hug him. I knew that God was inspiring me to do this, and instead of ignoring the impulse, like I usually do, I followed it."

When Mr. Burt finally opened the door to empathy and compassion for his son-in-law, his spirituality was awakened. The Imago processes helped him to trust something other than himself and his old ways—control and manipulation. The spirit became freed in these letting-go processes, and the beauty and depth of his African ancestry replaced the suspicion and mistrust he felt toward the European-American culture.

Mr. Burt did get the answer to his question: Steven could indeed be trusted with Mr. Burt's grandson. As we ended our Imago sessions, Mr. Burt said to Steven, "I am glad I got to know you, and I want us to stay in close touch, like we are now. My grandson is ready to go home, and I know you are ready to make a good home for him."

His powerful words still echo in our minds. We were a part of a healing process that has ramifications for our entire society, a society of peoples so separated by their differences that their similarities, and the spiritual connection that unites them, have been overlooked.

We learned much from our experiences with these African-American couples, and so offer several suggestions for therapists interested in working with couples from cultures other than their own. First, we believe it is vitally important to elicit the assistance of an African-American therapist before undertaking work with a family like the Burts, even though Imago therapy has the power to transcend cultural differences. Although there are few empirical studies of the effectiveness of therapeutic processes with African-American clients, one thing does emerge in the literature: the therapist's race is extremely important to the successful outcome of any therapeutic intervention with African Americans (Weiser, 1985). Clearly, in addition to being culturally sensitive themselves, European-American therapists should bring into the circle African-American therapists who show an interest in the Imago processes.

The success we enjoyed was a combination of Imago work and our empathic identification with our clients, which paved the way for trust. In summary, respect their culture as different from your own, but meet the couple with your heart and your spirit.

BIBLIOGRAPHY

Africa: A history denied (1995). In *Time Life*'s Lost Civilizations Series. Alexandria, Va.: Time Life Video & Television.

Akbar, N. (1991). *Visions for black men*. Nashville: Winston-Derek.

Berlin, I. (1974). *Slaves without masters: The free negro in the antebellum South*. New York: New Press.

Colin, R., & Bahn, P. (1991). *Archeology: Theories, methods and practices*. New York: Thames & Hudson.

Courlander, H. (1962). *The king's drum and other African stories*. New York: Harcourt, Brace, Jovanovich.

Dennis, D. (1984). *Black history for beginners*. New York: Writers & Readers Publishing.

Felder, C. H. (Ed.) (1991). *Stony the road we trod: African American biblical interpretation*. Minneapolis: Fortress Press.

Hendrix, H. (1988). *Getting the love you want*. New York: Holt.

Hopson, D. S., & Hopson, D. P. (1993). *Raising the rainbow generation: Teaching your children to be successful in a multicultural society*. New York: Fireside.

Isom, D. I., Jr. (1992). *When Jesus was betrayed* (audiotape). Youth and Young Adult International Convention, Christian Methodist Episcopal Church.

Kunjufu, J. (1986). *Motivating and preparing black youth to work.* Chicago: African American Images.

Lakey, O. H. (1985). *The history of the C.M.E. church.* Memphis: C.M.E. Publishing.

Lakey, O. H., & Stephens, B. B. (1994). *God in my mama's house: The woman's movement in the C.M.E. church.* Memphis: C.M.E. Publishing.

Lewis, M. C. (1988). *Herstory: Black female rites of passage.* Chicago: African American Images.

McMillan, T. (1987). *Mama: A novel.* New York: Pocket Star Books.

Satir, V. (1987). The therapist story. *Journal of Psychotherapy and the Family, 3*(1). 17–23.

Stephens, R. L. (1993a). *Afro-American male empowerment network* (unpublished). Peace Baptist Church.

Stephens, R. L. (1993b). *Figtrees and mountains* (unpublished). Peace Baptist Church.

Stovall, A. G. (1991). *Poverty, perceptions, and attitudes* (unpublished). Walden University, Minnesota.

Thompson, C. D. (1994a). *Cultural identity development of African-American women* (videotape). Midtown Mental Health Association.

Thompson, C. D. (1994b). *The pride of slavery: An explanation of the emotional heritage.* Kansas City, Mo.: Dreams Unlimited.

Thompson, C. D. (1994c). *Psychological effects of racism* (audiotape). Midwest Christian Counseling Center.

Weems, R. J. (1988). *Just a sister away: A womanist vision of women's relationships in the Bible.* San Diego, Calif.: LuraMedia.

Weiser, H. E. (1985). *The effects of counselor race upon therapeutic outcome* (unpublished). University of Missouri, Kansas City.

Welsing, F. C. (1991). *The Isis papers: The keys to the colors.* Chicago: Third World Press.

EDITORS' COMMENTARY

Only recently has the therapeutic community begun to recognize how much a person's cultural inheritance affects the ways people function in their close relationships. An example of this is provided by the Irish myth about leprechauns stealing away with children who are good. As a result, Irish parents have the tradition of withholding praise from their children for good behavior!

Likewise, all too often, therapists underestimate how much ancestral traditions contribute to how romantic partners view and treat each other. As Weiser and Thompson point out, such is often the case with therapists who work with African-American couples.

It is no surprise that the African-American culture, having been manipulated for so long by the mainstream culture, would be suspicious of mainstream therapies, including couples therapy approaches. For African Americans, relying on their own community and extended family feels far safer. This is evidenced by the fact that African Americans underutilize mental health services, as well as by the extent to which African Americans are underrepresented in the therapeutic professions.

This is not to imply that African Americans do not and will not seek couples therapy, even with a non-African-American therapist. Weiser and Thompson note that it is not so much who the therapist is, but who the therapist represents to the African-American couple. Imago therapists, the authors point out, have an advantage over others, since Imago therapy principles mesh well with those of the African-American culture. With its emphasis on empowerment, interpersonal connection, and placing the responsibility for healing in the hands of the couple, the Imago approach seems congruent with the needs of persons suspicious of mental health approaches. The versatility with which Imago can be used—for example, in including extended family members in the dialogue process, as we saw in this chapter—is also a plus when working with persons from minority cultures.

As increasing numbers of therapists do Imago work with ethnically diverse couples, the Imago approach is likely to grow in acceptability, and in the order of the stages Weiser and Thompson propose. Initially, therapists, communities, and families might feel suspicious. Once they recognize Imago's emphasis on safety, they can discover how it can empower them. And once they feel empowered, they are able to achieve the spiritual sense of connection. Thus, Weiser and Thompson deliver good news: Imago therapy shows promise as a vehicle that African-American couples can use in their return to the richness of their ancestral roots.

Chapter 7

IMAGO THERAPY WITH HISPANIC COUPLES

Homer Bain

My Hispanic practice consists of Mexican and Mexican-American clients, as well as some who are Latin American or Caribbean. My wife and passionate friend of 40 years is Mexican, and I owe much of my appreciation of the culture to her and her family. As a workshop presenter, I am often very moved by the enthusiasm with which participants respond to Imago precepts and exercises. It strikes me that many of the prevalent themes of Hispanic culture resonate powerfully with Imago therapy, beginning with the theme of emotionality.

THE WEAVING OF FIVE PROMINENT THEMES

Emotionality and Privacy

Expressive emotionality, so evident in my workshops, is key to Imago work. In Imago, we stress attention to feelings, owning and sharing our own, and validating and empathizing with those of our partner. The assumption in Imago, as in Hispanic cultures, is that feelings are where we live.

The theme of privacy—or of safety—emerges as an important balance to emotionality in both this cultural and this therapeutic context. The protection of boundaries builds in a quality of respect, which, in turn, frees us from a need for secrecy, a need that often becomes destructive. The language shift from *usted*, the polite form of "you," to *atu*, the familiar form, provides a quiet symbolic acknowledgment of the shift from privacy to intimacy. In my workshops, respect for privacy is the natural segue to the provision of safety. If couples do not want to share, their choice is upheld. Paradoxically, this approach tends to create a feeling of safety among the couples so that they become more likely to be able to share freely.

Communality and Authority

Alongside emotionality and privacy, the attributes of communality and authority reflect the context of the clan. In a culture that emphasizes tight communal bonds over, say, rugged individualism, rituals and gestures that reinforce privacy serve to protect a sense of individual space. Authority, on the other hand, is used by the culture to promote or sanction opportunities for emotional expression.

The workshop might be viewed as a sanctioned opportunity by some. During one demonstration, a woman vented her feelings about being an impotent captive of her husband's extended family. In response, the patriarch of another family stated that he had learned something from her about his own situation. A young man in the group talked about a self-integration exercise, in which one contrasts behaviors of the false self, such as conforming to one's caretakers in order to please them, with those of the true self, such as acting with a sense of freedom and dignity. The exercise clarified his determination not to adhere reflexively or unthinkingly to his parents' values while underscoring his belief that family solidarity and individual integrity can and should go together.

If, for a culture, communality and authority exist at opposite ends of a continuum, for the individual, differentiation and connection stand at each end. Our struggle then is to balance two opposing tendencies—to cut off and to merge. In the balance, there is well-being. Imago uses the terms "symbiosis" and "dialogue" to represent immaturity and maturity in the development of the individual and the couple.

The early romantic phase of the relationship is considered a symbiotic period, just as the earliest period in individual human development during infancy is called symbiotic. The couple relationship then moves into the still-symbiotic power struggle, which can be said to mimic adolescent rebellion where one strives for personal freedom but remains dependent on the caretaker. Couples, through the use of dialogue, can become better and better able to step away from the power struggle, gradually evolving a mutual interdependence, in which the need for connectedness exists in tandem with self-determination. Again, this parallels closely the period in human development during which the person negotiates the tasks and stages of individuation. And, once again, Hispanic culture and Imago share an emphasis: connectedness and individuation are seen as mutually inclusive.

Spirituality

Finally, spirituality is an essential thread in this multidimensional weave. The experience of the spiritual or sacred, as reflected in religious symbols and rituals, is a crucial feature of Hispanic cultures. The early communal tribal faiths became gradually overlaid with Spanish versions of Roman Catholicism. More recent influences range from Protestant Evangelical to Eastern and New Age trends. Regardless of the couple's particular orientation, the spiritual belief system, along with family and personal histories, serves as an important source of wounding, healing, and growth for most Hispanic couples and thus warrants exploration.

MARCOS AND SYLVIA

After a course of individual therapy with another therapist, Marcos, a 45-year-old television executive, began seeing me for couples therapy along with his wife, Sylvia, a 40-year-old homemaker. They have five children, ages 10 to 20. One of their presenting problems was that Marcos, who was often away on business, felt lonely and neglected by his wife; Sylvia, having become used to being on her own with the children, felt smothered by Marcos' demands for attention and affection.

The following conversation took place during an early session, before the couple had learned to dialogue.

> **Marcos:** *I can't stand it anymore. You're so cold and indifferent, you're even hostile whenever I ask you for anything. I feel totally rejected, like I don't count for anything, like I'm repulsive to you. I wait for you to call when I'm on the road, but I'm always the one who makes the call. Then when we talk, you sound distant, like I'm intruding. Sometimes I think you'd like to get rid of me, but not the income I provide. I'm drying up and dying inside from loneliness. I wonder, do you love someone else?*
> **Sylvia:** *No, I don't. I just can't stand your clinging. You're insatiable at home, and then you want me to call you night and day when you're away. I feel suffocated, like nothing is ever enough. It's like you want to possess me body and soul. You got so jealous on that cruise just because I was friendly with the other couples. I can't even tell how I feel about you. I just need space. And I need to be treated like I have some intelligence. Why don't you show me some respect, like giving me more control over handling Alfredo's problems at school? You just decide things on your own, without even asking my opinion.*

After some discussion in this vein, I introduced Marcos and Sylvia to the Parent–Child Dialogue. In this exercise, each partner takes turns listening while the other speaks as though he or she were a child talking to a parent.

Marcos was first in taking the role of the child. Sylvia listened and mirrored, taking on the role of his mother, as Marcos requested.

> **Marcos:**   *You never appreciate me or show me any affection. You give my brother all the praise. I never hear anything about my good grades in school. And you are so cold. I can never remember a time when I sat in your lap. I never remember your caressing me or even taking my hand. I'm just so hungry for you to touch me, to say to me, "Son, I love you."*

When it was Sylvia's turn to be the child, Marcos listened in the role of her father.

> **Sylvia:**   *You ignore my feelings; it doesn't matter what I think or want. I want so much for you to take me places, to buy me candy, to show me you care about what I like. I want you to be proud of who I am. I think you wanted a boy instead of me, but there's nothing I can do to make up for that. So I ignore you, too. I won't chase after you.*

In our therapy and workshops with couples, my wife and I have developed a special technique that highlights the key theme of a partner's childhood wounding and the healing he or she needs. We have couples create slogans that reflect each partner's vulnerabilities and desires—what hurts the most and what helps the most, what the person doesn't want and most wants. A phrase starting with "Don't" is written on the back of a T-shirt; the positive alternative, beginning with "Do," goes on the front.

After experiencing the initial Imago processes, Marcos wrote on the back of his T-shirt, "Don't Ignore Me," and on the front, "Pamper Me!" Sylvia chose the slogans, "Don't Dominate" and "Consider my Feelings!" I noticed that both Marcos' and Sylvia's slogans reflected the stereotypical notions, common to many cultures, of male authority and female servility, as well as the Hispanic emphasis on personal feelings and privacy.

In a subsequent session, Marcos and Sylvia were introduced to the Couples Dialogue and Behavior Change Requests, the Imago processes that help partners express understanding and make behavioral changes.

Marcos wanted to hear from Sylvia first. She agreed, but was quiet for a while before starting.

Sylvia: *I just can't do this. Talking about this hurts too much. And I'm not good at talking; you're the one who's had all the therapy. You can express yourself so much more fluently.*

Marcos: *You're feeling inadequate and pressured to do something that's painful and hard for you.*

Sylvia: *Yes.*

Marcos: *Is there more?*

Sylvia: *Yes. This is just how I feel at home. You are asking me to do the impossible. I'm on the spot and your demands are too much. I can't do it.*

Marcos: *You feel that I'm in control and you're helpless, and nothing you do is going to satisfy me.*

Sylvia: *Yes, so why try? I want to just turn away, like I did with my dad. Just give up.*

Marcos: *You want to react to me the same way you did to your dad.*

Sylvia: *It's just too much for me right now.*

Both were silent for a few moments.

Therapist (to Marcos): *You might ask her if she prefers not to talk now.*

Marcos: *Are you saying you want to stop?*

Sylvia: *Yes. I don't mind listening to you, but I just can't say any more. Maybe later, or maybe little by little, but not now.*

Therapist (to Marcos): *Can you name that feeling, and say it back to her with the same force as you're hearing it? Then validate it, tell her how her feelings make sense, even if just in part.*

Marcos: *I can hear and it makes sense to me that there's too much pain and this is new for you. You don't want to be pressured to dig all this up right now. You're feeling very vulnerable. It's like I'm controlling and having my way again while you're submitting. And you want to stop.*

Sylvia: *Yes. Thank you.*

After a break, Marcos became the sender.

Marcos: *Well, when you didn't want to talk to me, I figured, here we go again, the brush-off; what else is new?*

Sylvia: *You felt shut out, like I didn't have any interest in working this out with you.*

Marcos: *Yes, I felt unimportant, and I also felt hopeless. I think to myself, what can I do? If she doesn't love me, she doesn't love me. Even when we make love, I feel like I'm a bother to you. I ask myself, is that what I'm married for? To be starving while you withdraw from me? I can't go on like this.*

Sylvia: *You think I don't love you because I don't call, and I'm not warm enough when we make love.*

Therapist (to Sylvia):   *Try to name his emotion and mirror back how strong it is.*

Sylvia: *You're angry. You're ready to give up.*

Marcos: *Yes. Why go on like this? Is it too much to want my wife to want me? Why should I relive my mother's absence and indifference? Things have just become worse and worse, and now it's intolerable.*

Sylvia: *You feel desperate; things are getting worse and there's no way you're going to put up with the same treatment you got from your mother.*

Marcos: *Yes.*

Sylvia: *Is there more?*

Macros: *I'd be happy even if you just made a gesture, gave a sign of wanting to be in contact with me. Something not compelled. It has to come from you, it has to be your own.*

Therapist (to Sylvia):   *Could you validate any of this and capture the deep feeling?*

Sylvia: *Well, there's discouragement and pessimism about my really caring for you. It makes sense, because I've talked about resistance and hopelessness about filling needs that are so extreme. I think I love you, but I can't feel it right now.*

Therapist: *So there's a lot of discouragement on both your parts.*

Therapist (to Marcos):   *You mentioned that, if there were just a gesture on Sylvia's part, that would count. This is where a Behavior Change Request could be helpful. Would you be able to spell out, very concretely, three small things she could do that would relieve those feelings you've been expressing?*

Marcos formulated three requests, and Sylvia accepted all three:

1. Call me once on my next trip.
2. Initiate lovemaking after one of my trips during the next month.
3. Buy me a small, inexpensive gift.

In a later session, Sylvia began to dialogue about her perceptions of Marcos, his jealousy, possessiveness, and control. She felt heard and validated by him. She then followed with some Behavior Change Requests of her own.

1. Make calls to me from out of town only during my waking hours.
2. Give me flowers on my birthday.
3. Give me a voice in decisions affecting our home.

Although Sylvia had begun to fulfill Marcos' requests, he remained hungry for greater reassurances of her love. I pointed out that the urgency of Marcos' needs was related to his perception of scarcity, quoting Harville Hendrix's observation that when the cafeteria is always open, the hunger is not so great. Marcos observed, in response, that for him, the cafeteria is not open.

Throughout the succeeding weeks, Marcos and Sylvia kept dialoging and continued to make requests of one another. Months later, both agreed that, most of the time, their cafeteria was open. Sylvia credited Marcos with stretching to include her in decision making and in responding to her tastes. She told him, "I have decided to give you the phone calls, the presents, the gestures of affection willingly, not under compulsion, but as gifts, knowing they mean that much to you." For his part, Marcos said, "I have decided that I really do love you. I am staying calmer in those moments when I used to panic, when I start doubting your love. I'm able to avoid overreacting at times, and more and more often, you are reassuring me of your love."

This case demonstrates the Hispanic cultural themes of privacy, emotionality, communality, and authority. It also illuminates the personal wounding that all partners bring into their relationships, and that Imago therapy targets for healing, regardless of the couple's cultural heritage.

DIANA AND GEORGE

Diana and George represent a variation on our theme: a Hispanic-Anglo union. Diana, a Hispanic, is a high school teacher; George, an Anglo, manages a furniture store. They are in their mid-50s and have three children. Marcia, their youngest daughter, who is unmarried and in her 20s, is the focus of the couple's current conflict. The family belongs to a conservative Protestant denomination. George and Diana have been in Imago therapy for several years. They reported to me this conversation, which had taken place at home.

> **Diana:** *I don't like Marcia's attitude toward boys. I think we should talk to her. Until she's married, she's our responsibility, and we have to guide her.*
> **George:** *Wow, I gave that up when she went off to college.*

In doing her Imago work, Diana, the youngest of seven siblings, had written on the back of her T-shirt, "Don't Discount Me," and on the front, "Value My

Contribution." Diana's personal wounding became intertwined with Hispanic cultural expectations that parents will remain responsible for their offspring, even adult offspring, and that children, regardless of their age, should respect their parents' advice.

Not surprisingly, Marcia, in a conjoint family session, came up with her own T-shirt slogan. Also a youngest child, and having been heavily exposed to the Anglo culture, she wrote "Don't Control Me" and "Respect My Competence." In Marcia's case, then, personal, generational, and cultural wounding become manifest.

An eldest son, George's key desire is expressed by "Don't Criticize" and "Believe in Me."

Following is Diana and George's shift from their impasse to true dialogue.

> **Diana:** *Yes. When I was brought up, kids actually lived at home until they were married. There was none of this leaving home as soon as possible, trying to get away from your parents' values.*
> **George:** *You're offended that I would just wash my hands of any responsibility for Marcia now that she's an adult.*
> **Diana:** *Yes. Why should we just give in to whatever lifestyle she wants or whatever a particular man wants to do, if we don't believe in it?*
> **George:** *So you're scared and angry that we, or mainly I, would stand back and watch her make choices that we don't believe in, when it is our responsibility to help her avoid that?*
> **Diana:** *Yes. It's not the way my family was. We were all very open in telling each other what we thought. The other person might not accept it, but that didn't stop us from saying what we thought, out of concern for the other person. They were always our family.*
> **George:** *It sounds like you feel isolated, like I'm abandoning you, and you're alone in this Anglo environment, where everybody thinks a different way.*
> **Diana (in tears):** *Yes.*
> **George:** *I can see why you would feel that way. With me as your only ally, you sometimes feel deserted and alone. It makes sense that, for you, if we love somebody, we should never stop trying to help them, using our best judgment of what they need. Am I getting it? Do you feel understood?*
> **Diana:** *I think so, except that it makes me furious to think we would sit back and not protect our daughter from danger.*
> **George:** *You're furious with me, and you feel helpless and desperate about this situation.*
> **Diana:** *Yes.*

George: *Is there more?*

Diana: *Not right now.*

George: *Well, the fear I have is that I don't want to destroy communication with Marcia by telling her things that she's asked us to quit repeating. It makes me mad to think that you might be trying to satisfy some sort of parental conscience, whether it drives her farther from us or not.*

Diana: *You want us to help her, but you want me to go about it in a way that is less antagonistic to Marcia, and it makes you mad to think I might not care about our rapport with her, but am more concerned with being a responsible parent.*

George: *Right. It upsets me to hear you say, "This is the way it was in my home," as though we hadn't had our own home for 20-some years. You know, at times, it's seemed like you've said whatever you wanted to the kids, and it's been my job to pick up the pieces.*

Diana: *You also feel let down by my talking about my former life in Costa Rica. And you have felt burdened and resentful over having to be the one who's skillful with the kids, while I've just blurted out whatever was on my mind.*

George: *Yes. I have felt like I have to do the impossible, to control things I can't control, like the kids' behavior. It's not that I think I have all the answers and all the skills. I have always felt unsure of myself with kids, especially adolescents. I need help.*

Diana: *You have felt overburdened and not always sure of yourself with the kids. You want to feel like I'm a helper for you, so you don't have to be strong all the time.*

George (in tears): *That's right.*

Diana: *I can understand why you have felt there were things you couldn't control and that maybe nobody could control. It makes sense that you, as the father, would feel very responsible, especially since you were the oldest son and was supposed to lead the way. It also makes sense that you feel you need my help. I am hearing that your need is very deep sometimes, and that you feel scared and lonely. Is there more?*

George: *There is no more. Right now, I don't care very much about any differences we might have in our goals for Marcia. I feel heard and understood by you, so the sting is gone. I feel more comfortable about any talks we might have in the future about what to do or not do.*

Diana: *I still have something more to say, if you'd be willing to hear me.*

George: *All right.*

Diana: *I'm glad you said what you did. I also feel you have shown more consideration for my feelings and opinions, like you and I are more like a team working together as parents, instead of your working against me.*

I just want you to know that I have restrained myself with the kids a lot more than you realize, sometimes more than I think I should have. I've wanted to cooperate with you, wanted to do it your way with the kids, but I just get tired of waiting for you to do or say something. I end up being the bad guy, and you're the good guy.

George: *You want me to know you have restrained yourself and tried to cooperate with me, but you get desperate when I don't take more initiative and talk to the kids. You want me not to try to be the good guy at your expense.*

Diana: *That's right.*

George: *It makes sense that you don't want to be the bad guy due to my passivity. And it sounds like you feel very hurt at not being appreciated for the efforts you've made to work with me.*

In this dialogue, both personal/cultural styles were heard and validated by the partners, yet they did not achieve agreement. Their understanding and empathy did not include promises of behavior change. However, each partner's experience of respecting and being respected in their differences was transforming in itself.

Respecting differences could be referred to as the morality of therapy. For an Anglo therapist, counseling Hispanic couples, or any couple, means engaging in dialogue with them as they do with one another. Doing therapy involves taking turns empathizing with others' values while asserting one's own, being open to a new creation, a metacultural vision that incorporates and transcends both viewpoints.

We can never be sure whether our acceptance of some aspect of another's culture reflects that transcendent vision or comes out of our own symbiosis or conformity. Likewise, we can never be sure whether our critique of another's culture results from that vision or from our symbiosis or parochialism. We do know that offering empathy and validation places at risk our cultural as well as our individual assumptions. For example, becoming more appreciative of the privacy theme in Hispanic culture has caused me to question my Anglo tendency toward more direct and confrontational expression. Conversely, I resist the authority theme, as it seems directly counter to the Anglo emphasis on personal choice and growth, which I prefer. On the other hand, it is the authoritative structure and guidance of Imago therapy that appeals to many Hispanic clients, as well as to me.

The notion of transcending our present viewpoints, personally or culturally, is related to a spiritual theme that crosses cultures: that of humility and trust in wisdom and resources beyond our own. The evolution of more mature levels of connectedness and individuation involves risk, as we and our partners partly support one another and partly rely on a larger universal matrix or process. Both couples introduced in this chapter alluded to their own sense of God as being supportive of their taking risks with each other. And Imago theory speaks of nature, the universe, or the process, as a way of pointing to this larger context for personal and cultural healing and growth.

EDITORS' COMMENTARY

Few therapists have expertise in working with clients from each and every minority culture. Fortunately, what is most important about counseling minority-group members, as Homer Bain notes, is to understand the general themes underlying a given culture. The best and, in fact, easiest way of learning about those themes is to ask the minority client. Most people are pleased to be asked about the beliefs and rituals that reflect the uniqueness of their culture. They are delighted that someone is interested enough in them to wonder about the cultural thinking that shaped their childhood. Therapists need not be ashamed of their ignorance, and should, when they are in doubt, ask. When working with a culture different from one's own, there often is no other way to gain the information that is necessary to provide culturally relevant therapy.

The importance of cultural awareness is underscored by Dr. Bain's discussion of the five cultural themes he discovered in working with Hispanic couples. What strikes us about these themes is how elegantly they merge two polar opposites: privacy and emotionality, communality and authority. This tension of opposites provides a balance within the Hispanic culture. Consequently, when working with Hispanic couples, the therapist must recognize the couple's need to integrate both ends of the polarities and to express these opposing tendencies in their relationship—both privacy and emotionality, communality and authority, and so forth. Without any understanding of these seemingly contradictory tendencies, therapists would be, at best, stymied in their ability to assist Hispanic couples.

Perhaps the most fundamental of all polarities is that of connectedness and individuation. As Dr. Bain states, connectedness and individuation are mutually inclusive—a statement that seems internally inconsistent. Particularly given the North American culture's proclamation of individuation as the goal, how can anyone claim that connection and individuation are mutually inclusive? According to Imago theory, to validate rather than dismiss another's thoughts and feelings is to say, "You exist." When we are connected on the basis of our empathic understanding of one another, regardless of our disagreements, we can be connected while remaining separate at the same time. If you can see why I have my outlandish cultural beliefs and still hold on to your own, which I view as equally outlandish, we are connected, and we are separate from one another.

Maintaining a fully alive intimate relationship, regardless of our culture, demands that we take risks, and lots of them. When asked in therapy to take a risk, say, to speak out of one's vulnerability, a client might counter, "I don't think I want to go down that road." It is not that the road is so hard to go down; in their private thoughts, the couple has been down it many times before. Rather, what's scary is going down that road accompanied and witnessed by the partner. The fear is, "Once you really know me, you will use it against me." The fear is of someone really understanding our weaknesses, exploiting those weaknesses, and finally controlling us. To discover that this fear is by and large unfounded is itself risky. Indeed, the truths about ourselves and our partner can be more daunting than any of the lies.

We have been advised to "feel the fear and do it anyway." By announcing who they really are and asking for what they need, both in the therapy room and on their T-shirts, Dr. Bain's couples found strength alongside their vulnerability and courage hidden beneath their fear.

Chapter 8

LIVING IN THE "NOT KNOWING"

Maya Kollman

Toward all that is unsolved in your heart, be patient.
Try to love the questions
Do not seek the answers
Which cannot be given
You would not be able to live them.
Live everything
Live the questions now
You will then gradually without noticing it
Live into answers
Some distant day

Rilke

What does living in the "not knowing" mean? Simply put, it means being able to suspend judgment about what is best for ourselves, for our partners, for the clients with whom we work. The need to be certain that what we hold to be true is, in fact, the truth makes it impossible to be respectful and receptive in the presence of others whose sense of truth opposes our own. When we associate our truth with our survival, we will stop at nothing to ensure that our truth survives. We become closed to new possibilities; we become stuck in old, sometimes dangerous patterns. This can be seen in any relational situation—between romantic partners, between countries, between parents and children, or in the therapy room. The beauty of Imago theory (Hendrix, 1988) is that it offers a way out of this rigid defensive stance; it provides a way to live in the "not knowing."

Perhaps this aspect of Imago resonates with me in part because of my own history. When I was married, my husband and I sought therapy for some problems in what was in many ways a strong relationship. The central issue for me was that I was attracted to women. Over the course of time, we went to five different therapists, three of whom actually did a version of the Couples Dialogue. However, all of the therapists viewed my attraction to women as stemming from my fear of and my resistance to doing the work necessary to improve my relationship with my husband. None saw the attraction on its own terms, as a legitimate entity that should be addressed in and of itself.

The "work," as described to my husband and me, included such tasks as developing friendships with heterosexual couples, finding ways to be more romantic, and examining our inability to express anger as we explored our childhood wounds. Unfortunately, this course of treatment had little to do with the fact that I continued to have powerful feelings for a woman with whom I had had an intimate relationship a few years earlier. At that time, I had become so frightened by my feelings that I decided to end the affair immediately and recommit to my marriage. I had gone into therapy then as well and was told that my homosexual feelings were a symptom of my neurotic attachment to my mother.

Had this therapist, and later the therapists with whom my husband and I worked, considered the situation and my position with a sense of curiosity, rather than by relying on analysis and judgment, healing could have started sooner. Had the approach been to mirror rather than interpret, a context might have been established in which I felt safe enough to express my real feelings and my husband felt free enough to respond. If the goal of keeping the couple together was reframed into a goal of allowing the partners to speak the truth to one another no matter what it was, we would have been able to face it and then to move on to grieve for the loss of what had been and to show compassion both for ourselves and for each other. For circumstances to have unfolded in this way, however, the therapy would have had to begin from a place of "not knowing."

The following is an excerpt from my first session with a couple who came to me with similar questions around one partner's sexuality. I began this session as I begin every session—from an open, respectful position in which I do not presume to know their dilemma before I am told.

> **Therapist:** *What is it that brings you both here? Anyone can start. I'd like to hear from both of you.*
> **Susan:** *We've been married for four years and have two children. I recently told John something because I couldn't keep it a secret anymore. When I was in college, I had an intimate relationship with a woman, Stephanie. I felt compelled to be with her. I felt like I loved her. But I knew*

it was wrong; my parents and my church would have been horrified. I ended that relationship because I felt so guilty, and I told myself that I would forget about my friend. Then I met and married John. For the first year, things were all right. I worked and stayed very involved with our church. I got pregnant and had our daughter. But then I began to dream about Stephanie, and over the past three years, my feelings for her have become stronger and stronger. Last Christmas, I ran into her at a party. My feelings were so powerful that I could hardly contain them. I finally confided in John. I am terrified, and so is he. I love him, but I've never felt about him the way I feel about Stephanie. I can't be intimate with John anymore. Before I told him, I became so depressed that I actually thought of killing myself. I don't know what to do.

Therapist (mirrors, validates, and empathizes with Susan): *So, John, tell me your experience.*

John: *When Susan told me, in some ways I was relieved. I thought she didn't want to be physical with me because something about me disgusted her. I am very deeply in love with her, but I've always felt something standing in the way of our being completely connected. I still don't know what to do. It hurts like hell not to feel loved for being the man I am. Susan has tried in the last month to show me what she gets from Stephanie that is missing with me. I have been doing exactly what she says she wants, and yet she still doesn't feel attracted to me. I don't know how much more of this I can take.*

Therapist (mirrors, validates, and empathizes): *I am touched by your dilemma and by how respectful you are of one another. Even in the face of all this confusion and pain, you are not blaming each other, but you are able to feel your partner's pain as well as your own. You obviously care a great deal for each other. Would you be willing to move over to these chairs and face each other while you continue to explore what is going on with both of you?*

(The couple moves their chairs in order to face one another.) *Since Susan started earlier, John, would you finish this sentence stem? "As I sit here, getting ready to talk with you, what I am experiencing is..."*

John: *As I sit here getting ready to talk to you, what I am experiencing is frustration, sadness, fear, and confusion.*

Susan: *(Mirrors)*

Therapist: *And now, Susan, if you would finish the sentence, "As I sit here getting ready to talk with you, what I am experiencing is..."*

Susan: *As I sit here getting ready to talk with you, what I am experiencing is shame, guilt, love, fear, and sadness.*

John: *(Mirrors)*

Therapist: *Now either of you can begin to share more. I am going to ask the one who is not speaking to mirror what your partner says and to check to see if you got it accurately.*

John: *I want so much to make this work for us and the kids, but no matter what I do, it doesn't work.*

Susan (mirrors):   *Did I get that right?*

John: *Yes, you got it.*

Therapist: *Ask him if there is more.*

Susan: *Is there more?*

John: *No.*

Therapist (to John):   *Say more about what it is like to try so hard and have nothing change.*

John: *I end up feeling so inadequate. I know that the only thing that would work would be to turn myself into a woman. But still, a voice in my head says, "If you were more of a man, better in bed, a better provider, Susan would be attracted to you, not to Stephanie."*

Susan (mirrors):   *Did I get it? Is there more?*

John: *I feel really hopeless and scared, and I get really angry that you knew and didn't tell me.*

Susan (mirrors):   *Is there more?*

John: *No.*

Therapist: *You're both doing wonderfully. I'm inspired, John, by your willingness to let Susan really see your pain, and Susan, by your willingness to hear him. Now, let's reverse, and Susan, you speak while John mirrors back.*

Susan: *It is so hard for me to hear you, even though I know you are being honest. When I hear your pain, I just want to pretend that my feelings for Stephanie are gone and that you and I can go on with our life together.*

John (mirrors):   *Is there more?*

Susan: *Yes. As much as I want to move forward with you, I know I can't. We have had romantic dinners, communicated better, tried to become more sexual, and talked more about what we need from each other. Nothing works. It seems like the more I try to make my feelings for Stephanie go away, the more powerful they become.*

John (mirrors):   *Is there more?*

Susan: *I guess I feel the same way you do. No matter what I try, it doesn't seem to change things, so I end up feeling bad, guilty, and hopeless that we can ever be happy together.*

John (mirrors):   *Is there more?*

Susan: *No.*

Therapist (to Susan):   *Say more about the guilt and hopelessness.*

Susan: *I wish I could make this all go away. I don't want to hurt you, but I also don't want to live without feeling alive and connected, and the only time I ever felt that way was with Stephanie. I don't understand how something that is about love can be bad in the eyes of God.*
John (mirrors): *Is there more?*
Susan: *I need you to know how much I care about you.*
John (mirrors): *Is there more?*
Susan: *No.*

They dialogued this way until the end of the session. I continued to use sentence stems to help them deepen their affect and connect their current frustrations with their childhood experiences. Although, by the end of the session, there had been no resolution and Susan and John remained in pain, they both stated that it felt good to finally talk openly about their feelings.

Therapist: *Let's end with each of you finishing the sentence, "As we end this session, what I am experiencing is..."*
Susan: *What I am experiencing as we end this session is gratitude— gratitude for a safe place in which to talk about this and gratitude for your willingness to stay connected with me.*
John (mirrors): *What I am experiencing is a mix. Talking like this makes me even more confused, because it reminds me of how close we can feel, and then I don't understand why it can't work. When we are angry and distant, it hurts less but actually feels much worse. Overall, though, I too am grateful that we can talk like this.*
Susan: *(Mirrors)*
Therapist: *I am enriched by your vulnerability and your courage. If you would be willing, I would like to suggest that you move slowly and keep exploring, rather than decide anything right now. I would like to invite you to come here once a week to dialogue with each other about what direction to take with your relationship. I would also suggest that you take a couples' workshop and participate in a couples' group.*

At the workshop they attended about two months later, Susan and John decided that each of them needed to start a new life. In their sessions with me after the workshop, they went through some "goodbye" processes. They also joined a group of couples who were struggling with similar issues.

They are now divorced, although they are still living under the same roof for financial reasons. John had opted for the divorce so that he could feel free to see other women. Susan wanted to renew her relationship with Stephanie and is dating her, although she hasn't yet introduced her to her children. Susan and John dialogue weekly to work out the logistics of their living arrangements.

WORKING WITH SEXUAL-PREFERENCE ISSUES

One of Imago theory's core building blocks is the creation of a sense of safety for our clients. This sense of safety is facilitated especially by the therapist's willingness to come into the therapy unencumbered by preconceived ideas of what will and will not work for the couple. "Not knowing" is an exquisitely powerful force when we are working with sexual-preference issues.

A partner who acknowledges some confusion regarding his or her sexuality may feel very frightened about what this self-doubt means about himself or herself and how it will affect the future of the marriage. The first step in working with this couple is to use the dialogue process to alleviate some of the fear and to promote sharing. By using sentence stems, the therapist gently encourages partners to look beneath surface content and to uncover vulnerabilities and hurt. The partners should be guided to move slowly, to take the time they need in order to explore. They should be assured that they need not do anything about what they discover, and that whatever the outcome, they will ultimately benefit from their work together.

If, after a period of exploration, the questioning client accepts that he or she is gay, both partners should be encouraged to explore the literature and to seek out gay/lesbian resources in their community. Joining a group of similar couples where they can share their confusion, anger, hurt, and terror with others in the same situation can be a powerful healing experience.

Even when the question as to whether one is gay or bisexual has been adequately addressed, other questions remain: Although I am indeed gay/bisexual, do I really want to leave the life I've established? What about my children? What if my job would be endangered by my coming out? What if I really love my opposite-sex partner and don't want to see him or her in pain? What if I have elderly parents who might suffer a stroke or heart attack if I were to leave my marriage for someone of the same sex?

The therapist must not respond to a couple's pressure to provide a quick fix. It is crucial instead that he or she help the couple to recognize the complexity of their situation, validate their discomfort with being in it, and support their moving slowly and carefully.

The therapist should also help the couple, when they are ready, to grieve the loss of their dream. Using the "goodbye" process, the partners say goodbye to what was wonderful as well as to what was difficult about their relationship. They say goodbye to their dream and then they greet the future. I recommend that couples who are separating do this exercise many times to assist themselves in letting go. Each time they go through the process, they will grieve another piece of the lost dream and move a bit closer to a new life.

SUMMARY

It is the case in all of our clinical work that we must balance the knowledge we have with that which we do not presume to have. One technique that helps me build on this paradox with clients is to ask each partner to use this phrase in dialogue: "As I sit here looking at you, getting ready to talk with you, what I am experiencing is... ." This sentence stem can have profound effects, both on the interactions between partners and on those between therapist and client.

Imago therapy offers a toolbox of techniques to help bring couples into connection. These techniques are particularly conducive to allowing the couple's own truth to emerge, as the therapist mirrors and becomes a container for their experience. Where sexual preference is an issue, this truth may take time to evolve, and its implications may be very far-reaching. However, if we serve as witness, replacing judgment with interest, assumption with acknowledgment, and rigidity with wonder, we can help partners move away from surface content toward deeper feelings. Only if the truth is revealed will they be able to grieve and let go of what was, and thus find their own peace.

BIBLIOGRAPHY

Hendrix, H. (1988). *Getting the love you want: A guide for couples.* New York: Holt.

Mahler, M., Pine, F., & Bergman, A. (1975). *The psychological birth of the human infant: Symbiosis and individuation.* New York: Basic Books.

Stern, D. (1977). *The first relationship: Infant and mother.* Cambridge, Mass.: Harvard University Press.

EDITORS' COMMENTARY

Maya Kollman reminds us that, regardless of how skilled, highly experienced, or well intentioned any therapist might be, ultimately the couple is the expert on their own relationship. Citing her own experience of trying to decide whether to leave her marriage for a relationship with a female lover, Kollman has us consider the possibility that a couple could be hurt, rather than helped, by an inflexible approach to couples therapy. By clinging to preconceived "truths" about relationships—insisting, for example, that all couples stay together "no matter what"—therapists risk overlooking the unique realities and limitations of the couple sitting in their office.

Ironically, the partners' childhood wounding, which is reactivated by the couple's relationship and thus leads the couple into therapy, can be further amplified by an "all-knowing" therapist. A rigid therapeutic stance could lead the therapist to pathologize a couple if, say, the partners have not changed in ways that Imago therapy, or any other therapy, predicts they will. Not all couples are alike. As Kollman implies, the therapist's interpretations, however brilliant, impose a specific meaning on the couple's experience, a meaning that may be more about the "truth" of the therapist than about the "truth" of the couple.

The case example of Susan and John underscores the importance of the therapist's taking a "not knowing" stance. We see how tentatively and respectfully the therapist intervenes with the couple during the dialogue. She allows painful emotions to emerge, not interfering with the couple's sharing of confusion, fear, guilt, and sadness over Susan's sexuality. She facilitates the couple's dialogue without aiming them toward any solution or outcome. In essence, she trusts the dialogical process despite her uncertainty over what will come of it. By establishing an utterly safe and open atmosphere, and by modeling full acceptance of the partners as they are, the therapist sets the stage for the partners to discover their own "truth."

For Susan and John, this discovery led to their ending their relationship. Clearly, the tolerance and openness established by the therapist did not cause the couple to break up, nor would a rigid or shaming attitude on the part of the therapist have inspired them to permanently remain in their relationship. Rather, the openness that the therapist provided and modeled for the couple made possible their fearless exploration of themselves. In turn, they found the courage to acknowledge and to act in congruence with their authentic selves.

By contrasting the treatment in this case with her own experiences in couples therapy, Kollman raises some sobering concerns over how therapists conduct therapy. For instance, being gay or lesbian in our culture, even by today's enlightened standards, results in an overlay of shame and guilt. The therapist who interprets homosexual desires as indicating some form of psychopathology—as was the case when the author sought couples therapy—only adds to the burden of self-loathing suffered by many gays and lesbians. In sum, this type of therapeutic stance does more than provide a disservice to clients: it harms instead of helps.

Both the couple and the therapist need to tolerate the "not knowing." It is all too easy for a therapist who is uncomfortable with ambiguity to transmit this discomfort to the partners, who consequently draw conclusions based on some preordained set of "shoulds" and "musts." Although this process might alleviate some of the therapist's and the couple's discomfort, it will not alleviate the couple's core issues. Even Imago processes can be misused to meet the unconscious needs of the therapist, rather than to enhance the growth of the couple. This chapter argues eloquently for the need to transform not only the dynamics of the couple, but also the attitudes of couples therapists.

Chapter 9

MULTIPLE MIRRORING WITH LESBIAN AND GAY COUPLES: FROM PEORIA TO P-TOWN

Sharon Kleinberg and Patricia Zorn

Our workshops for gay and lesbian couples in Cape Cod's Provincetown, the major gay resort in the Northeast, always attract participants from diverse settings: large cities, small towns, rural hamlets. The P-Town workshops teach Imago theory and communication skills while enabling couples to understand and explore the effects of homophobia on their relationships. Although these workshops are process rather than subject oriented and couples may pick whatever issue is relevant to them, frequently those of homophobia and lack of mirroring while growing up are responsible for many of the problems that arise between couples. As therapists, who are themselves lesbian, we believe it is important to help couples become aware of the impact of these two issues on their relationship. Imago techniques offer a unique way to bring their often covert influence into the couple's consciousness and to help partners come to terms with the need to create opportunities for mirroring and other support.

ROBERTA AND COLLEEN

Roberta and Colleen arrived late in Provincetown, both in an irritable mood, for the gay and lesbian couples workshop. Their conflict had begun as they drove through Cape Cod and Colleen suddenly announced that she was going to detour through a small town where her grandmother used to live. She said she wanted to see what her grandmother's house looked like now, so many years after Colleen had spent a memorable summer there when she was 10 years old. "That was the summer I decided to become a nurse, you know," she told Roberta.

Roberta was dumbfounded. Colleen had never mentioned the summer with her grandmother, or the reasons why she had become a nurse. Both topics seemed to come out of nowhere. When Roberta asked Colleen about this, Colleen explained that her grandmother had been a midwife, and that when she saw how proud she was that she had helped deliver so many babies and how appreciative the women were of her efforts, Colleen decided to go into nursing. When asked to say more, Colleen shared how she had witnessed her grandmother's bonding with women and her true enjoyment of the company of other women. Since Colleen had experienced her own mother as aloof and had no women friends of her own, being privy to her grandmother's openness and joy made her feel less lonely and more hopeful. The story startled Roberta as she had always thought that she knew Colleen very well after living with her for 20 years. But perhaps not.

The couple lived in a small New England village where they were not "out," had no gay friends, and were relieved that their neighbors thought of them as sisters. The P-Town workshop, recommended by Colleen's straight therapist, was the first gay event they had ever attended. When they arrived at the gay guest house where the workshop would take place, they were so nervous that they had to practice deep breathing for several minutes before getting out of the car. During the couples' introduction segment of the workshop, Roberta and Colleen sat on the side, volunteering very little information about themselves. Only as the safety of the group became more evident were they able to relax and begin to participate more fully.

When the participants were asked to select an issue on which to work while learning the dialogue process, Roberta brought up Colleen's visit to her grandmother's house. Roberta admitted how shocked she'd been to realize how ignorant she was about one of the most memorable summers in Colleen's life. Had Roberta never picked up Colleen's hints about her grandmother's influence on her? Or was it possible that Colleen had never mentioned it? Colleen ultimately replied that she had not, in fact, mentioned it before.

NON-REFLECTION OR DISTORTED REFLECTIONS AND LESBIAN AND GAY COUPLES

From a gay or lesbian therapist's perspective, it is understandable why Colleen never revealed her summer with her grandmother. She had become an expert at hiding her feelings, her need for the things that meant most to her, and, in fact, much of her whole self. Her true self was forced underground while she was trying to survive being a gay child in a conservative Catholic family. As she gradually realized her growing desire to be affectionate toward other girls, Colleen kept her longings hidden deep within her. She knew that telling anyone meant real trouble. As she related in the dialogue, she even tried to erase all lesbian thoughts from her mind because, as a good Catholic girl, she feared that God could read her thoughts and would punish her. In fact, in Colleen's attempt to hide her loving feelings for other girls, awareness of her thoughts and feelings in general became hazy. What became apparent was that Colleen had learned early that to share personal feelings was dangerous because she had to be vigilant about keeping her "special" feelings hidden. Her vigilance spilled over to all aspects of her life. Better to be "safe than sorry," so little of her inner life was shared with anyone.

From an Imago perspective, Colleen needs a way to explore and rediscover her authentic self, sharing her hidden thoughts and feelings with Roberta without fear of being judged. She needs a framework in which such communication is safe, which it rarely was while Colleen was growing up.

Colleen's socialization was similar to that of other lesbians, as well as gay men, who, in the absence of positive mirroring from parents, family, peers, and society, learn to hide who they are. Gay children experience either no mirroring at all, rendering them invisible, or distorted mirroring in the form of faulty, grotesque, negative images of gays and lesbians. They see "distorted images reflected back in words like: perverse, sinful, immoral, infantile, arrested, inadequate, or (they see) no reflection at all—a peculiar silence." (Buloff & Osterman, 1995, p. 95). Rarely do gay children see positive role models of same-sex couples who treat each other intimately and affectionately. When gay children look for a reflection of themselves in their parents and society, they do not see it. Instead, they often see hostility in their parents' attitudes and behavior toward gay people. Gay children who are members of minorities suffer even more severely from lack of mirroring than do straight children from minority groups; the latter, at least, are able to find mirroring through their parents, relatives, and neighbors, and occasionally through movies, television, and magazines.

Gays and lesbians learn to assess, at a given moment, how safe it is to be visible and how much of their authentic self can be revealed. Having desires that are forbidden by society produces shame because the messages reflected back are that those desires are not "normal." Living with shame forces individuals to retreat into a world of isolation, where their feelings and desires will never be discovered. Over time, gays and lesbians become experts at stifling expressions of their true self. Living with such self-deception further increases their sense of isolation and lowers their self-esteem.

Keeping one's feelings under wraps over long periods of time also has disastrous effects on intimacy. As Cavallaro and Zevy (1987) put it, "Intimacy involves the ability to disclose the essential, most inward parts of oneself to another person and have them equally disclose themselves." If all goes well, we develop our capacity for intimacy during childhood, which allows us to build on this capacity as we move into adulthood. However, if a child learns not to reveal intimate aspects of himself or herself due to "deceptive patterns of communication," then, as these authors rightly maintain, "intimate relationships cannot be developed until the layers of invisibility are peeled away and the essential person emerges" (p. 91).

Since identity develops early and in an interpersonal context, growing up in a homophobic society creates challenges for gays and lesbians in developing self-esteem, a positive self-image, and a strong identity.

Roberta's story is similar to Colleen's: as a child she was not seen nor was she valued for the person she really was. There are, however, some significant differences. Roberta's mother was a narcissistic woman who needed a great deal of mirroring to sustain her own view of herself as beautiful and feminine. Roberta's younger sister was the favored child who could provide this function. The impact of this dynamic was revealed when it was Roberta's turn to dialogue.

> **Roberta:**   *Colleen, I can't believe you never told me about the summer at your grandmother's house. How could you have kept something so important from me?*
> **Therapist:**   *Keep the focus on yourself. How do you feel about not knowing? Start with "I feel..."*
> **Roberta:**   *I feel so angry and frustrated and exasperated! It makes me crazy that I don't know about something that was so important to you.*
> **Therapist:**   *Colleen, mirror that back.*

Colleen mirrors and asks, "Did I get it?" Once she's told Yes, she asks, "Is there more?"

> **Roberta:**   *Yes. I'm not just frustrated about not knowing about the special summer at your grandmother's. I'm frustrated about all the times you don't include me in the important or even unimportant aspects of your life. For example, I really get frustrated when you come home from work or from dinner with a friend and rarely share much of your experience with me.*
> **Colleen:**   *So what I'm hearing you say is that it's really frustrating for you when I have experiences at work or dinner with a friend and share very little of it with you. Am I getting that right?*
> **Roberta:**   *Yes, that's it.*

Therapist gives Roberta a sentence stem to encourage her to go more deeply: "And what scares me about that is. . ."

> **Roberta:**   *And what scares me about that is that it feels like I'll never get to really know what's important in your life and that I'll continue to feel alienated from you.*

Colleen mirrors.

Therapist, continuing to help her go deeper, says: "And what hurts me about this is. . ."

> **Roberta:**   *And what hurts me is that I feel shut out and unspecial. I've known you for 20 years and I feel you treat me like a stranger. I love you so much; you're the most special person in my life, yet I don't always feel special to you. I know you choose to live with me and build a home together, but when I keep finding out all that you don't share with me I feel like you don't really care.*

Colleen mirrors, then asks, "Did I get it? Is there more?"

> **Roberta:**   *Yes you got it. No, there's no more.*

Therapist offers stem, "And what this reminds me of in childhood is . . ."

> **Roberta:**   *You're just like my mother. She used to take my younger sister, Shelly, to the mall with her. Shelly was her favorite. My mom loved buying my sister all those frilly dresses with matching accessories. Once they even came home with those "mother–daughter" outfits. Mom didn't like to go shopping with me because I liked wearing comfortable clothes. . .you know, pants and polo shirts. Shelly told me that after they finished shopping, they'd go for ice cream sodas and Mom would tell her all these personal things about how she felt about Aunt Kathy and Aunt Tess. I felt so hurt and left out. Mom never shared anything personal with me. I wanted so much to be closer to her, to be as special as Shelly was. But nothing I did worked. I wanted her to love me enough to share stuff with me. I guess it's like I feel with you.*

Colleen mirrors.

> **Therapist:**   *Colleen, do you have enough information now that it makes sense to you why Roberta gets frustrated? And can you imagine how she might feel?*

Colleen: *It really makes sense that when I didn't tell you about the summer at my grandmother's you got frustrated. It must have been especially upsetting because you frequently experience me as not sharing with you about events in my life. And in light of your growing up with a mom who was very close to your younger sister and never shared stuff with you, I imagine when I'm not forthcoming, you probably feel angry, unspecial, unloved, alienated, and alone. Is that what you feel? Did I miss anything?*

Roberta replied that Colleen got it all.

What Roberta needs, then, is an opportunity to be valued as a trusted friend who is special to her partner. She needs a safe context in which she and her partner can mutually share their desires, hopes, and dreams as individuals and as a couple.

For those who discover their homosexual feelings during adolescence, the issue of peer group participation is excruciating. As Malyon (1985) points out, "Peer group validation is of fundamental importance in the development of autonomy and self-esteem. Conformity brings acceptance, while differences, especially stigmatized divergences, result in alienation. To consolidate an identity, there must be the freedom to engage in peer interactions that incorporate the expression of needs, values, interests, and proclivities" (p. 60). While there are now groups for gay and lesbian adolescents in most major cities, the choice too often is still between remaining isolated from other adolescents or developing a false self to fit into a group—clearly two undermining alternatives. Recent studies suggest that up to one third of the skyrocketing incidence of teen suicides are associated with questions of sexual orientation (Miller, 1992). This is a painful reminder that homophobia can kill. In a recent growth seminar, a conservative couple shared about the tragic suicide of a beloved teenage nephew. Tearfully they admitted that they had been shocked and did not understand why such a lovable, wonderful boy had taken his own life. On the surface, it made no sense. It later came out that this boy had confessed to a guidance counselor that he was experiencing feelings for other boys, and that he was terribly ashamed and felt he would be punished and ostracized if anyone knew. The guidance counselor told him that it was a phase and that he would grow out of it. One can only wonder at the dismay and isolation he must have felt with no one to validate his experience as a young gay man. The tragic reality is that gay children are invalidated and unmirrored. They often become throwaways: children who are forced to leave home because their caretakers cannot accept them.

But even those gays and lesbians who become aware of their homosexual feelings later in life have introjected homophobic attitudes much earlier, leading to the development of internalized homophobia (Margolies, Becker, & Jackson-Brewer, 1987, p. 230). "To one degree or another anti-homosexual attitudes become embedded in all persons who live in unaccepting cultures" (Falco, 1991, p. 71). Internalized homophobia is ever present, and results when these negative attitudes take up residency within the selves of lesbians and gays (Margolies et al., 1987, p. 230).

Internalized homophobia is also brought into the relationships of gays and lesbians. For example, partners may take too much personal responsibility for relationship problems, in response to the widely held notion that lesbian and gay relationships are faulty and canot survive—itself a homophobic point of view.

Other examples of internalized homophobia can be more subtle and difficult to recognize. Several examples are evident in the case of Roberta and Colleen. Their desire to pass as straight in society, even in situations where it is not objectively dangerous for them to be out, believing that others would not accept them, is exemplified in many ways: never taking each other to family holiday gatherings because, supposedly, it would be "boring"; failing to recognize their partnership as itself a family; referring to themselves as single and checking that category on forms; using the pronoun "I" rather than "we" when discussing events attended with the partner; not identifying as lesbian, even after being in a committed relationship for over 20 years; never announcing their anniversary to straight friends with whom they are intimate because anniversaries aren't as "important" for gay and lesbian couples; suppressing any public displays of affection together, while being very affectionate with friends, colleagues, and family; not having gay friends, claiming they have never met a gay person they really liked (avoiding guilt by association).

Internalized homophobia can become part of the power struggle for gay and lesbian couples. One partner, for example, might criticize the other for looking too "butch" or too "femme." One might be upset with a partner who tries to look and act straight in order to be more socially acceptable. Two partners might keep their money and possessions separate, fearing the inevitable breakup, because it is commonly believed that gay relationships don't last. Or one partner might resent the other's resistance to introducing the partner to his or her family owing to the belief that the family would never accept them as a couple. All couples need to dialogue about these issues, relating them to each partner's own internalized homophobia. The therapist can establish a safe context in which the couple can work on the issues as a team, but if this is done only within the relationship, it can put a severe strain on the couple and the relationship itself. As Toder (1992) puts it, combating the pressures of homophobia on a daily basis requires enormous strength that "comes from inner resources and from the love and support of our partners." But this might be asking too much, as "it is very easy to drain these resources and to feel overwhelmed by the huge obstacles we face" (p. 53). Working within a gay environment, however, can provide mirroring and support for gay couples and an ability to understand their struggles in the context of a larger society.

THERAPEUTIC IMPLICATIONS

Successful therapy with gay and lesbian couples has two requirements: a therapist who has done his or her "homowork,"and is familiar with and sensitive to gay issues; and ongoing contact by the couple with a gay and lesbian community. For gay people, their sexual orientation is not just another therapeutic issue; it is often the major issue.

Viewing sexual orientation as a non-issue, or treating it as though it were similar to other issues, is detrimental to gay and lesbian clients. Because gay people must constantly monitor social situations for indications of how safe or unsafe it is to reveal their gay identity, they can approach therapy, as Colleen approached her relationship, with a reluctance, built up over years, to reveal their true selves. It is essential that the therapist not reinforce such silence. Gay and lesbian couples should not be expected to look like heterosexual couples.

For example, lesbian couples may seem to lack individuation, with partners appearing more closely merged with each other than typical heterosexual partners. This is due, in part, to the fact that gay partners are of the same gender, but more significantly, it is a result of the mirroring role each partner performs for the other. Buloff and Osterman (1995) call this "double-jointed mirroring," which provides the validation lacking from society (p. 99). Without positive role models in society or in the media, same-sex couples have to derive mirroring from their relationship, thus appearing as too close or symbiotic to therapists who are unfamiliar with the inner workings of gay relationships (Kleinberg & Zorn, 1995).

Therapists must become aware of, and sensitive to, the different issues that affect gay couples. Not only must they identify the external sources of stress on a gay couple's relationship, but they must also strongly affirm the gay client's love for another person of the same sex. Such affirmation is especially crucial because of the lack of affirmation that has characterized the client's entire gay life.

Carl Rogers (1980) was the first to recommend mirroring as the primary means for enhancing one's understanding of the experience of another. He discovered that mirroring facilitates the other's healing and increases his or her self-esteem. He also found that being mirrored allows a person to access more of her or his thoughts and feelings, leading to a more congruent sense of self.

Mirroring is, therefore, the essence of our work with gay and lesbian couples. As therapists, we attempt to mirror our clients as much and in as many different ways as possible. The Couples Dialogue is an ideal tool for lesbian and gay couples because it is structured to provide the mirroring that clients have been missing in their lives.

THE WORKSHOP: AN EXPERIENCE
OF MULTIPLE MIRRORING

Some of the lesbian and gay participants in our couples workshops come because they are on the verge of breakup; others attend for a tune-up. Most say that they need better communication skills. What many of the couples are unaware of is the extent to which homophobia, especially insidious internalized homophobia, profoundly affects the issues between partners. We've discovered that as these issues emerge during the workshop, they provide opportunities for multiple mirroring.

For example, as "out" lesbian facilitators, not only are we able to teach communications skills, such as the Couples Dialogue, but we also can give examples of the effects of homophobia from our own experiences. Participants, therefore, quickly realize that it is safe for them to reflect on and talk about their own experiences. Eventually, partners begin to pay attention to the more subtle forms of internalized homophobia that have had an impact on their own relationship.

We've found that gay and lesbian couples, especially those who have few or no gay friends, are hungry to hear other couples' stories. They want to share about gay life, and when they do, they are experiencing a form of mirroring. Such experiences enhance a couple's intimacy. In the Provincetown workshop, multiple mirroring also takes place outside of the workshop room: going out for meals or seeing other gays in town allows participants to feel comfortable enough to continue to be visible as a couple on the streets and in the restaurants. In less gay-friendly locales, we suggest that the workshop participants dine or spend the evening together, so that individual couples won't be confronted with the negativity or hostility that causes gay partners to become aloof toward each other. For many gay and lesbian couples, spontaneous signs of affection in public, such as hugging and holding hands, have been stifled for so long that the couple has difficulty being loving spontaneously in private as well. The workshop becomes a safe place in which to experiment with such outward signs of intimacy.

Ron and Jess

Ron and Jess had been together openly, as a gay couple, for 12 years. Both are politically active in gay organizations. Their relationship issues emerged during the Brag exercise, right after the workshop began. In the Brag exercise, each person introduces his or her partner to the group by enthusiastically describing, in approximately 60 seconds how he or she is the perfect partner. The Brag exercise allows couples to acknowledge, in public, the positive, healing, nurturing qualities of their relationship. It is a rare experience for many gay couples.

They talk about how wonderfully generous, attractive, sexy, warm, kind, and special their lovers are to them. When they do this exercise, often one or both partners will say how touched they were to hear such positive statements made publicly. Sometimes they cry. In one workshop, when a woman said that her lover was wonderful because she had stayed with her, even when the going got rough, for 25 years, the entire group burst into spontaneous applause—a clear indication of how hungry gays are for positive mirroring of long-term gay relationships.

When Jess and Ron got up to brag, Jess seemed angry while Ron looked terrified at being in front of the room. Later, during a break, they got into an argument. Jess was upset that Ron had barely spoken during the bragging exercise. Jess told Ron that he looked stilted and uncomfortable and said very little to the group about what a perfect partner Jess was. Jess had hoped that Ron could say publicly all the loving things he said so easily in private, and that then they would watch as the group members smiled, applauded, and expressed delight in their relationship. Jess said he was tired of Ron's always being unassertive and passive around other people. He said, "Ron, you have opinions about things, but you just won't express them."

Ron replied, "I'm afraid that if I speak up, you'll get angry and be critical of me." Jess responded that he knew he sometimes got angry at Ron, but never for saying how he felt. "I may not like everything you say," Jess said, "but that's okay. I like how bright, creative, witty, and caring you are, and I want other people to see how great you are too."

During the Couples Dialogue, Jess agreed to mirror Ron so that they could both learn more about this issue. Ron remembered having similar feelings during his childhood. He was always afraid to speak up in public or even to express himself in private, because he was often criticized for what he said. "When I was in sixth grade, the school librarian wrote a note to my teacher because I didn't want to read the biographies of football players or war heroes that she had picked out for me. I wanted books about people who were kind and helped others, like

Florence Nightingale, Albert Schweitzer, and Eleanor Roosevelt." Ron recalled that he enjoyed helping his sister coordinate outfits for her Barbie doll and that he had asked for one for himself for Christmas. His parents and grandfather were shocked and criticized him for this for weeks, hounding him to play instead with the toy soldiers they had given him. Ron also remembered how he liked going with his older sister to movies or shopping in the mall; she would let him tag along and she loved and accepted him for who he truly was.

Ron realized, through this dialogue, how he had adapted to his family life during childhood. "I stopped asking for things I wanted, for fear of being criticized and not fitting into the rigid sex-role stereotypes that my family and teachers demanded. I stopped speaking. I stopped telling people what I thought and felt because I knew they would be critical. So I went around with people who didn't make these demands on me. It was my strategy for avoiding criticism and disapproval because I didn't meet the image of the son that my family wanted."

Ron and Jess were relieved to discover that what had seemed like a problem rooted in their relationship was, instead, a result of Ron's growing up in a homophobic family. From Jess, then, Ron needed safety and support, so that he could begin to speak truthfully about who he really was.

When it was Ron's turn to mirror Jess, Jess recalled how, as a boy, he had become aware that he was different from other boys, and, by the time he reached adolescence, he knew that he had feelings toward other boys. During his teen years, he had no male peer relationships; he never felt like he was one of the boys, and he was viewed as aloof and felt isolated. Because he was frequently alone, there was no one there to mirror him for who he was. He yearned to become part of a group. So when Ron resisted going up to brag about Jess because he feared being criticized, it restimulated in Jess the feelings of isolation and shame that he remembered from adolescence.

Jess remembered times in the locker room after gym class, being aware of how the other boys joked and bragged about the pretty girls to whom they felt attracted. When a guy gave his ring or letter sweater to a particularly popular girl, he was seen by his peers as sexy and desirable. The adolescent girls would sneak out to the handball courts and spray-paint a red heart with their initials linked to the initials of a boy they liked. Who you were going steady with that week was proudly announced to your friends for their approbation. Jess could participate in none of this. He had no outward validation from his peer group as a desirable, popular, sexy young man. The shame and isolation he felt here were profound. Once Jess and Ron were able to hear about each other's painful childhood experiences, they were compassionate and loving with each other.

As a Behavior Change Request, Jess asked that at the next dinner party they attended, Ron would put his arm around Jess and tell at least two people something he had enjoyed about Jess that week. Ron's request of Jess was that the next time he suggested something that Jess didn't like, Jess would initiate a dialogue by saying, "Something just got triggered for me and I would like to understand it better. Could we do a dialogue?" This approach would help Ron feel less criticized and less likely to shut down.

The results of this couple's work culminated in the candle ceremony that concludes these weekends. We developed the ceremony as a ritual in which couples acknowledge, and are acknowledged for, their relationships. A large candle is lighted in the front of the room to represent the light and energy of all gay relationships. As each couple comes up, each of the partners lights a small candle from the large one. Then, holding their candles and facing each other, the lovers tell each other one thing they learned about the partner in the workshop and one thing they appreciate about the other. There are many intense and profound moments as couples witness each other's testimonies.

During the candle ceremony, Ron and Jess looked uncomfortable. Finally, Ron got up, grabbed Jess's hand, and led him to the front of the room. Ron beamed at Jess and told him that he was the sexiest and most desirable man he'd ever known, and that he was proud to be in a relationship with him. Then, reaching into a bag, Ron pulled out a T-shirt he had purchased during the lunch break. Painted on the back was a big red heart with both of their initials inside. Ron said, "This is for the world to know that you're number one and you're mine." Jess had tears in his eyes as he let himself experience the validation he had craved all his life. When he was finally able to speak, he took Ron's hand and told him how much he appreciated Ron's struggle to be open, visible, and vocal in light of the constant cirticism he had received as a child. He restated his commitment to take responsibility for his tendency to become critical when he was scared or hurt.

AFTER THE WORKSHOP: RETURN TO A WORLD OF DISTORTED REFLECTIONS

At the end of every workshop, couples spontaneously exchange phone numbers, and often plan to visit each other or to stay in touch in some way. Participants have invited each other to spend Chanukah, Christmas, or Thanksgiving together, thus forming an extended loving and accepting peer group. In addition to such informal contacts, we encourage couples to establish support groups in which they can continue the dialogue skills and multiple mirroring they learned in the workshop. In New York City, where we live, we offer a weekly couples therapy group for this purpose. Support must be ongoing if couples are to live in a homophobic world while still maintaining the positive energy and hopeful enthusiasm they derived from the weekend.

The nonsupportive, antigay world can quickly intrude into couples' lives. After the Provincetown workshop, we got a call from one of the participants, Marcus, who was very upset and angry. He and his partner, Lee, had left the workshop feeling close and connected. During the trip home, they pulled into a rest stop to get jackets from the trunk of their car. Lee lifted a suitcase and hurt his back. The pain was excruciating, so they rushed to a nearby hospital. In the emergency room, Lee was whisked away. The admitting clerk assumed that Marcus, who is black, and Lee, who is blond and blue-eyed, had no family relationship. Marcus was not allowed any say in Lee's treatment, nor was he even allowed to see Lee.

Had this same incident occurred with a heterosexual couple, married for one hour and setting off on their honeymoon, they would have had more rights and privileges regarding each other's welfare than did gay partners who had been living together in a committed relationship for over 15 years (Berzon, 1990). Marcus called us to get some validation for what had happened at the hospital. He also needed us to reflect back, once again, the reality and the value of their loving relationship.

Several months after the workshop, Roberta and Colleen wrote to let us know of their progress. They had been able to locate a lesbian support group 30 miles from their hometown, which they attended twice a month to socialize and participate in various events. Additionally, there were often break-out groups where interested couples shared mutual concerns that affected their lives. Roberta volunteered for the events committee and Colleen became involved in doing mailings.

They reported how much closer they felt with each other as a result of being able to be more open with other lesbians. In addition, they taught their therapist the Couples Dialogue process so they could continue to do their personal work in therapy.

CONCLUSION

The discrimination that all gay and lesbian couples must confront in our homophobic society creates ongoing stresses (Greene, 1995, p. 11). We believe that these couples need the continued support, safety, and multiple mirroring of a gay group to overcome this negativity. The group becomes a holding environment in which the teaching and practice of the Couples Dialogue becomes a powerful and healing experience.

When couples begin to mirror, validate, and empathize with their partners and other gay couples, they also begin the journey toward healing as individuals and as a couple. The journey can bring about a reawakening of the sense of full aliveness that most gay partners lost in childhood, and it can provide the support and inspiration needed by lesbian and gay couples from Peoria to P-Town.

BIBLIOGRAPHY

Berzon, B. (1990). *Permanent partners: Building gay and lesbian relationships that last.* New York: Penguin.

Buloff, B., & Osterman, M. (1995). Queer reflections: Mirroring and the lesbian experience of self. In J. Glassgold & S. Iasenza (Eds.), *Lesbians and psychoanalysis: Revolutions in theory and practice.* New York: Free Press.

Cavallaro, S. A., & Zevy, L. (1987). Invisibility, fantasy, and intimacy: Princess Charming is not a prince. In Boston Lesbian Psychologies Collective (Eds.), *Lesbian psychologies: explorations and challenges* (pp. 229–241). Urbana.: University of Illinois Press.

Falco, K. L. (1991). *Psychotherapy with lesbian clients: Theory into practice* (p. 71). New York: Brunner/Mazel.

Frommer, M. S. (1994). Homosexuality and psychoanalysis: Technical considerations revisited. In *Psychoanalytic dialogues* (vol. 4, pp. 215–233). New York: Analytic Press.

Greene, B. (1995). Addressing racism, sexism, and heterosexism in psychoanalytic psychotherapy. In J. Glassgold & S. Iasenza (Eds.), *Lesbians and psychoanalysis: Revolutions in theory and practice.* New York: Free Press.

Hawkins, R. L. (1992). Therapy with the male couple. In S. H. Dworkin & F. J. Gutierrez (Eds.), *Counseling gay men and lesbians: Journey to the end of the rainbow.*

Hendrix, H. (1988). *Getting the love you want: A guide for couples.* New York: Harper & Row.

Hendrix, H. (1992). *Keeping the love you find: A guide for singles.* New York: Simon & Schuster.

Kleinberg, S., & Zorn, P. (1995). Rekindling the flame: A therapeutic approach to strengthening lesbian relationships. In J. Glassgold & S. Iasenza (Eds.), *Lesbians and psychoanalysis: Revolutions in theory and practice.* New York: Free Press.

Malyon, A. K. (1985). Psychotherapeutic implications of internalized homophobia. In J. C. Gonsiorek (Ed.), *A guide to psychotherapy with gay and lesbian clients* (pp. 59–89). New York: Harrington Park Press.

Margolies, L., Becker, M., & Jackson-Brewer, K. (1987). Internalized homophobia: Identifying and treating the oppressor within. In Boston Lesbian Psychologies Collective (Eds.), *Lesbian psychologies: Explorations and challenges* (pp. 229–241). Urbana.: University of Illinois Press.

McWhirter, M. D., David, P., & Mattison, P. (1985). Psychotherapy for gay male couples. In J. C. Gonsiorek (Ed.), *A guide to psychotherapy with gay and lesbian clients.* New York: Harrington Park Press.

Miller B. J. (1992). From silence to suicide: Measuring a mother's loss. In W. J. Blumenfeld (Ed.), *Homophobia: How we all pay the price.* Boston: Beacon Press.

Morin, S. F., & Garfinkle, E. M. (1978). Male homophobia. *Journal of Social Issues, 34,* pp. 29–47.

Rogers, C. R. (1980). *A way of being.* New York: Houghton Mifflin.

Toder, N. (1992). Lesbian couples in particular. In B. Berzon (Ed.), *Positively gay: New approaches to gay and lesbian life.* Berkeley, Calif.: Celestial Arts Press.

EDITORS' COMMENTARY

When we refer to mirroring, we usually are thinking about the listening skill, discussed throughout this casebook, that Imago therapy teaches couples to use. We rarely consider that our culture mirrors us from the day we're born. When parents wheel an infant through the shopping mall and are greeted by admiring comments, both the parents and the child are mirrored. When our teenager is dressed and ready to go to the prom, and we proudly shoot several rolls of film, the teenager is mirrored. When we return to work after getting a haircut and a colleague comments, "Nice hair style," we are mirrored. When others compliment the meal we cooked or the flower arrangement we produced or the chapter we wrote, we are mirrored. Mirroring tells us that we're doing what is acceptable to our culture. We are passing the test.

But many groups are not mirrored by our Western culture, which stigmatizes and, in many instances, rejects those who don't pass the test—who are, quite simply, different from the rest of us. Those affected by such cultural attitudes include members of minorities, such as African-Americans, Asians, Native Americans, and Hispanics. Especially affected is the group Kleinberg and Zorn discuss: gays and lesbians.

According to estimates, up to 10 percent of the population is exclusively homosexual. Gays and lesbians cut across all ethnic, racial, and socioeconomic lines. They commonly grow up with parents who have little understanding of homosexuality or, even worse, openly ridicule homosexuals. Thus, gays and lesbians enter adulthood deprived of the cultural mirroring that most of us receive, and that teaches us that it's okay to be who we are.

Kleinberg and Zorn illustrate how gay communities, such as Provincetown, provide a healing environment for gay and lesbian couples. There, partners who have spent a good part of their lives hiding their true identities experience mirroring of their entire selves—not just the parts that our culture accepts. This enables their authentic selves to finally emerge, giving them the courage to confront deeper issues, such as the internalized homophobia that keeps them from fully accepting themselves and their partners.

The couples groups that Kleinberg and Zorn describe provide a mirror, and thus a means of healing, for gay couples. But a few isolated groups in a segregated community such as Provincetown are not enough to give gays and lesbians an equal place in our culture. First and foremost, empathic understanding—the kind that Imago therapy teaches partners to give each other—is needed by both cultures, the gay and the straight. To understand a culture is not to give it one's stamp of approval. Rather, empathic understanding implies an acknowledgment of the other's right to exist, to be different, and to express one's differentness. For the gay child, this could spell the difference between a lifetime of self-love and one of self-hatred. For all of us, it could mean the difference between living in a culture of intolerance or a culture of "liberty and justice for all."

Chapter 10

WHEN A PARTNER HAS AIDS: THERAPY WITH GAY/LESBIAN COUPLES

Patrick Vachon

Whether partners are of the same sex or opposite sex, most committed love relationships are difficult. All of us, gay or straight, carry into our relationships childhood wounds, unmet needs, and character defenses that serve as fuel for the power struggle. Successful relationships demand that partners give up or alter the character defenses they developed as children and that are no longer adaptive as they reach adulthood. Unwilling or unable to make this transformation, most couples eventually break up or divorce.

As far as the Imago model is concerned, there are few differences between same-sex and opposite-sex romantic relationships. Any differences that exist lie not in the content of childhood wounding, but in the greater intensity and duration of the wounding suffered by gays. Those character defenses that gay partners bring to their relationships are often more rigid than those among opposite-sex partners and thus are more difficult to change.

For same-sex couples, in addition to past wounds, there are also the ramifications of living in a heterosexist culture. As children, we are socialized to act in ways that will ensure our acceptance by our family, our community, and mainstream society. We learn gender roles, leading us to embrace or deny certain parts of the self. From early childhood, children are bombarded by homophobic messages from the familial, social, political, cultural, and religious structures. Such messages become part of children's belief systems, resulting in an "internalized homophobia" that affects them whether they are destined to become straight or gay as adults.

Thus, the familial, social, and cultural sanctions that generally exist for heterosexual relationships are absent for most gay relationships. This lack of support makes sustaining a gay relationship even more challenging than maintaining a healthy straight one.

An additional factor complicating gay relationships is the presence of human immunodeficiency virus (HIV) seropositivity or acquired immunodeficiency syndrome (AIDS) in one or both partners. Some sources estimate that approximately 50 to 55 percent of the gay population is HIV-positive. Given these figures, it can be assumed that the seropositive status of one or both partners will likely need to be addressed when a gay couple comes to therapy.

It is important for therapists to understand the unique challenges of treating HIV-positive gay couples. Since wounding in such partners is likely to be intensified owing to both the stigma of being gay and the pervasive effects of HIV, the opportunity for greater relational healing is also enhanced. Therapists need to understand the therapeutic issues—and the possibilities—of working with such couples, so that optimal growth and healing can take place.

My own process of coming out as a gay male began in the early 1970s. In 1978, I met my first lover, with whom I would spend the next eight years. Less than a year into our relationship, he began showing symptoms of HIV-spectrum disease, then called AIDS-related complex (ARC). He had night sweats, diarrhea, and repeated high fevers. We did not know what was happening to him until two years later, in 1980, when he was hospitalized and diagnosed with GRID, the term previously used to refer to AIDS. During the five years leading up to his death in 1985, we struggled with our relationship problems as well as with his illness. During a period when little was known about AIDS, we tried unsuccessfully to communicate with each other about what we were going through. Afraid to show our vulnerability, my partner and I never spoke of his impending death until two weeks before he died. Because of our ignorance, the opportunities for sharing our pain and supporting one another through it were lost forever.

It does not have to be so for others. This is one reason I work with couples like Jeff and Andrew.

JEFF AND ANDREW

Jeff and Andrew, who have been together for five years, are both in their early 30s and have been "out" since their early 20s. Jeff has been HIV-positive for eight years; Andrew continues to test as negative. Except for one episode of pneumonia related to his HIV, Jeff has shown no other obvious HIV-related symptoms. Both partners are employed full-time, but Jeff makes significantly more money than does Andrew.

The couple came to me for therapy several months after attending a "Getting the Love You Want" couples workshop. They stated that they had become more and more reactive with each other and complained that they "just couldn't seem to get along about anything anymore." They wanted to try therapy as a last resort.

In our initial session, I focused on creating safety through the dialogue process. This was done so that the partners could express their presenting issues, and then move beyond them to allow the emergence of more important underlying themes related to childhood wounding.

Five minutes into the first session, Jeff began to criticize Andrew for his "irresponsible behavior," complaining that while Andrew "played around" and went to the gym, he had to do all the housework. After allowing them to escalate into their typical reactive state, I invited them to begin to dialogue instead.

> **Jeff:** *What I am frustrated about is the fact that you never help with anything around the house.*
> **Andrew (mirrors):** *Is there more?*
> **Jeff:** *I always have to pick up after you, clean the house, and pay all the bills.*
> **Andrew (mirrors):** *Is there more?*
> **Jeff:** *Yes, there is more. All you do is go to work, come home, go to the gym, and then off to bed you go. I end up having to do all of the work around here while you go and show off your body.*
> **Andrew (mirrors):** *Is there more?*
> **Therapist (to Jeff):** *And what hurts about that is . . .*
> **Jeff:** *And what hurts about that is that we used to do all of those things together, and now we don't. We don't do anything together anymore.*
> **Andrew (mirrors):** *Is there more?*
> **Jeff:** *Yes, you go to the gym and work out, and you have all of those guys looking at you, and I look like shit.*

Andrew: *What do you mean, you look like shit?*

Therapist (directs Andrew):   *Just mirror that.*

Andrew: *Oh, sorry. Is there more?*

Jeff: *Well, my body looks horrible, my muscles are soft, and I look dead!*

Andrew (mirrors):   *Is there more?*

Jeff: *Why would anyone want to stay with me the way I look?*

Andrew (mirrors):   *Is there more?*

Therapist (to Jeff):   *And what I'm afraid of is . . .*

Jeff: *And what I am afraid of is that you will find someone else at the gym and leave me.*

Andrew (mirrors):   *Is there more?*

Jeff: *Yes. Every time I look at you, I see a hot sexy guy. All the guys at the gym look like that, and I don't fit in anymore. I've never fit in. You're going to dump me and find someone else.*

Andrew (mirrors):   *Is there more?*

Jeff (begins to cry):   *I'm scared that you're going to leave and I won't have anyone to take care of me when I get sick.*

Andrew (mirrors):   *Is there more?*

Jeff: *No, there isn't any more.*

Therapist: *And what this all reminds me of from my growing up is . . .*

Jeff: *And what this reminds me of is my whole fucking life. No one was ever around to take care of me. I was always the outcast. No one ever wanted to be around me. I had to do everything for myself and by myself. My dad pushed me aside to pamper his favorite son, the butch one, while I got cast aside. Now the only person I've ever loved is going to leave me too. I'm going to die alone. (Jeff began to sob.)*

Andrew: *(After a pause, mirrors) Did I get that right?*

Jeff: *(Nods his head)*

Andrew: *Is there more?*

Jeff: *(Shakes his head)*

At my direction, Andrew summarized what Jeff had said so far. He offered validation and expressed empathy. I next said to Jeff, "Is there anything that you would like from Andrew right now?"

Jeff: *A hug would be nice.*

Therapist: *So, would the two of you be willing to do the Holding Exercise that you learned in the workshop?*

Jeff: *Sure, but I forget how.*

I helped the couple get into the proper position for holding. Then I asked, "Jeff, is there anything else you would like to tell Andrew about your fear or about what it was like growing up in your family?"

Jeff: *It was painful and incredibly lonely. I always felt so alone. (He began to cry again.)*
Andrew: *It will be O.K., I won't leave you.*
Therapist (to Andrew): *Maybe you could just hold Jeff silently and listen to him talk about his pain.*

Andrew nodded silently. He held Jeff for about 10 minutes.

Therapist: *Whenever you are ready, you can sit up and take a moment to get grounded back into this room and this moment.*

The two slowly returned to an upright position.

Therapist: *Would the two of you be willing to work on some Behavior Change Requests, which might help heal some of Jeff's pain?*

(Both nodded.)

Therapist (to Jeff): *Do you remember from the workshop how this works? First state a global desire, then state three requests. Andrew will choose one of them.*
Jeff: *Well, my global desire is that we will be together until the day I die, that you will never leave me, that you will always find me attractive, and that you will always take care of me when I am sick.*
Andrew (mirrors): *Did I get that right?*
Jeff: *Yes.*
Therapist (to Jeff): *Now state three specific requests that could help heal both your old and your current hurts and fears.*
Jeff: *Well, the first one would be to have you promise you will take care of me when I'm sick.*
Therapist: *Remember, your request needs to be measurable and specific, and you should include when, where, and how Andrew could meet your request. What would that look like?*
Jeff: *Well, you don't even know what is going on with my illness. So next week, when I go to the doctor, I would like you to come along to meet her and the nurses, so you can get to know them.*
Andrew: *(Mirrors)*
Therapist: *Now for your second request.*
Jeff: *The second request would be to spend every Saturday morning for the next month helping me do things around the house. That way, if I get sick, you'll know how to do the things I've been doing.*
Andrew: *O.K., so every Saturday morning for the next month, you would like me to help you do things around the house, so I can get to know the things you've been doing. Is that it?*

Jeff: *Well, I wouldn't want you to work for an hour, and then quit!*

Therapist (to Jeff):   *You might want to make the request more specific and more measurable.*

Jeff: *Then, for two hours every Saturday morning this month, I would like you to spend time with me doing things around the house, so that you can take over if I get sick.*

Andrew: *(Mirrors)*

Jeff: *And my third request would be to have you take me out on a surprise date, the way you used to, at least one time in the next two weeks.*

Andrew: *(Mirrors)*

Therapist: *Now, Andrew, you get to choose one of these three requests to give as a gift to Jeff. The one you choose should be a stretch for you, but possible to do.*

Andrew: *I will go to the doctor with you next week.*

Therapist (to Jeff):   *Say to Andrew, "Your giving this to me will help me heal my childhood wound of..."*

Jeff: *Your giving this will help heal my wound of not being important enough and not being cared about.*

Andrew: *(Mirrors)*

Therapist (to Andrew):   *And my giving this to you will help me grow by...*

Andrew: *And by giving this to you, I will grow by... (Andrew paused.) By having to look at something I don't want to look at—your illness. And also by making me work on my self-centeredness.*

Jeff: *(Mirrors)*

Later in therapy, Andrew and Jeff revisited this issue, this time with Andrew as the sender and Jeff receiving.

Andrew: *I got really frustrated when you accused me of going to the gym all the time and insinuating that I don't help you around the house. I do a lot of work, maybe not as much as you, and maybe not the way you like it done, but I do a hell of a lot of work around that house.*

Jeff (mirrors):   *Is there more?*

Andrew: *Just because you don't want to go to the gym anymore doesn't mean I can't go. I love going to the gym. It's the only place I can go and feel good about myself.*

Jeff (mirrors):   *Is there more?*

Therapist (to Andrew):   *And what hurts the most about this...*

Andrew: *And what hurts the most is that I am never good enough for you. You always find something wrong with me. At least at the gym, I know I am good. I work hard at it, I look good, and I am proud of my body.*

Jeff (mirrors):   *Is there more?*

Andrew: *No, there is no more. It just pisses me off when you criticize me like that.*

Therapist (to Andrew):   *And what scares me the most about this is . . .*

Andrew: *And what scares me is that you will try to take away all the things I like to do, just because you don't want to do them anymore. Then I will shrivel up and die just like you.*

Jeff: *(Taking a deep breath before mirroring this time) Is there more?*

Andrew: *I don't think so.*

Therapist: *And what this reminds me of from my growing up is . . .*

Andrew: *Well, it is kind of like when I was little, when the things I liked to do were never good enough for my dad. He wanted me to play football, baseball, and all those things, the way my brother did. I couldn't have an identity of my own; it was like my father wanted me to be a clone of himself. He used to call me a wimp and a sissy and a mommy's boy. He used to tell me to go play with the girls, where I belonged. He would say he wanted a son, not a little fruitcake. Then, when I would try to be more like him, I was never good enough. He eventually left me, just like you will!*

Jeff: *(Mirrors, then speaks softly) Is there anything more you would like to tell me about that?*

Andrew: *No, that's all.*

Therapist (to Andrew):   *And what I learned to do to keep myself safe back then was . . .*

Andrew: *Well, I used to just stay to myself. Sometimes I would ride my bike for hours; sometimes I would go for real long runs in the woods. Sometimes I would spend hours after school at the gym. I was determined not to let the other kids beat up on me, so I kept in shape. I also used my looks to connect with the girls. I had a lot of girlfriends who thought I was real cute. (He laughed sheepishly.)*

Jeff (mirrors):   *Is there more?*

Andrew: *No. I think that is really all of it.*

Therapist (to Jeff):   *And what makes sense to me about all of this is . . .*

Jeff: *And what makes sense to me is, well, all of it.*

Therapist: *Especially the part about . . .*

Jeff: *Especially your feelings about being criticized. It makes sense to me that, if you hear my requests to help around the house as criticism, it would remind you of all the criticism your dad gave you. It also makes sense that you would be reminded of not being good enough.*

Therapist: *And I would imagine all of that makes you feel . . .*

Jeff: *I would imagine you would be feeling inadequate, angry, frustrated, hurt. Did I get those feelings right?*

Andrew: *Yes. And I'm also scared.*

Jeff: *Is there more about that?*

Andrew: *Yes, I'm scared you will die and leave me, just like my dad left me.*

Jeff (mirrors):   *Is there more?*

Andrew: *No, that's it.*

Therapist (to Andrew):   *So, to help heal all this, what would you like to ask from Jeff?*

Andrew: *Well, I would like you to always support me and let me be me. I want you to promise to always stay with me and give me continuous praise and admiration. (He grinned.)*

Jeff: *(Mirrors)*

Therapist: *Now make three Behavior Change Requests, Andrew.*

Andrew: *The first one would be to compliment me a lot. Compliment me about something I do well, at least once a day for, say, the next week.*

Jeff: *(Mirrors)*

Andrew: *The second would be to go with me to the gym and work out with me.*

Therapist: *You might want to quantify that.*

Andrew: *How about if, one time a week this month, you go with me to the gym and we work out together for one hour?*

Jeff: *(Mirrors)*

Andrew: *And the third would be for us to spend every Sunday afternoon this month doing something fun and new together, something exciting.*

Jeff: *(Mirrors)*

Therapist (to Jeff):   *And the one I will gift you with is . . .*

Jeff: *Well, the one that would be the biggest stretch for me is to go to the gym with you, so I will do that one.*

Andrew: *Thank you.*

Therapist (to Andrew):   *And so, by giving me that gift, you will help me heal my childhood wound of . . .*

Andrew: *You will help me heal my childhood wound of not having my identity supported.*

Therapist (to Jeff):   *And giving this to Andrew will help you grow by . . .*

Jeff: *By giving this to you, I will grow by supporting you, in spite of my insecurity about my body. I guess it will force me also to invest in life, rather than death.*

Jeff became teary-eyed.

Andrew (mirrors):   *Thanks.*

Through dialogue, Andrew and Jeff were able to discover the childhood-based fears that drove their conflicts and that were, in fact, similar for both. Each had felt abandoned by his father, resulting in a fear of being abandoned by his partner. Dialogue provided the safety they needed to explore the roots of their problems as a couple and to take ownership of their own contributions to those problems. This, in turn, allowed them to take steps to help each other feel more secure. They became enabled to make choices to override reactivity and to stretch in the direction of the other's needs, thus achieving a greater degree of self-growth and promoting healing in the other. Although earlier attempts to resolve their issues had resulted in a stalemate, with each resisting compromise for fear of losing his identity, the use of dialogue transformed the former lose–lose situation into a win–win situation for each partner and for the partnership.

In a later session, Andrew and Jeff delved into an issue that can be highly sensitive, and even explosive, for HIV-positive couples. Their sexual relationship had changed dramatically since Jeff's HIV disease progressed, which led to many fights. They agreed to try to dialogue about the issue instead. First, Andrew was the sender.

> **Andrew:**   *This is pretty scary for me to talk about.*
> **Therapist:**   *What makes this so scary?*
> **Andrew:**   *Well, whenever we've tried to talk about this before, we have always gotten into a fight.*
> **Jeff (mirrors):**   *Is there more?*
> **Andrew:**   *It's always been a scary topic with us, just like at home. I could never talk about sex or my sexuality.*
> **Jeff (mirrors):**   *Is there more?*
> **Andrew:**   *Well, we just don't have sex anymore. It's been months since we made love.*
> **Jeff (mirrors):**   *Is there more?*
> **Andrew:**   *We used to have a great sex life together. When we first met, we couldn't stop. Now it seems like you don't want to touch me, or you don't want me to touch you.*
> **Jeff (mirrors):**   *Is there more?*
> **Andrew:**   *Yeah, it makes me feel dirty. When you push me away, I feel dirty, like you don't really love me. If you loved me, you would want to have sex with me.*
> **Jeff (mirrors):**   *Is there more?*
> **Therapist (to Andrew):**   *And what hurts the most about this is . . .*
> **Andrew:**   *And what hurts the most is that, if you don't want to have sex with me, then you must not love me. I know I'm good at sex, and if you don't want me sexually, then I must not be good for anything.*
> **Jeff (mirrors):**   *Is there more?*
> **Andrew:**   *No, I don't think so.*
> **Therapist (to Andrew):**   *And what scares me the most is . . .*

Andrew: *And what scares me the most is that you will toss me aside for someone else. If I am no good sexually and also no good around the house, why would you want me around?*

Jeff (mirrors):   *Is there more?*

Therapist: *And what this reminds me from my childhood is . . .*

Andrew: *And what this reminds me of is what my dad used to do to me. He would say that if I was going to act like a girl, he would treat me like one. He would say that right before he would make me have sex with him! Then he'd say that sex was all I was good for. When he finished, he would just push me aside and go back to his business. I learned real young to be good at sex. It was the one way I seemed to be able to please him, at least for a little while. Then, when I got older, I would have sex with kids in the neighborhood—well, it was more like I'd service them. They eventually took advantage of me and would threaten me and force me to do it. When I came out and began to meet other gay men, I had sex with a lot of them. It was a way for me to feel important and good at something, even though a lot of them quit calling me and dumped me.*

Jeff (mirrors):   *Is there anything else about any of that?*

Andrew: *Just that I can see now where it all comes from, why I'm scared you will do the same thing they all did to me—use me and throw me aside.*

Jeff: *Is there any more?*

Andrew: *No, not for now. But thanks for listening. I've never really told anyone about this before, how I was taught to be sexual, then condemned for it. I would like to hear what all this sexual stuff between us is about for you.*

Jeff: *Well, I just haven't felt very sexual lately.*

Andrew (mirrors):   *Is there more?*

Jeff: *Yes. I used to feel very sexy and very sexual with you, but I don't anymore. I don't like the way I look. I've lost weight, my muscles are flabby, and I don't think I could get an erection all the time, anyway.*

Andrew (mirrors):   *Is there any more?*

Jeff: *When I look in the mirror, I get disgusted. I feel dirty. I am dirty. I have this virus in me that can kill me and you. I'm scared to have sex with you. I feel like I'm your enemy.*

Andrew (mirrors):   *Tell me more.*

Jeff: *This is hard to say, but when I hold you, I'm reminded of what I used to be. You are in shape, solid, sexy, and you're still cute. When I look at you, I remember the sexual part of me that is dead and might never live again. You are everything I am not.*

Andrew (mirrors):   *Is there more?*

Jeff: *Sex is what got me this fucking disease in the first place. Sex is* *dirty, sex is deadly, sex is bad, sex is going to kill me, and maybe you. It's not a fun thing anymore; it's scary. I'd finally reached the point where I could feel pretty good about being gay, then this happened. My dad always told me that being gay would kill me some day. In fact, he told me he'd rather see me dead than gay.*

Andrew (mirrors):   *Is there any more?*

Jeff: *I got the same message from church. The preacher would say that homosexuals were going to go to hell. So I had my dad telling me I didn't deserve to live, I had the preacher telling me I would be damned after I died. I kept my sexual side hidden inside me for years. Then I came out, started feeling good about myself, and got AIDS. Now a part of me believes I deserve to die, and I don't deserve to have a sex life anymore.*

Andrew (mirrors):   *Did I get all of that?*

Jeff: *Yes, you got it all. I really want you to know that I love you very much, and that my lack of sexual interest right now is not about you. In my eyes, you are still a very sexy man.*

Andrew: *(Mirrors, with tears in his eyes) Is there anything more?*

Jeff: *No, I just wish all of this would go away!*

As these dialogues demonstrate, for gay HIV-positive couples like Jeff and Andrew, both surface issues and the deeper woundedness underlying those issues become magnified. For them, as for many straight couples, attachment is a major concern. But because our culture generally does not recognize same-sex marriages, there are no legal parameters to motivate gay couples to tough it out during the hard times. Therefore, the fear of separation—a fear underlying a great deal of the conflict in romantic partnerships—is especially prominent for gays.

Also like most couples, Andrew and Jeff shared similar areas of wounding. Both had distancing fathers. As children, their nonconformity to sex roles had left them with feelings of incompetence that lingered as they grew into manhood. Because they were not allowed to develop their own identities as young gay males, but rather were expected to conform to social, cultural, and familial norms, their identity development was thwarted. This created a time bomb, forcing identity issues to stay below the surface until they exploded later in life.

Jeff had developed into an extremely responsible and competent person, but as the HIV disease progressed, he began to fear the loss of his competence. He also feared that, as he lost his ability to function, Andrew would be unable to pick up the slack. Andrew, for his part, feared the loss of his gay identity because, as Jeff became more ill, Andrew had to make adjustments that made him feel he was sacrificing parts of himself. Because he had less physical energy than Andrew, for example, Jeff also had less desire for sex or for going out. In response, Andrew invested more time into going to the gym—the very thing that threatened Jeff most, because the gym symbolized what Jeff had lost as a result of having HIV.

The themes Jeff and Andrew expressed during their dialogues are typical of gay men living with HIV disease. At first, such arguments revolve around the typical issues that most couples, regardless of their sexual orientation, fight about: work, money, sharing responsibilities, sexual attractions to others. The Imago processes, however, helped Jeff and Andrew to uncover their "real" challenge: not the HIV, as daunting as it is, but striking the balance, as all couples must, between being connected to each other while remaining separate and differentiated persons.

Ironically, Jeff and Andrew became healthier as a couple, not despite the HIV, but because of it. Against the backdrop of what inevitably must be an HIV-shortened life for one partner, their power struggle intensified, allowing their deeper issues to emerge and take center stage. Through the safety of the dialogue, they were able to understand and empathize with each other's woundedness and unmet needs, leading them to a stronger, more intimate connection.

My own hope is that, through sharing my personal and professional experiences, I can assist other therapists in helping HIV-positive couples embrace, rather than reject, their crisis, reframing it as a unique opportunity for individual and relational healing.

EDITORS' COMMENTARY

This glimpse into the workings of a long-term gay relationship leaves us with this realization: gay couples deal with the same issues that are faced by straight couples. Feeling loved despite one's flaws, being desired and cherished, fear of being abandoned—this is the stuff of romantic relationships, whether gay or straight. Straight readers might feel uncomfortable listening to two men discuss their sex life, but this is real-life work, no different from Imago work with any other couple, except that Jeff and Andrew are both males. When we are able to dispense with our moral judgments, we simply see two people who are in love and struggling to cope with a disease process that might very well be fatal. As Maya Kollman (personal communication, 1992) points out, "As far as how good a person I am, what possible difference could it make that I love another woman?"

Like all couples, Jeff and Andrew were wounded during childhood. They were wounded long before they knew or cared about their sexual orientation. Their self-hatred developed well before they could understand why their fathers shamed them for having "feminine" traits. By the time they comprehended the notion of homophobia, Jeff and Andrew had already internalized it, leading them to develop the self-loathing they unearthed in their dialogue. Through dialogue, they began to make sense of their feelings, connecting them to the abandonment wounds they had sustained as children ("If you are gay, I will leave you and never come back").

The presence of HIV in one or both partners has complex effects on a relationship. Without question, the effects of the virus on one's health and the struggle to adhere to elaborate treatment regimens put severe stress on any couple's relationship, no matter how sound. But even more profound are the effects of the virus on the couple's unconscious issues, which seem to be magnified when a partner is HIV-positive. This leads us to wonder whether, were HIV not present, the topics of sex, attractiveness, abandonment, and childhood wounds would have surfaced as intensely and as powerfully as they did for this couple. Perhaps for couples affected by HIV, or any other life-threatening disease, Imago therapy becomes a more concentrated and contracted process that results in a greater intensity of healing. Vachon's case indicates that this may be so. Although no one is expected to give thanks for a serious illness, couples facing the crisis of HIV can, as the Chinese meaning of "crisis" ("opportunity") implies, reap benefits that "more fortunate" couples never dream about or hope for.

Chapter 11

GOING BEYOND AIDS: THERAPY WITH HETEROSEXUAL COUPLES

Donna M. Ritz

For the last three years, I have been doing a great deal of work with HIV-positive clients and others affected by the AIDS epidemic. I have also been fielding questions from colleagues, family, and friends about why I would choose to work with clients who, sooner or later, most likely will die of AIDS. It's a fair question: as one person said to me, "It's not like there's going to be a happy ending."

According to the New Jersey Department of Health's Division on AIDS (June 1996), in the preceding year alone, almost 20,000 people died of AIDS. Yet working with those affected by HIV and AIDS is not as much about dying as it is about experiencing the power of connection. It's about weeding through the nonessentials and getting down to the really important stuff of life. I've witnessed HIV-positive clients using their remaining time to join with others, to say what's been unspoken, and to heal in ways they had never thought possible.

ISABELLE AND WALT

Isabelle and Walt were referred to me through a community AIDS organization. Walt was HIV-positive; Isabelle was HIV-negative. They had an unusual history. They had fallen in love with each other some 20 years earlier, and after a brief period together, had separated when Walt moved across the country. When he left, Walt had not known that Isabelle was pregnant. She decided to keep the baby, a girl she named Marina, who is now 19 years old. Walt later heard about Marina, but avoided both the mother and child for almost two decades. However, when he found out he was HIV-positive, he moved back to the area to try to form a relationship with his daughter. While doing so, he reconnected with Isabelle.

Typically, I see people responding to an HIV-positive diagnosis in one of two ways: with denial ("I won't die; I have a long time before I go"), or with a sense that time is of the essence ("I need to do and say it all now, because I am dying"). Either reaction leads to major life struggles, both for the infected person and for his or her loved ones.

When Isabelle and Walt initially contacted me for therapy, they were still in the romantic love phase of their renewed relationship. They had rented an apartment, moved in together, and planned a future, meanwhile ignoring Walt's HIV status. Initially, I spent some time reviewing the facts of HIV transmission and assessing how knowledgeable Isabelle and Walt were about the virus. Frequently, with a discordant couple, in which one partner is HIV-negative and the other is positive, the negative partner's guilt over being negative can lead him or her to engage in risky behavior. I have heard women say they were afraid their infected lovers would feel rejected if asked to use a condom, and so they practiced unsafe sex and subsequently became infected. An alarming number of women take sufficient precautions 98 percent of the time, yet merely ask their partner not to ejaculate inside of them the other 2 percent of the time. I was convinced, however, that Isabelle was not taking inappropriate risks. She was committed to raising her son, Sammy, an eight-year old from an estranged relationship, and so was careful to avoid infection.

In the early stages of our work together, I taught Isabelle and Walt the three-step Couples Dialogue. They spent a lot of time mirroring each other, and the usual theme of their dialogue was, "I am so lucky to have you." Especially in couples struggling with HIV, however, the theme soon becomes, "Will you still be here tomorrow?" This makes the romantic period of crucial importance for these couples: it allows time for them to bond, to use the therapy to practice the art of mirroring and to develop rituals that support their relationship.

At about session six, Isabelle came in refusing to talk at all. Walt complained that she had been moody; to Isabelle, nothing he did seemed right anymore. They had been fighting all week. I asked Isabelle if she would be willing to tell Walt why she felt unable to talk to him. Initially she resisted, saying that nothing she said would matter: the situation was hopeless. I asked Walt to mirror her. Although Isabelle was unwilling to talk to or mirror Walt, when Walt mirrored Isabelle's message to me, he became the receiver, the one hearing Isabelle's distress.

Walt and Isabelle's Dialogue

> **Walt:** *What I hear you saying is that this situation is hopeless and no matter what you say, and no matter what the therapist says, nothing will change. Did I get that?*
> **Isabelle:** *Yeah, and you can sit here and pretend all you want that you're hearing me, but the fact is, when we get home, you aren't about to make any changes. So there's no use in us mirroring about it in here.*

At this point, I asked Isabelle to say more about her frustration.

> **Isabelle:** *What frustrates me about that is that it is all pretense. What frustrates me is that we can sit here mirroring all day and all night, but in the end, nothing is going to be different. You're going to die and I am going to be alone. And I am tired of being alone. I am tired of being the only person who does everything for these kids, the only one who is working. Now you say you are going to lose your job, and you say don't worry. That's easy for you to say. You haven't had to work and then come home and take care of kids every day. As soon as the men I know find out how hard it is to be a single parent, they are gone. And you'll be gone, too.*
> **Therapist:** *And what that reminds me of from my being a kid is . . . . .*
> **Isabelle:** *What that reminds me of from being a kid is that my goddamn father was almost never there for me. Even when he was, he was always telling me how I was doing everything wrong. Even today, he never says anything great about the work I do, or about how hard it must be for me to raise my kids. It reminds me of how much he loved my sister but ignored me.*

Isabelle began to cry. She cried for the relationship she didn't have with her father, for the relationship she'd lost when Walt left 20 years earlier, and for the relationship with Walt she'd be losing once again.

Isabelle began to talk about how hopeless she felt upon hearing that Walt's work hours would soon be cut back. For Isabelle, Walt's working outside of their home served to validate her own years of working hard as a single parent to raise their daughter. Now that Walt was back, he owed her this type of support as a payback, and if he really loved her, he would be willing to do it. At the same time, Isabelle felt guilty asking Walt to work harder than he wanted to; after all, he was dying.

AN IMAGO-SYSTEMS APPROACH

According to systems theory, all members of a family are mutually interdependent: each one affects how the others function, both within the family system and in the world outside. As a systems therapist working with HIV-affected couples, I work to normalize the family's difficulties, empowering them to deal proactively with the illness rather than resign themselves to a situation they might view as hopeless. Gillian Walker (1991), in *In the Midst of Winter*, says, "As we have experimented with using family therapy to help people with HIV infection, certain principles have emerged. The first is: *The therapist should empower the family to believe in its own capacities for the problem solution and illness management.* Then, by carefully helping family members explore and define beliefs about illness and death, hopes for alleviation or cure, and skepticism about the limits of medical interventions, the therapist encourages them to resume control of their lives in relation to the illness" (p. 39).

Walker's statement reflects a systems perspective that holds that, as long as clients view "the problem" as the HIV infection, it is impossible for them to believe they are capable of solving their problems. By focusing all their attention on the medical impact of the virus, family members become disempowered while, at the same time, they overlook other important dynamics going on within the family. For example, the noninfected partner might be avoiding expressing any negative feelings; after all, why bring up such things when the HIV-positive partner could die anytime?

Certainly, at best, life with HIV is uncertain. Although some clients defy the odds, living well beyond the average life expectancy for persons with AIDS, others die relatively soon after diagnosis. I have known clients with T-cell counts of 100 (1,000–1,200 is normal) who have continued to live for years; others with higher counts have died within a year. Only recently have combinations of various drugs hinted at the possibility of halting or significantly slowing the progression of HIV. Eventually, such treatments could allow us a more optimistic and accurate estimate of how long an HIV-infected individual might be expected to live. At present, however, it remains impossible to predict the course that the disease might take in any given individual.

Despite its profound impact on a couple's relationship, HIV is usually not the core issue. Rather, HIV and other life-threatening conditions become the backdrop against which core issues are played out. Isabelle, for instance, had been wounded by parents who were inconsistently available. Her father was often away on business, and her mother, whom Isabelle described as chronically depressed, was physically present but not emotionally available to her daughter. It makes sense, therefore, according to Imago theory, that Isabelle would unconsciously choose a man who would physically leave her during their early relationship but return when his physical health undermined his ability to be with her for the long term. Clearly, abandonment issues would have emerged for this couple regardless of their HIV status.

The first therapeutic task was to sort out the problems related to Walt's HIV from those stemming from other aspects of Isabelle and Walt's relationship. To begin, I asked Isabelle if she would work on relating to Walt without being preoccupied by his HIV status. She could, for example, pretend for a period of six weeks that he was not going to die. Walt's T-cell count was about 600; he had no signs of AIDS-related conditions, his weight was fine, and he was symptom-free. We discussed the fact that, given that he might expect to lose around 100 T-cells per year, we could safely assume that he would not die of AIDS in the next six weeks. Isabelle was willing to make this contract. Once she began to treat Walt as though he were not terminally ill, she became able to view their problems from a different perspective. Her message now shifted from, "You are leaving me because you are dying," to "You would be leaving me whether or not you were dying." Since Walt was "no longer dying," we could now grasp and work on the core issues of the relationship.

> **Isabelle:**   *It's not fair. You left when Marina was born and now you're back, but you're not really back. If you were really back and really wanted to be with me, you would want to marry me. And we would buy a house. How is that supposed to happen when you aren't even going to be employed throughout the winter season?*
>
> **Therapist:**   *Isabelle, can you say some more about how Walt would be if he "really cared" about you?*
>
> **Isabelle:**   *Well, he would take care of me.*
>
> **Therapist:**   *Would you say more about what taking care of you would look like?*
>
> **Isabelle:**   *Well, he would work. And he would come home at the end of the day and we would have dinner together. We would both be there for Sammy for soccer and just do stuff as a family.*
>
> **Therapist:**   *And could you say a little more about what being together might be like?*
>
> **Isabelle:**   *I don't know—we would just be together.*

I began to suspect both that Isabelle wasn't sure what emotional support would look like, and that, in any case, she would probably be unable to receive it. Because Isabelle couldn't visualize support in concrete terms, Walt was likely to fail her, no matter what he did.

I worked with Isabelle and Walt to explore how each of them was contributing to the conflict in their relationship. Although Walt could mirror Isabelle when she became upset, Isabelle seldom went to Walt to intentionally dialogue. She would eventually have an outburst, which would be followed by a period of isolating herself from Walt. When the isolation became unbearable, Isabelle would have another outburst, followed by more isolation. Walt, on the other hand, was so contained that he seldom revealed his feelings or intentions to Isabelle.

As with most couples, I had asked Isabelle and Walt to spend 10 minutes at the end of every day mirroring each other. During one session, they reported that, although they were becoming more successful with the mirroring exercise, they were also experiencing an increase in conflict between sessions. Walt said that Isabelle seemed mad at him most of the time and he was feeling attacked. I asked Isabelle to mirror him as he shared more about that.

> **Walt:**   *I feel like you blame me for everything, whether it's my fault or not. You used to like it when I went to work; that was the thing that was important to you. Now, if my boss calls me in to work, you get mad. If I'm at home not working, you get mad. And even if I spend my time cleaning and making dinner and getting Sam from school, when you get home, you still get mad.*
> **Therapist:**   *And what that reminds me of from my family of origin is . . .*
> **Walt:**   *What that reminds me of is how my mother used to get on us boys to do things, no matter how much we did. We would just be finishing one thing and she would be on us for the next thing. It felt like we would never be done with the list of things she had for us to do.*
> **Therapist:**   *And my reaction to that frustration was . . .*
> **Walt:**   *Well, you're not going to believe this, but I used to pick a job, like cleaning the bathrooms. I would first clean the bathrooms upstairs, then I would go downstairs to clean the bathroom there. When I was done cleaning, I would climb out the window and go play with my friends. I knew I would be in big trouble when I got home, but it was worth it, because at least I'd have time with my friends if I sneaked out. If I stayed, I never knew if she would ever let me go.*

"*If I stayed, I never knew if she would ever let me go.*" This statement summarized the theme of Walt's life. He had left Isabelle all those years earlier to avoid living his life without fulfilling his hopes and dreams. This theme accompanied him wherever he went during the 20 years he was gone. He traveled a great deal, seeing the country, exploring alternative cultures, never settling into a relationship for very long. Not until he learned his HIV status did he begin to examine what he really wanted out of life, which led him to return home to his daughter and, finally, to Isabelle.

> **Therapist:** *Can you say more about how knowing you are HIV-positive has influenced your wanting to leave again or stay?*
> **Walt:** *Well, I've always thought there'd be time to go back, but if I stayed, I might end up being trapped. Well, now I am trapped—by the HIV. Even though I'm not exactly dying right now, there's no more bathroom window to climb out of. This HIV is always going to give me another task to do. Another piece of unfinished business, another chore.*
> **Therapist:** *And what scares me about this is . . .*
> **Walt:** *Is that, if I don't keep doing the chores, I might die.*
> **Therapist:** *And the way the chores keep me from dying is . . .*
> **Walt:** *Well, if I can just keep doing stuff I should have been doing all along, maybe I won't die as soon. Maybe then I won't die alone.*
> **Therapist:** *And my biggest fear is . . .*
> **Walt:** *My biggest fear is not dying; it's dying alone. I don't want to suffer, either, but I really don't want to die alone.*

I don't use interpretation much with couples. I believe that their own interpretation is more important and probably more on target than mine. In this case, however, I had an interpretation to offer.

> **Therapist:** *Walt, I heard you say a minute ago that you used to climb out of the bathroom window as a way to escape your mother, who always had a list of chores for you. Then I heard you say that the HIV always has another emotional chore for you to do. Is it possible that the HIV has become to you like your mother with her constant lists? And is it possible that you are recreating with Isabelle that experience of having an unsatisfied mother?*
> **Walt:** *Well, it is true that no matter how much I do, either to make up for the HIV or to make up to Isabelle, it isn't enough. I feel like I am trying to outrun both of them.*

I was cautious not to allow the focus of the dialogue to shift away from their core issue and settle on the HIV again.

In exploring further, Walt and Isabelle became aware of their own contribution to the distance that would creep into their relationship. Isabelle wanted Walt to step into the role of her early caregivers and to experience being taken care of by him. But whenever Walt attempted to take care of Isabelle, she would tell him that his efforts did not meet her expectations. Anticipating Isabelle's displeasure, Walt would then isolate himself from her. After finishing some task Isabelle had requested of him, he would leave the house, staying away for hours to avoid learning whether or not Isabelle was pleased. Isabelle couldn't understand why Walt would leave, since his presence was far more important to her than the chore he'd done, and she would criticize Walt for his absence. Over and over, the couple reenacted this cycle.

By this point, it had become clear that both partners had difficulty asking for what they wanted from the other. I invited Isabelle to be the first one to use the Behavior Change Request process since, in contrast to Walt, she seemed fairly clear about what she wanted from the relationship.

> **Therapist:** *Isabelle, could you describe a frustration that is particularly difficult for you?*
> **Isabelle:** *Well, I feel like Walt doesn't really want to work. If he really wanted to take care of me, to make up for the years he wasn't there, he would look harder for a job, or at least find one that wasn't just seasonal.*

One of the frustrating parts of working with this couple was that, even when progress had been made in dialoguing about a certain frustration, soon afterwards they would return to the same complaint. I often had to remind myself that changing a relationship is a process that takes time. Walt began to mirror Isabelle.

> **Isabelle:** *When I was a kid, my father always worked. I go to work, and my girlfriends' husbands and lovers work, too. All the guys I know work, but their wives don't have to work. In fact, these guys work overtime so that their wives won't have to work.*
> **Therapist:** *What frustrates me most about your not working is . . .*
> **Isabelle:** *What's frustrating is that if you really cared, you would be worried about how your not working is affecting me.*
> **Therapist:** *And what makes me angry about that is . . .*
> **Isabelle:** *And what makes me angry about that is that I am goddamn tired of taking care of you and doing the things you should be doing for me! I am tired of raising kids, I am tired of not being like other moms who go to their kids' school during the day and go to the plays and are able to do things because they can stay at home. I am angry because I missed out on the childhood of one of my kids, and now I going to miss out on Sammy's, too.*
> **Therapist:** *And what hurts so much about this is . . .*

Isabelle: *And what hurts so much about this is . . . Nothing hurts about this, it just makes me so goddamn angry. It doesn't hurt; it makes me furious!*

I walked a fine line at these times with Isabelle. Although I believe that under all frustration and anger are buried childhood wounds, I knew that Isabelle would not acknowledge that she was hurt as well as angry. I knew from experience and my Imago training that pushing her to acknowledge her buried feelings would only make her more strongly resist seeing them and would cement her position.

Therapist: *Try this one, Isabelle, and see if it fits. If not, no problem. What this reminds me of from my family of origin is . . .*
Isabelle: *What this reminds me of from my family of origin is . . . nothing. Well, it does remind me of this one time when my sister took my prom gown without even asking me. She just took and wore it, as though it belonged to her, and like I didn't pay for the dress entirely by myself from my baby-sitting for hours and hours. When I told my parents about it, you know what they said? They said, since I had already worn it and Cindy didn't have anything to wear or any money to buy something, they didn't see what a big deal it was that she was wearing it. It was a big deal to me, though. How come they made me get a job and save money to buy the damn dress, and then Cindy got to wear it free of charge?*
Therapist: *And what hurt me about that back then was . . .*
Isabelle: *What hurt me about that was that they didn't care about me or my feelings. What hurts is all my hard work went down the tubes, like it didn't mean anything to them.*
Therapist: *So the way that fits with Walt's not working is . . .*
Isabelle: *And the way that fits with your not working is that it makes me believe you don't care about me, either, just like my parents. All my hard work down the tubes again. It's just not fair.*

Isabelle began to cry, sobbing quietly. This was an ideal point for having the couple do the holding exercise.

In the holding exercise, one partner reexperiences painful childhood memories while being held in the arms of the other. The partner being held talks about childhood memories, recreating his or her experiences with a childhood caretaker, whom the holding partner represents. However, because the holding partner practices intentionally hearing and empathizing with the other's pain, the childhood scenario is recreated, but this time with a different outcome. It is the different outcome that promotes the healing of childhood wounds.

I asked Walt to position himself on the floor. I always help the holder to become physically comfortable so that he or she can hold the other long enough while concentrating on what the partner is expressing. The holding position elicits regression, meaning that painful childhood experiences, with their accompanying emotions, are recreated.

I moved Isabelle and Walt quickly and quietly into position, wanting Isabelle to continue concentrating on painful childhood memories. Walt supported Isabelle in his arms.

> **Therapist:**   *Isabelle, would you say more about how hurt you were when your parents didn't acknowledge the work you did?*
> **Isabelle:**   *I hated them that day; I swear I did. It was like all the other times they took me for granted. My dad didn't know half the things I did, because he wasn't home most of the time. He told me once that having me saved their marriage. Huh! Some marriage. They didn't love each other, and they sure didn't love me. I remember pretending that I was adopted and that my real parents were going to come and get me and take me away. I remember thinking there must be someone out there who really loved me and who would come get me. I had a friend who was adopted, and she used to wish she knew her real parents. I wished I had real parents, too, instead of those two. I wished they would love me, just once.*

During the holding exercise, the holder listens with empathy but doesn't mirror. This proved difficult for Walt, as his mirroring back Isabelle's intense emotions helped him feel safe. Likewise, during the holding, the holder doesn't use comforting gestures like stroking or patting, because those can halt the other partner's experiencing of painful feelings from childhood. I had to coach Walt simply to listen and remain emotionally present to Isabelle. I suggested phrases that would support Isabelle's affective experience, such as, "It's okay, I'm here for you."

> **Therapist:**   *You've both been doing very hard and wonderful work, and I'd like you to take your time to experience your feelings together. Feel the safety you have created for one another, and just stay with it and with your feelings.*

After the couple had remained in the holding position for about 10 minutes, and when they seemed ready, I asked them to move out of the position to begin the next phase of the process.

> **Therapist:**   *Isabelle, I'd like you to suggest to Walt three behaviors which, if he did them for you, would help to heal your wound of feeling*

unimportant and unloved. You need to be able to state these requests in positive and specific terms, so that anyone hearing your request would understand exactly what you want. Walt, you are going to pick one of Isabelle's three requests and make a commitment to give it to her as a gift. I'd like you to pick the easiest one, the one you are absolutely sure you can do.

Therapist: *First, Isabelle, start with a global request, which means pretending you're a kid in a candy shop, and you can have anything you want. Walt, you are under no obligation to give her this global request, but hearing it will give you an idea of what Isabelle has wanted for a long time and hasn't gotten.*

Isabelle: *Well, I really want you to get a really good job, one that pays lots of money. Then I want you to come home and insist I quit my job. Insist that no wife of yours will work, and that I have to stay home. You want me to be the room mother for Sammy's classroom and to take Spanish lessons, like I have always wanted to.*

Therapist: *And now for your three real requests.*

Isabelle's first request was that Walt make three phone calls a day to look for full-time employment. The next request was that he hold her while lying on the couch and ask her about her day, without making sexual advances toward her. Her last request was the most interesting. She asked Walt to take her out dancing. As she made this request, she seemed completely transformed and childlike, an image she did not usually allow others to see.

Isabelle: *Well, on Friday night, you would be all dressed up when I came home from work. Sammy would be with someone else and not at home. You would have Steely Dan on the CD player, and you'd pour us a glass of Pelligrino. You'd be wearing that blue suit you have, the one with the French cuffs, and your pig cufflinks. When I came home, you would kiss me and hold me and then tell me you were taking me out for a surprise. Then we would go dancing at Astor's.*

I was gratified to hear Walt choose number three, the request to go dancing.

As a result of the Imago work, Walt and Isabelle demonstrated Walker's (1991) principle: they began to believe in their ability to problem solve. They finally moved away from focusing on the fear of AIDS and the fear of dying, thus becoming able to embrace the current issues that were present in their lives. By putting aside the issue of the HIV, they had more energy to work on the core issues in their relationship. By working to change behaviors and to form new patterns of relating, they began to take charge of the health of their relationship.

Isabelle and Walt also began to change their perspectives toward Walt's illness and their relationship. As Walker (1991) writes, "The therapist changes the problem-generating narrative about the patient, the family, and the disease itself. A fundamental principle of systemic therapy is that it provides an alternative paradigm to Western thought, which depends on practices of scientific classification and the objectification of individuals. Systemic therapists see behaviors not as fixed and classifiable, but as relative, flowing from the contexts which they in turn shape, subject to change as new information changes those contexts" (p. 42).

This couple was lucky to have begun treatment while Walt was still symptom-free, so they could focus on their relationship without feeling overwhelmed by the disease. When Walt's health began to decline, the work they had done helped them to stay connected, even though their life became much more stressful and difficult.

Isabelle and Walt came back to therapy to do some more intensive work at about the time he was diagnosed with "full-blown AIDS." For several weeks, they dialogued about their emotional responses to Walt's deteriorating health. We also made plans to get them connected to others in the community, to overcome the effects of AIDS isolation.

One of the unique difficulties of contracting and dying of AIDS is that the diagnosis itself has an isolating effect. I have heard of a situation in which a church group came to visit and comfort a member whose gay son died of AIDS, while the son was not permitted a funeral service in that same church. Frequently, family members, aware of such discrimination, pull away from anyone who might subscribe to it, which, in turn, contributes to AIDS isolation. Thus, it is crucial to help clients make connections with individuals and groups who are empathic with and respectful of persons with AIDS and their family members.

WALT AND ISABELLE: SAYING GOOD-BYE

As Walt became sicker, we began to work on what he wanted to see happen during his remaining time. We also started discussing his death.

Therapist: *I know these are the hard times, the hardest of times, and you have a lot left to do. You have worked together so hard to build what you have between you. Let's do some work on what you want for the future.*

Walt: *Well, I don't know what I want. I don't want to lose my control of my body. That's what I am most concerned about.*

Therapist: *Would you say a little more about that.*

Walt: *Well, I just don't want to be one of those people who are dying and who smell bad and don't have people coming to see them and have all those bags all over the bed. I just can't stand that. I want to be shaved every single day. I don't want to look sick.*

Therapist: *How do you imagine your death might be?*

Walt: *I've been thinking about that. I think I want to die in my sleep. Actually, I would like to die sleeping next to Isabelle in my bed at night, lying there like we were just a regular couple, and then just drift away. That would be the best way, but I don't think it is likely that that will happen.*

I wondered if he had any wishes for his daughter and his stepson. "Asking the dying person to participate in planning an optimistic future for the people he or she will leave is an immensely healing experience" (Walker, 1991, p. 55).

Therapist: *We can come back to that at another time. Would you be willing to say something about what you want for Isabelle, Marina, and Sammy?*

Walt: *Well, as for Marina—she's grown up now. There isn't much I can say to her.*

Therapist: *Well, what might you hope and dream for her? Whether or not you actually say it, what message might you want her to get from you and from your dying?*

Walt: *I want her to know that I always loved her. I want her to know that I messed up real bad. Her mother did the right thing by her, but I was a bum father. I hope she forgives me for that, and maybe can even understand that some day.*

(He paused, and then became enthused.)

I know what I want for her! I want her to go on vacation. Isabelle will get insurance money, so I want Marina to have some of it to go on vacation. I never did right by her while she was growing up, but I can do right by her now that she is an adult. Maybe she could go somewhere that she would never be able to afford, like an island or Europe or somewhere really wonderful. I would like that very much. I would look down from Heaven and smile, knowing that, at least in my death, I did right by her.

Therapist: *Is there more that you want to say or do for Marina?*

Walt: *No, that's all.*

Therapist: *What might you want for Sammy?*

Walt: *He's my boy. I want him to practice his goddamn pitching. I keep telling him that he could be a great pitcher if he would just practice a little bit every day after school. But he's a big shot, you know; he doesn't listen to his old man anymore. I want him to keep playing sports and to do well in school. I'd like him to do something during the summers so that he stays out of trouble. Maybe some baseball clinic with his friends. Isabelle, maybe you could send him and Clayton to that Phillies camp next summer. He could have that to talk about for a long time. And give him my backpack, in case he has a bit of the wanderer in him. Tell him that backpack kept me alive a lot of nights.*

Therapist: *Is there more you want for Sammy?*

Walt: *Yeah, tell him to go to college, or I'll come back and kick his ass for him! Other than that, that's it.*

Therapist: *What might you want for Isabelle?*

Walt: *Oh well, sweetie, what can I say? What do I want for you? I want you to be happy. Isn't that stupid? I brought you all this unhappiness for all those years, and now that I'm dying what I really want is for you to be happy. I don't want you crying by my bedside. I want to die knowing you're going to be okay. I can't stand the image of you standing there crying while I die.*

Therapist: *What is your image of Isabelle while you are dying?*

Walt: *Well, I want you to have with you all the people who are important to you. Don't worry about all those dumb funeral arrangements right away. Instead, I want you to call all those folks you really love, and the hospice folks, and ask them to be with you. I don't want you to be alone when I die.*

Therapist: *Walt, you said you don't want Isabelle to be alone when you die. Do you want to be alone when you die?*

Walt: *You know what I want: I want Isabelle and the kids and the nurses and our friends and maybe our families to all be there when I am dying. I'd like to say goodbye to them when I know it's time, if I know it's time.*

Therapist: *And my wish for Isabelle as I take my final breath is . . .*

Walt: *My wish for you when I take my final breath is for you to stay with me or walk away from me, but to just let me go. I swear, Isabelle, it won't matter. A few more minutes or days for me won't make any difference. I want you to be okay.*

Therapist: *And I'll know you're okay if . . .*

Walt: *I'll know you're okay when . . . I don't know. I guess when I am looking down at you and I see it.*

Therapist: *My wish for you while I am looking down is . . .*

Walt: *My wish for you while I am looking down is . . . for you to use some of this money and pay off a big piece of the house. Take a leave* *of absence from your work and volunteer at Sammy's school. Better yet, I'll know you're okay when I look down and see you dancing! Promise me you'll go dancing. Even if you don't go right away, promise me you will go.*

Isabelle promised. It was a difficult promise to keep, she later told me; after Walt died, she didn't feel like going dancing for a very long time.

The last phase of his illness was difficult for Walt. His neurological system began to shut down and he began to lose his sight. His death was, however, a peaceful one, which was comforting to Isabelle. Although by that time Walt had been in a coma, his family gathered around him, held hands, and sang. Isabelle and Walt's daughter, Marina, began to sing a Beatles song called "Still." The others joined in. At some point during that song, Walt died. Isabelle told me she was certain that, during the song, she saw Walt smile.

Walt died about six weeks after our last session. Before he died, he wrote letters to both of his children, telling them he loved them. He told them about the dreams he had for them, and he left them the money to go on a vacation and to a baseball clinic.

Isabelle and I made one last contact. She called me for an appointment several weeks after Walt's death. She was grieving deeply but was expressing her emotions freely. When she came, she brought me two pins that Walt had wanted me to have. Both were circles, one with the word "love" inside the circle, and the other with the word "peace." He had arranged to wear the pins at his funeral and then to have them removed from his suit and given to me, with his thanks. I consider these pins only two of the many gifts I received from Isabelle and Walt.

My colleagues wonder why I work with the HIV-positive population. I wonder why they do not.

BIBLIOGRAPHY

Sontag, S. (1989). *AIDS and its metaphor.* New York: Doubleday.

Umbarger Carter, C. (1983). *Structural family therapy.* New York: Harcourt Brace Jovanovich.

Walker, G. (1991). *In the midst of winter.* New York: Norton.

EDITORS' COMMENTARY

People rarely have the opportunity to prepare for death as Walt and Isabel did. The specter of dying early of AIDS shifted Walt's perspective on life, leading him back to the family he'd abandoned years before. AIDS brought much heartache to Walt and Isabel, and it robbed Walt of many years of living. But the disease also enabled this couple to see, for the first time, who their partner really was. AIDS opened their eyes to the real person buried beneath the anger and rejection and self-hatred. With wisdom and compassion, the therapist guided Walt on his journey toward death, which was, for this couple, a journey toward healing.

Ritz's chapter illustrates some basic guidelines for working with couples affected by a chronic or terminal illness. First, the therapist must be aware of the stages of the illness and its effects on the patient's body, mind, and emotions. Second, the therapist must understand how the patient's illness has an impact on the family system. Finally, the therapist needs to use this awareness and understanding in deciding how to intervene at various disease stages with the patient, the family, and other members of the patient's support network.

As suggested by clinicians who work with HIV-positive patients, people cope with HIV differently, depending on the stage of the disease. When he was first diagnosed, for example, Walt was deeply shaken and almost immobilized, even though he was symptom-free. Immediately after diagnosis, shock and denial are normal, and in most instances, the therapist should simply allow the couple whatever time they need to come to grips with the reality of the diagnosis. Eventually, however, the therapist should help them to focus on the objective facts about the disease, its effects, and its likely progression. This is especially important for HIV-positive persons: HIV seropositivity is, in and of itself, no longer an automatic death sentence, although the prognosis for any given individual remains uncertain.

As we saw in the case of Walt and Isabel, as HIV disease progresses, the affected couple has to make more and more accommodations in order to cope with its effects. Medical appointments, fatigue and other side effects of medications, pain and discomfort, and feelings of depression and discouragement eventually take their toll on the patient and, consequently, on the relationship. During the middle stages of HIV-related illness, couples need to dialogue about their needs, frustrations, and fears. Doing so paves the way for the more difficult work of saying goodbye—to past mistakes, to unfulfilled dreams, to the innocence and assurances of the past. Safely dialoguing about their life together prepares the couple to dialogue about death and about the fact that, sooner or later, like all couples, they will say their final good-bye.

Ritz demonstrates how the dialogical process can infuse the last phase of a couple's life together with a deep sense of spirituality. Through dialogue, couples can deal with death, not as a feared and unspeakable issue, but as an integral part of living. Walt died knowing that his wife and family fully understood him, his strengths and his shortcomings, his joys and his regrets, his desires and his dreams for them. He left this world known by those who loved him and whom he loved the most, turning the tragedy of death from AIDS into an awakening that few of us experience during our lifetime.

Chapter 12

THE IMPACT OF ADULT ATTENTION-DEFICIT DISORDER ON COUPLES

*Kathleen Kelly and Marianne Luquet**

Attention-deficit disorder (ADD) has become the hottest diagnosis of the 1990s. Current estimates show that as many as 20 million Americans—children and adults alike—may suffer from this syndrome whose widespread coverage by the media has engendered both controversy and confusion. And now, with so many adults beginning to feel that they might qualify for testing and diagnosis, some questions arise: Is adult ADD being misdiagnosed, overdiagnosed, or maybe even underdiagnosed? Is it a myth? A fad?

ADD is not a new disorder, but rather one that has undergone many changes through the years. Its clinical diagnosis has experienced a metamorphosis—from "minimal brain damage" in the 1950s to today's "attention-deficit disorder." Its diagnosis was originally limited to children but, as a result of more children being so diagnosed in the 1980s, many parents of such children became aware that they,

---

*In our efforts to present the information for this chapter, we were faced with our own challenges and struggles, as one of us is an ADD adult and the other is the partner of an ADD adult. Since one of us has ADD, by using the dialogue process with one another, we were able to maintain our connection as authors so that each of our voices could be heard and understood.

I, Marianne, was diagnosed in 1990 with ADD without hyperactivity. It has presented numerous challenges in my marriage. Ongoing couples' therapy, education about ADD for myself and my partner, and attendance at workshops specifically on ADD and the couple have proved immensely helpful. Extensive use of the modified Couples Dialogue has been a necessary tool for staying connected through difficult conflict.

too, presented the interacting cognitive, behavioral, and biological symptoms that they saw in their children.

Research in the field is now demonstrating that ADD is a hereditary neu-robiological disorder manifested in childhood by myriad symptoms—attentional difficulties, impulsivity, hyperactivity, and restlessness, to name but a few—that puts its sufferers at a great disadvantage. And because the symptoms of ADD can so affect an adult's functioning, the disorder can wreak havoc on relationships. This is part of the reason why it is essential for therapists treating couples to be aware of what adult ADD is and to know how best to treat the particular difficulties it presents to the dyadic relationship. Often, the couples therapist will consult with other practitioners responsible for a patient's ADD care—generally a psychiatrist or neurologist who specializes in the diagnosis and treatment of adult ADD. If the ADD partner has been prescribed medication by another practitioner, such a consulting relationship is highly recommended.

What is most significant about working with a couple with ADD, where either one partner or both have the disorder, is the disconnection that continually occurs. The goal of the Imago model is to promote connection and intentionality in a committed relationship while helping couples to move from an unconscious to a conscious marriage. We aim to heighten the clinician's awareness by illustrating the obstacles presented by the syndrome for couples with ADD that may interfere with their consciously achieving connection.

THE COUPLES DIALOGUE

The Couples Dialogue is a communication tool and way of being that seems tailor-made for ADD couples and individuals, as it provides an external structure that compensates for the lack of internal structure experienced by those with ADD. Although practicing the Couples Dialogue is particularly difficult for ADD couples, this process is the key element of therapy in assisting the couple to achieve and maintain connection. It will be evident to the therapist early in treatment that such couples initially struggle with various components of dialogue. In our personal and professional experience, we have found that through the use of a specially modified approach to the Couples Dialogue process, connection can be achieved. Without modification, the dialogue can be painful and frustrating for these couples.

Several case vignettes in which one or both partners have been diagnosed with ADD, or in whom we strongly suspect this diagnosis, illustrate some of the common relational themes that couples therapists will observe in their offices. The accompanying checklists will give the reader an understanding of the classic problems for the ADD- and non-ADD partner in the Couples Dialogue process, both as *sender* and as *receiver*, and we will provide a brief review of the literature on how the syndrome affects couples in the areas of intimacy, communication, and relationships.

WHAT IS ADD?

ADD is an invisible disorder. As Sari Solden (1995) writes, "ADD is not a psychological or characterological but neurobiologically-based disorder that is chronic in nature and severely impacts on one's life. With ADD, one is not brain damaged, but rather the individual's brain functions differently."

Two theories currently support the biological basis for ADD. The first theory hypothesizes an absence of the neurochemicals—specifically, dopamine and norepinephrine—that are necessary for the transmission of impulses across various areas of the brain, in that they may be firing inconsistently or inefficiently. This dysregulation of the neurochemicals could be an explanation for the cognitive, physiological, and behavioral symptoms that manifest in ADD.

The second theory, which hypothesizes a "disinhibition" of the frontal lobes of the brain, may explain the impulsivity, hyperactivity, and distractibility related to the disorder. The frontal lobes are responsible for cortical control, meaning that they are the gatekeepers for all of the impulses coming from the lower brain. If the frontal lobes are unable to regulate these impulses, this will ultimately interfere with one's ability to process information accurately, control one's emotional reactivity, and postpone or delay one's responses, thus making it difficult to carry out plans. What can also occur is that impulses may reach the frontal lobes, but because the gatekeeper literally is not available, the impulses may enter and exit rapidly. This is more likely to be seen with an adult who is experiencing attention-deficit/hyperactivity disorder (ADHD) than with the hypoactive form of the disorder.

Russell Barkley (1991), a noted researcher in the field of ADD, believes that ADHD involves a failure to control motor activities or behaviors (a problem with the output of messages from the brain), and that ADD without hyperactivity involves sluggish cognitive processing (a problem with the brain's receiving and processing information quickly and accurately). In ADHD, the prefrontal and limbic portions of the brain are believed to be the major sites with neurotransmitter problems. Some researchers believe that ADD, inattentive type without hyperactivity, involves problems in a different section of the brain—the posterior cortical area (Zeigler Dendy, 199.).

Barkley also maintains that ADD, inattentive type without hyperactivity, includes problems with focused attention and cognitive processing speed, rather than with sustained attention and impulse control as observed in ADHD. Slow cognitive functioning tends to make individuals with this type of ADD feel extremely frustrated. Even though they are bright, and know it, they have the experience that the information is trapped inside their brains. Difficulties include slow processing of information, slow response to requests, poor recall, slow completion of work, and great difficulty with getting started on tasks and sustaining their efforts. A person with this type of ADD may appear low in energy, apathetic, and unmotivated, and depression and anxiety may be more common.

Alan Zametkin et al. (1990) at the National Institute of Mental Health did a study with adults that proposed that there is a biological basis for ADD. The study proved that there is a difference in energy consumption at the cellular level between parts of the brain that regulate attention, emotions, and impulse control in subjects with ADD, as compared with those without ADD (Hallowell & Ratey, 1994, p. 71).

Hallowell and Ratey, authors and clinicians, both of whom have ADD, have written about and worked with more than 1,000 adults with ADD. They have brought a great deal of understanding of the dynamics of adults with ADD and the difficulty they have in establishing and maintaining relationships. They propose that these adults are thwarted by the *biology of intimacy*—"those physiological, behavioral, cognitive, and affective symptoms of ADD that act as a barrier to forming healthy relationships" (Nadeau, 1995, p. 219). Hallowell and Ratey have based their theory of the biology of intimacy on the conceptualization of the two models of ADD described above—the dysregulation of the neurotransmitters and frontal lobe disinhibition.

Harville Hendrix (1988) illustrates the effect of the old brain/new brain theory in relation to the conscious versus the unconscious marriage, proposing that couples are often operating unconsciously from responses of the old brain. With the evolution of the new brain, we have available to us our cerebral cortex, which is the site for our conscious thinking and problem solving. The old brain, which originates in the brain stem, is cradled by the limbic system, which is the center for our emotions. The limbic system links the brain stem and the cerebral cortex. The interaction that takes place between the old brain and the new brain is a complex endeavor. Because we have our old brain available to us, we have to combat its powerful emotions. For example, when we experience a threat or perceive danger, our old brain kicks into a fight-or-flight mode. This is the unconscious part of our old brain that cannot make a distinction, but responds on a primitive level. A comment such as, "You're never ready on time!" could elicit a fight-back response,

"What do you mean, I'm always late?!" And if the message doesn't travel to our new brain, which is the seat of our consciousness, then we are apt to overreact and a fight will probably ensue. But if we respond to our partner, "So you feel that I'm never on time?" the response is rational. Since this response originates from the new brain, the cerebral cortex, the center for conscious thinking, we are less likely to perceive and react to attacks from our partner.

The Imago model seeks to assist couples in developing a conscious marriage, a partnership in which they feel safe and loved, and can work toward healing one another's childhood wounds, thus achieving aliveness and wholeness. The ADD adult's lack of awareness, inability to focus, and tendency to become emotionally flooded and overreactive—which are caused by the ADD brain's dysfunction—can be counterproductive to the achievement of these goals.

CHALLENGES FACED BY THE NON-ADD PARTNER

Just as the partner with ADD has many obstacles to face in identifying and understanding how the syndrome specifically affects his in her life, non-ADD partners are equally challenged to understand and appreciate the struggle of their partners. One of the biggest obstacles that partners with ADD face is that their behavior is not necessarily within their control. For example, when we see someone whom we feel has gained weight, the thought may arise that it would be hurtful to them if we mentioned it. A process occurs in our brain, through a series of steps that probably take a matter of seconds, that allows us to hold back our comment. But for many with ADD, the brain's impulsivity negates any opportunity for them to handle an unconscious mental task in a way that comes so naturally to a non-ADD partner.

For the non-ADD partner, it is difficult (if not impossible) to imagine that the behaviors manifest by the ADD partner may not be under the partner's control.

The film *Mrs. Doubtfire* shows what can happen in a relationship when ADD traits are unrecognized or misinterpreted. Robin Williams' character, exemplifies many characteristics associated with ADHD. In the opening sequence, he walks out on his job after a disagreement with his boss. As is characteristic of ADHD, he responds impulsively to the situation, becoming emotionally overreactive to his boss; acting on his impulses, he doesn't consider the consequences of his actions. He then proceeds to spontaneously throw a birthday party for his son without consulting his wife. She, however, gets a telephone call from the police and she goes home to find a mobile petting zoo is part of the celebration.

Dumbfounded and overwhelmed, she begins to lash out angrily at her partner. He says in return, "Honey don't get mad!" at which point, she replies, "I want a divorce!"

THE MODIFIED COUPLES DIALOGUE

When working with an adult with ADD, the dialogue provides an external structure that facilitates focusing and helps to minimize distractions. According to Rick and Jerilyn Fowler (1995), intimacy between a man and a woman requires focus. But when ADD is present, true closeness suffers from too many distractions. Since the adult with ADD lacks the internal structure, the external structure of the dialogue process is crucial. As one client with ADD expressed it, "This process helps me hear what you are saying because it's like taking a broom and sweeping out a corner of my brain to make room for the things that you are telling me. Then I have a place for them so that I can remember what you told me."

When partners with ADD are the receivers in the dialogue process, it is important that they receive only small chunks of information, because that helps them to stay focused. When the ADD partner receives too much information, it's like the police officer who is trying to direct traffic when the lights go out at an intersection. The officer, bombarded by honking horns, traffic backing up, and cars trying to get through the intersection, must decide which traffic to let through first. As a result, an inner, as well as an outer, traffic jam ensues, causing too much information to be sent to the officer's brain, which, in turn, causes him or her to panic. The officer, along with the traffic, becomes a gridlock. This situation is similar to what happens in the ADD brain; it is not able to process the information, and this creates a minipanic, leaving the person in an emotionally overreactive state. At this juncture, it is important for the therapist to slow the process down, allowing the ADD partner the opportunity to regain his or her footing.

Marital researcher John Gottman (1994) refers to a problem sign in a marriage when one or another spouse feels "flooded" almost continually. By flooding, he means susceptibility to frequent emotional distress. It is our perception that, due to difficulties with the prefrontal lobe, the person with ADD may be more vulnerable to the flooding Gottman describes, putting the relationship even more at risk for disconnection between the partners. According to Gottman, people who feel flooded cannot hear without distortion or respond with a clear head. They find it hard to organize their thinking and they fall back on primitive reactions. We believe that the Couples Dialogue is the key to helping ADD clients and their partners stay connected; however, as mentioned earlier, some modification should be considered in light of the difficulties with flooding for the ADD partner. The first modification is the inclusion of time-out breaks. When a situation becomes too heated and the ADD partner's feelings are so strong that they override everything else, mirroring and empathy deteriorate, and a 20-minute time-out may be needed to restore physiological balance before the couple is capable of continuing with the dialogue process. In order to truly mirror, validate, and empathize, it is necessary for the ADD partner's emotional reactions to calm down.

According to Daniel Goleman (1995), 20 minutes is, physiologically, the minimum time required for the body to recover from states of arousal. Relaxation techniques, aerobic exercise, and distraction are all effective ways of helping the ADD partner calm down. Ventilation of anger should not be encouraged at such a time, as this tends to increase the brain's level of arousal. Once a sense of calm is achieved, the ADD partner can resume the dialogue process.

The therapeutic posture in which partners face each other while maintaining eye contact is extremely useful for enhancing focus. The struggle that the ADD partner may experience as the receiver in the dialogue process involves recalling and integrating the chain of events. For example, reactivity to the information being sent makes it difficult to mirror, validate, empathize, and respond appropriately. At this point of reactivity, disconnection will occur.

One of the primary concerns for the ADD adult is that of being misunderstood. In order to facilitate connection, it is helpful for the therapist to understand the frustration experienced by both partners. For non-ADD partners, the struggle has been the repeated attempts to get their partners to listen and to pay attention to their needs, resulting in their feeling angry and resentful. This will lead to further disconnection because the non-ADD partner might not be able to hear or be interested in what the partner has to say. As one non-ADD partner stated, "Every time I try to get you to hear my feelings, you get distracted by your own feelings and I feel dismissed, like you're only concerned about your own feelings." Because of all that is operating biologically, it takes a great deal of energy and effort for the ADD partner to focus and pay attention.

Even when the connection can be made in the mirroring stage of the dialogue, the movement or shift to the next stage of validation could create difficulty for ADD partners. In order to validate their partner, they have to be able to remember what was stated in the mirroring stage. Difficulty with short-term memory and thought retrieval is a real problem for those with ADD. At this juncture, it is helpful for the therapist again to slow down the process, ask the non-ADD partner to repeat the statements that were missed, and allow the ADD partner the opportunity to regain his or her concentration and move successfully to the validation. It is equally important to support that success, as the adult with ADD has encountered many failures in communication and has often felt misunderstood or has misunderstood others.

Expressing empathy, the last stage of the Couples Dialogue, is the ability to reflect on one's partner's feelings. According to Hallowell, Miller, and Ratey (1995), the need for the ADD adult to discharge emotions all at once without being able to reflect because of processing difficulties puts the ADD adult at a disadvantage, as they are not able to consider the emotional state of their partner, which ". . . precludes them from a true sense of empathy" (Nadeau, 1995, p. 224). This does not mean that everyone with ADD will experience this difficulty; it is probably more prevalent in those with ADHD, because of the rapid fire of emotions and the inability to stop and think before acting. If the ADD partner cannot imagine how the other partner is feeling, the therapist can ask the non-ADD partner to share his or her feelings and then have the ADD partner mirror those feelings. Often this is sufficient to restore the connection between the couple. When the ADD partner really begins to understand why his or her partner is so angry, there can be a genuine connection. By providing safety and a place to be heard, the structure of the dialogue allows the ADD partner a sense of hope that, after years of being misunderstood, he or she can actually achieve an intimate connection to his or her partner in a way that the ADD partner may have thought impossible.

Modifications to the Couples Dialogue for the ADD Couple:

1. Have the couple maintain eye contact when sending and receiving.
2. If the ADD partner is having difficulty expressing empathy, have the non-ADD partner send what he or she is feeling one sentence at a time, to be mirrored back.
3. Initiate a 20-minute time-out whenever the ADD partner is feeling flooded or is unable to stay in the process.
4. If the ADD receiver is feeling too emotionally reactive, have him or her ask the sender's permission for the receiver to send three sentences about how he or she is feeling. He or she can then return to being the receiver after these feeling statements are mirrored back.
5. If the ADD partner is having difficulty with short-term memory, have the non-ADD partner send one sentence at a time.
6. List the steps of the Couples Dialogue on a poster or flipchart for a quick visual reminder to help the ADD partner with memory and sequencing.
7. Normalize the difficulty people have learning and practicing dialogue before beginning, so that the ADD partner does not feel that the dialogue will be yet another failure.

8. The therapist may need to check in periodically with the ADD partner as to his or her experience of safety in hearing the non-ADD partner's anger and frustration, and assist the ADD partner in feeling safe.

Checklists

The following three checklists will assist the clinician in pinpointing areas of challenge for partners with ADD in using Couples Dialogue.

Problems in the Dialogue Process for the Partner with ADHD.

- Is hypersensitive to what is perceived as criticism
- Interrupts sender for fear of losing thought
- Feels pressure to move on to next thought or idea
- A tendency toward self-absorption
- Feels overwhelmed when trying to remember what the sender is saying
- Difficulty with reflecting on partner's feelings
- Being impatient and easily becoming bored
- A short fuse, leading to emotional outbursts
- A need to be in control
- Impulsivity—blurts out comments
- Can be thin-skinned—feels things intensely
- Defensive posture—easily frustrated
- Seeks stimulation
- Can react excessively to normal stress
- Distractibility that interferes with staying on task during conversation
- Hyperfocusing
- Paying attention is exhausting
- Finds transitions difficult
- Misses verbal and nonverbal cues
- Hypersensitive to tactile stimulation
- Difficulty with short-term memory and thought retrieval

Problems in the Dialogue Process for the Non-ADD Partner.

- Exhaustion—lack of energy
- Frustration and anger
- A tendency to be reactive
- A defensive posture
- Feeling "forced to take control"

- Becoming overinvolved and lost in partner's problems—not attending to own needs
- Frustration with partner's "not getting it" and yet knowing the partner can't help it
- Feeling helpless and overwhelmed
- Continual struggle to get partner to pay attention
- Feeling unappreciated and dismissed
- Recipient of blame

Problems in the Dialogue Process for the Partner With ADD Without Hyperactivity.

- Difficulty moving from impulse to action
- Low energy
- Internal restlessness
- Works and thinks slowly
- Is easily frustrated and overwhelmed
- Shifting attention—interferes with completing tasks
- Emotionally overreactive
- Can be thin-skinned—feels things intensely
- Difficulty with short-term memory and thought retrieval
- Can react excessively to normal stresses
- A tendency to become lost in inner world
- Seeks self-protection
- Is disorganized
- A tendency to become overwhelmed by stimulation
- For women, hormonal imbalance can intensify ADD symptoms

CASE VIGNETTES

The following vignettes are illustrations of actual cases with names and various details changed to disguise the couples' identities. Their purpose here, rather than to suggest a particular intervention or course of treatment, is to heighten the clinician's awareness of the core issues that often arise for couples affected by attention-deficit disorder. We recommend that the reader pay particular attention to the types of interactions that repeatedly occur and the emotional experiences of the client couples as a response to these interactions.

The brief comments that follow each vignette provide a "current reality" perspective on the case—bringing the reader up-to-date on the couple's progress in working the process—and offers our clinical thoughts and insights.

Case 1: Mary and Jim: Male Partner with ADHD and Non-ADD Partner

Mary and Jim, who have been married for 30 years, presented with a lifelong history of marital discord. At the initial session, Mary's anger was palpable and she expressed ongoing frustration with Jim and his inability to listen and stay focused. She stated that she was "at the end of her rope" and wasn't sure if she wanted to put out the energy required to deal with the issues at hand. She further stated, "I'm tired of picking up the pieces," as a result of Jim's emotional outbursts, which she feels are directly related to Jim's loss of potential clients.

Jim countered by blaming others for his loss of temper and subsequent outbursts. He was generally confused and angry as to why these incidents keep recurring. It was obvious to the therapist that Jim was highly sensitive to Mary's anger but that it was unclear to Jim why his wife was "making such a big deal" of it.

As Mary continued to express her frustrations with the relationship, Jim became increasingly defensive and argumentative. Neither partner was able to hear the other. Mary described Jim as having a hair-trigger temper that could be touched off by the least provocation, and was generally an overreaction to the situation. What would typically occur when the pair had a disagreement would be that Jim would explosively dump his anger and leave the situation, only to return later feeling clueless as to why Mary was still angry. Mary's ongoing frustration with Jim was over his inability to take responsibility for his emotional outbursts and the impact that they had on her. She was feeling unheard and unacknowledged. What further complicated the situation was Jim's inability to remember their arguments.

Jim expressed frustration because he felt that Mary had an advantage over him, as she could recollect all the details, leaving him feeling confused and overwhelmed. In his struggle to respond to Mary, he would inadvertently come across as angry, which would further fuel the argument. At this juncture, Mary would be unable to remain calm and would also become emotionally overreactive.

The following is Mary and Jim's initial attempt at the Couples Dialogue.

Mary: *When I speak to you, I would like you to look directly at me, so that I know I have your attention.*

Jim: *So what I hear you saying is that you would like me to look directly at you when you are speaking to me. Do I have that? Is there more?*

Mary: *Yes, you have it, and there's plenty more. I feel that when I try to discuss something that has to do with my feelings, you will distract the conversation and somehow the focus is on you and your feelings. It leaves me feeling dismissed and angry.*

Jim: *I don't know what you're talking about, you're always throwing in things. It's like I always have to figure out a code, and just look at the expression on your face. You're really angry and it seems like I'm the one who is always doing something wrong.*

Therapist: *Jim, could you stop for a second and help me understand what's going on for you right now?*

Jim: *She really makes me angry. She's always criticizing and she doesn't understand my ADD and my struggles.*

Mary: *See what happens? The focus is always back on him and his feelings and I'm sick of it.*

Therapist (to both):   *What appears to be happening right now is that you are both feeling misunderstood and not heard. I'd like to take this opportunity to demonstrate how this dialogue process works. I will begin by mirroring what I heard each of you say to the other, and will invite you both to clarify or correct anything I say that doesn't fit exactly what you mean. (To Mary): Mary, what I hear you saying is that you would like Jim to look directly at you when you are speaking to him, so that you know he is paying attention. You also find that when you are speaking to Jim about your feelings, and concerns, he will become distracted and absorbed in his own thoughts and feelings, and that all of this leaves you feeling angry and dismissed and you are sick of it. Do I have that?*

Mary: *Yes, that's it. And I also get very angry and feel abused by his verbal attacks.*

Therapist: *And you also get very angry and feel abused by the verbal attacks.*

Mary: *Yes.*

Therapist: *It makes sense that when you're trying to get Jim to pay attention and he becomes preoccupied with his own thoughts and feelings it leaves you feeling very angry and dismissed because the focus is no longer on you, but back on him.*

Mary: *Yes, that's it exactly.*

Therapist: *I can imagine that leaves you feeling angry, frustrated, and alone, and maybe feeling hopeless that he will never hear you.*

Mary: *Yes, and also exhausted.*

Therapist: *It also leaves you feeling exhausted.*

Mary: *Yes, that's it.*

Therapist: *Jim, could you tell me more about what happens for you when Mary is trying to get you to pay attention?*

Jim: *She's always so angry and I don't know what she's saying. It's like somehow there's some secret code to what she is saying and I'm not getting it.*

Therapist: *So what I hear you saying is that you experience Mary as being angry and that you have difficulty trying to decipher the secret code as it relates to Mary's communicating with you. Do I have that?*

Jim: *Yes. It's like I start to listen, and then a thought comes up, and then that thought develops a tentacle of thoughts and then I get distracted by all these thoughts and I miss what Mary is trying to tell me. Then she gets that look on her face and I know I've missed it again.*

Therapist: *So what I hear you saying is that you get flooded with an array of thoughts that greatly interfere with your attempts to hear what Mary has to say. Do I have that?*

Jim: *Yes, and I feel so ashamed because I really want to hear what she has to say and somehow I've missed it again and I get so angry at myself.*

Therapist: *In addition, you feel ashamed because you really want to hear what Mary has to say and you're left feeling angry at yourself. Do I have it? Is there more?*

Jim: *Yes, that's what happens. No, there is no more right now.*

Therapist: *So what makes sense about all this is when you make an attempt to hear what Mary has to say, you become so distracted and overwhelmed by the intrusion of your thoughts and concerned with Mary's anger and facial expressions that you miss the message that Mary is attempting to convey. In addition, you're left feeling ashamed and angry that you have disappointed Mary. It also makes sense that you feel alone in your struggle with ADD. Do I have it?*

Jim: *Yes.*

Therapist: *I can imagine that all of this leaves you feeling frustrated and angry for missing what Mary is saying, and alone in your struggle when you get bombarded with your thoughts that interfere with your repeated attempts to hear your partner.*

Jim: *Yes, that's right.*

Therapist: *It is clear that you both are experiencing a great deal of difficulty each time you make an attempt to speak to each other about your mutual concerns. I have confidence that, through the use of the dialogue, you will both be able to achieve your goal. It is not uncommon for couples to initially experience difficulty in learning this process.*

Comments on Mary and Jim.* This vignette is an illustration of a couple struggling in their relationship in which one of the partners has been diagnosed with ADHD. Researchers in the field believe that it is in the area of establishing intimate relationships that the adult with ADD experiences the greatest difficulties.

Jim had made the initial call for treatment. During their first session, I attempted to gather information regarding his diagnosis and treatment course. Even though they both stated that they knew about ADD, it was evident that Jim did not have a clear understanding of his own problems related to the ADD and how they were affecting his relationship. Mary stated that she had read all there is to read, and that her husband's ADD was simply a fact.

The storm hit when Mary became overly reactive emotionally to a comment I made, and I immediately mirrored her statement and validated her. This diffused her anger and she asked what, specifically, I could do to help them.

I introduced them to the Couples Dialogue and we spent the remainder of the session practicing mirroring. Jim was enthusiastic about the prospect of finding a way to communicate with Mary that would help her to understand his struggle with ADD, and Mary was hopeful that she might be able to find a way to get Jim to pay attention. What quickly transpired in their initial attempt at the Couples Dialogue, though, was a sequence of events that allowed me to observe why their early attempts at dialogue had failed.

Although Jim initially was open, his becoming flooded and distracted by his thoughts created an internal chaos that was manifest in his becoming defensive, argumentative, emotionally overly reactive, and hypersensitive to Mary's anger. He was unaware of his behavior and its impact on the dialogue, and it set his blaming of Mary into motion.

Even though Mary was clear in her presentation of the issues, her anger toward Jim (reflected in her tone, posture, and responses) triggered his reactivity. Thus, her attempt at dialogue in this session turned out to be another failure in her repeated attempts to be heard.

My decision to intervene and demonstrate the dialogue process by mirroring, validating, and empathizing with each partner separately in the presence of the other was to give them both the experience of being heard, since they were unable to accomplish this task on their own. What this produced was decreased reactivity, which helped restore a sense of safety and connection. My hope was that they

*By Kathleen Kelly.

would return for future sessions confident that I understood their struggle with ADD and how it affected their relationship. My goal for the termination of this session was to instill some faith that they could, through the use of the dialogue, find a place of connection and communication where they could be heard in a safe, nonblaming, and nonreactive way. I'm not sure that they believed this was possible at the time, but I did direct them to the light that was peeking through at the end of the tunnel.

After the first few sessions, the couple began to trust that I understood the dynamics of ADD from the perspectives of both the ADD partner and the non-ADD partner. A kernel of hope emerged that maybe things could improve in their relationship.

The greatest obstacle for Jim was managing his ADD symptoms, which were clearly out of control. He had been prescribed Ritalin, three times daily, but it was ineffective in helping his emotional lability. After my consultation with Jim's physician, the doctor prescribed an additional medication.

The goal of treatment is to facilitate the connection between the partners. I believe that such connection depends on the non-ADD partner's getting his or her anger expressed, heard, and validated by the ADD partner, and that it is the therapist's responsibility to create a safe place in which this can occur.

At the time of this writing, I have worked with this couple for seven sessions and feel strongly that the dialogue process is crucial to their success in improving communication. It will take patience and tolerance on my part to stay in the struggle with them. Success in the process of the dialogue will provide the foundation for building the connection that is so important to both partners.

Case 2: Lynn and Mark: Both Partners with ADD

Lynn and Mark, who have been married for four years, presented with an inability to communicate in their relationship, difficulty with money management, and escalating fights with outbursts of rage by both partners. They were often late for their scheduled appointments or forgot them altogether, and often forgot their checkbook.

Lynn excelled in her work with computers, but when it came to meetings, she found it impossible to concentrate. This left her frustrated, and brought up old feelings of incompetence and a lifelong struggle and fear of not being able to reach her potential. While growing up, she was often accused of being lazy, daydreaming, and being unmotivated. She also experienced feelings of shame about her inability to keep her home clean and organized. She stated, "Clutter is everywhere, I keep trying to get it together, but it never happens." One of the couple's major arguments focused on Lynn's inability to pay the bills on time. To avoid conflict, for example, Lynn might tell Mark that she had paid the premium on their insurance policy, when in fact she had not, thus further inflaming the situation. Mark was emotionally overreactive to Lynn's poor money management and baffled as to why she was so disorganized, but her reason for assuming the task was Mark's inability to handle the finances himself. Both had contributed equally to their financial instability. Each was quick to react and to blame the other, and was, therefore, not able to hear the other's frustrations.

Mark is a successful salesperson who owns his own business and thrives on the stimulation of making deals. He excels at seeing the big picture, but has difficulty with the details. His wife experiences difficulty with his fast-talking, fast-moving, intense approach to life. She finds his intensity draining, as she moves and thinks slowly and often feels flooded and overwhelmed.

What further compromises the connection for this couple is Mark's hyper-focusing on projects. If he becomes involved in a business venture, it becomes all-consuming. Lynn's major frustration with Mark is that anything in which Mark gets involved becomes an all-or-nothing situation.

Mark's major frustration with Lynn is her seeming lack of energy. He also feels that she is not supportive, but Lynn contends that when she attempts to be supportive, Mark doesn't stay in the room long enough to allow her the opportunity to hear what he has to say.

Comments on Mark and Lynn.[*] At the onset of treatment, my primary goal was to initiate the dialogue process. The couple was receptive, but issues of defensiveness, emotional reactivity, and weak memory skills presented a challenge. This was the first couple with whom I had worked where my suspicion of ADD was a consideration in my assessment. My next step was to further explore this possibility. Lynn was open to it, as she had some information about ADD and was curious as to whether she might fit the profile. After further exploration, both partners agreed to consult a psychiatrist who specialized in evaluating adults with ADD.

Lynn was diagnosed with ADD without hyperactivity and started taking Ritalin. Her response to the medication was positive; she was especially amazed

*By Kathleen Kelly.

at her new ability to focus and concentrate at business meetings. Mark was subsequently diagnosed with ADHD, and started on a regime of Ritalin and an antidepressant. The combination of medications was effective in enhancing his focus and helping to modulate mood swings, which inadvertently reduced his emotional outbursts.

After the initial diagnosis of ADD, there is often a sense of relief. Lynn expressed a feeling of validation from the diagnosis because, as she explained, "I always knew that there was something different but I could never explain it." Mark had the same awareness: "Now I know why I felt so different from my peers while growing up. I would sit back and wonder why I couldn't get it as quickly as my peers, as I knew that I was not stupid." Mark was greatly affected by this new information, which left him with feelings of regret for the lost time and lost potential.

Empathy for each other's reaction to the diagnosis was a place of connection for the couple, as Lynn truly understood Mark and could, through the safety of the dialogue process, mirror and validate her partner's feelings from a nondefensive and nonreactive posture. In the telling and retelling of their specific experiences with ADD, they began to build the bridge of connection to each other.

After the evaluation, I continued to struggle with the couple's difficulty with remaining in the dialogue. Emotional reactivity continued to short-circuit the connection. Issues of safety became a focal point of their discussions.

As the therapist, I often imagined that there were loaded sticks of dynamite placed at strategic places at either end of the "bridge" between this couple that could be ignited at any given moment. As their emotional reactivity began to abate, I began to visualize giving the partners wooden planks with which to rebuild their connection, in place of the sticks of dynamite. As I began better to understand the cognitive, behavioral, and emotional characteristics of ADD, I was able to bridge my own connection to the couple, and to visualize the Couples Dialogue as the main support for their bridge.

Since this was my first experience in working with a couple where both partners had ADD, I encountered many obstacles. Once I had a clearer vision of what was occurring, I was able to be less reactive to the intensity and reactivity between the couple. I found that mirroring the partners individually was often useful. It was important that they experienced being understood, as they both had engaged in a lifelong struggle with feeling misunderstood and misunderstanding others. As each began to identify his or her own specific emotional and behavioral characteristics and how these were affecting the partner, each became more sensitive to the partner's frustrations.

I worked with this couple for about six months before they moved to Florida, where I referred them to another Imago therapist. My hope is that they have continued to build their connection with each other. I do believe that the couple's commitment to working within the framework of the dialogue process allowed them to create the necessary safety in which to restore their connection.

Case 3: Heather and Steve: Female Partner With ADD Without Hyperactivity and Non-ADD Partner

An example of the efficacy of Couples Dialogue in maintaining connection between partners is demonstrated in the case of Heather and Steve.

Heather, a 40-year-old mother of three, was diagnosed six years earlier with ADD without hyperactivity. She has a part-time psychotherapy practice. Heather's son, Christopher, age nine, also has ADD. The couple has another son, age seven, and a daughter, age three.

Heather has great difficulties with organizing and managing the domestic responsibilities that go with rearing a young family. Unlike those with ADD with hyperactivity, Heather's energy stores are low, and she has trouble getting started on tasks and seeing them through. The distractions of having young children in the household add to her already present attentional difficulties. Heather's premenstrual syndrome (PMS) is also aggravated by the ADD, as is often the case. Trying to balance the needs of family, work, her own ADD and that of her son adds to her stress and affects the marital relationship. Heather is not currently taking medication for her ADD because it has had adverse effects.

The following is an excerpt from one of the couple's dialogues that highlights the struggle of a woman with hypoactive-type ADD.

> **Heather:**   *I noticed that every month at this time we seem to be having our biggest fallouts. I really want to prevent that pattern from recurring.*
> **Steve (mirroring):**   *So, I hear you saying that you notice a pattern to our more difficult fights and you'd like to make sure we break that pattern.*
> **Heather:**   *That's right. What I'm noticing this week is that I'm really feeling overwhelmed with all that needs to be done before we go on vacation, and with the Easter holiday following as soon as we get back.*
> **Steve:**   *I hear you saying that you're feeling really overwhelmed with all that has to be done before we leave and with preparing for the holiday as well.*

Therapist (to Steve): *Is there more about that, Heather?*

Steve: *Is there more about that?*

Heather: *When I think about it all, and the short time period, I don't know how I can possibly organize it all. It sometimes feels like such an impossible task that I shut down because I don't know where to start on the list.*

Steve: *I hear you saying that you're afraid you won't be able to organize all that needs to be done, so you shut down and can't even get started. Did I get that right?*

Heather: *Yes.*

Therapist (to Steve): *What does that remind you of from childhood?*

Steve: *What does that remind you of from childhood?*

Heather: *Oh, I guess when I was in elementary school and I couldn't follow directions or finish the assignments in the allotted time. I'd get behind, then the work seemed impossible to complete. Sometimes it was so confusing, I just couldn't do anything.*

Therapist: *Steve, can you validate that?*

Steve: *That makes sense to me that when you were little you would get so overwhelmed you wouldn't be able to keep up with assignments. I can see how you might feel the same way now when there is so much organizing of work to do in a short time.*

Therapist: *Can you imagine how Heather might feel?*

Steve: *I imagine that you'd feel frustrated, confused, and overwhelmed.*

Heather: *Yes, and ashamed.*

Therapist: *Tell him about "ashamed."*

Heather: *Ashamed because I feel so inadequate. Other people would be able to manage the situation. I feel like there is something wrong with me because I can't. I just don't measure up.*

Steve: *I hear you saying that you feel ashamed because you can't manage like other people and you feel inadequate, like you don't measure up.*

Therapist (to Steve): *Can you validate that?*

Steve: *I can understand how you might doubt your abilities when others seem to do things more easily. It must make you feel sad when you can't keep up.*

Heather: *Yes, it does.*

Therapist (to Steve): *Can you hold her while she tells you about the sadness?*

Therapist (first to Heather): *Just take it in. Let him hold you and tell him how it hurts. (then to Steve): Steve, just softly mirror from time to time.*

Comments on Heather and Steve.* Prior to working on dialogue with their therapist, Heather and Steve had experienced difficulty around Steve's lack of empathy regarding Heather's problem with organizing family packing for an upcoming trip. The couple tried to resolve the issue at home, but Heather became flooded, Steve became very reactive, and they had to call a time-out. In a subsequent therapy session, I coached them in discussing the issue using the modified Couples Dialogue. The result was that both partners came away with a greater understanding of Heather's ADD and its impact on Steve and on their marriage, and they had a deeper level of empathy for each other.

At the completion of the above dialogue, the couple did a full holding exercise. Afterwards, Heather made a Behavior Change Request of Steve that for one week a month—the week of her PMS—they would dialogue every night for a maximum of one hour. This nightly dialogue would help them stay connected during particularly rough episodes when Heather's ADD is aggravated by her monthly hormonal imbalance. Prior to the institution of regular dialogue at this time of the month, Heather and Steve's arguments would escalate. Each would become reactive and defensive and their talks would ultimately end in verbal attacks, followed by withdrawal on both sides. The Couples Dialogue, once in effect, averted this typical negative outcome.

Dialogue has also been helpful in alleviating stress, especially during the premenstrual phase of Heather's cycle. Ongoing couples therapy, attendance at workshops regarding ADD and the couple, and education about ADD have all helped Heather and her non-ADD spouse maintain their relationship.

OTHER SPECIAL CONCERNS

Women with ADD: Hypoactivity Is the Norm

Sari Solden (1995), in *Women with Attention Deficit Disorder*, states that ADD without hyperactivity is the most common form of ADD diagnosed in girls. Until recently, most experts quoted the standard ratio of ADD boys to girls as between 6-to-1 and 10-to-1. This disparity is most likely seen because the studies have not included the quiet, nonhyperactive child. Kate Kelly and Peggy Ramundo (1993), believe that the ratio would approach 1-to-1 if girls without hyperactivity

---

*By Marianne Luquet.

were included. Larry Silver (1994), also agrees that the ratio of boys to girls is much closer to equal, feeling that, with this type of ADD, girls are more likely to be overlooked and seen as either depressed or disinterested.

Among typical characteristics of females with ADD without hyperactivity, Kathleen Nadeau (1996) lists being shy, introverted, easily embarrassed, anxious to conform to expectations, hypersensitive to criticism, very reactive to stress, nonassertive, forgetful, inefficient, and prone to daydreaming. Often these difficulties are compounded by their trying to manage the symptoms of anxiety and depression as well. The rapid give-and-take of group interactions may cause the ADD woman without hyperactivity to feel isolated socially. She tends to do better one-on-one. Hormonal fluctuations can exacerbate the neurochemical problems caused by ADD. The combination of these imbalanced systems can result in hypersensitivity, hyperirritability, emotional overreaction, and dramatic mood swings. A major challenge for the ADD woman is managing the overwhelming sense of inadequacy she feels in trying to live up to her own expectations, as well as to those of her family and society. Most women are still expected to be caretakers at work and at home. They are expected to manage, support, and oversee the activities of others, even though they themselves struggle with planning and organization. Men with ADD have a great advantage, as wives and assistants often do any organizing that is necessary. Few women have access to this support system, since society has traditionally expected women to be the support system themselves. Life-management skills Kathleen Nadeau recommends to a woman with ADD include:

- Giving herself a break.
- Educating her partner about ADD and how it affects her.
- Using humor.
- Simplifying her life.
- Avoiding superefficient homemakers who can't understand her problems.
- Building a support group for herself.
- Building in daily time-outs.
- Not placing herself in a "burn-out" situation.
- Eliminating and delegating tasks.
- Learning child-behavior management techniques.
- Looking for positive experiences to share with her kids.
- Getting help for PMS or menopausal symptoms.
- Focusing more on the things she loves.

The most helpful and compassionate gifts the ADD woman can give to herself are to gain the best understanding of ADD that she can and to learn to accept it in herself without judgment. Educating family and friends about ADD will help to build support and increase understanding. Psychotherapy can greatly enhance self-esteem and provide one with coping strategies. Joining ADD support groups helps alleviate feelings of isolation. And let's not forget to focus on the positive aspects often associated with women with ADD: creativity, spontaneity, humor, and a caring nature.

Sexual Intimacy

Inasmuch as communication provides connection for ADD couples, the ADD partner's distractibility, preoccupation, and impulsivity can create disconnection, especially in the realm of sexual intimacy. ADD presents many challenges to the couple that may interfere with their enjoying a fulfilling sexual relationship.

Lynn Weiss (1994) has found that touch can be a barrier for the ADD partner, as rhythmic touching (such as stroking and patting) can be experienced as annoying rather than arousing. It is crucial for non-ADD partners to understand that this is not a reflection on them, but rather a problem related to the ADD partner's neurobiological hypersensitivity. For some, it may be more helpful firmly to grasp a finger, an arm, or a toe, rather than to hold the partner's hand. Some adults with ADD might experience touching or hugging as painful at times. This can lead to frustration for the non-ADD partner who does not understand how his or her hug could be uncomfortable. It can be helpful for the ADD partner to communicate clearly that he or she is feeling sensitive, and that a brief hug or just sitting next to each other would feel more comfortable. Direct, honest communication and sensitivity and understanding on the part of the non-ADD partner will restore the connection.

For some adults with ADD, hypersexuality can be an issue, as one woman married to a man with ADHD commented, "I just don't understand why my husband always wants sex." Sex can provide a great stimulation for the ADD partner, in that it will create a release of neurochemicals in the brain that facilitate the reduction of stress, block out distractions, and allow a state of good feeling and a sense of aliveness. Tom Hartmann (1996, p. 87) states that once the brain has found stimulation that provides relief, it will continue to seek that source of stimulation.

Solden (1995) has discovered in her work with women with ADD that many have difficulty focusing during sex because they are distracted by thoughts concerning things that they need to do, rather than because of a lack of involvement with their partners. Clinicians who have worked with such adults have found that medication can help to eliminate these distractions and to facilitate focus.

Weiss (1994) advocates that the non-ADD partner be sensitive to the needs of the ADD spouse who requires new and novel sexual activities to become stimulated and maintain arousal. She further clarifies that it is also important for the ADD partner to be respectful of the needs and wishes of his or her partner, and that together they work toward a mutual consensus on how to achieve sexual satisfaction.

The Grieving Process

After an adult is diagnosed with ADD, there is often an initial sense of relief. The diagnosis helps validate what the person had suspected all along—that he or she was "different." Then what usually follows is shock, excitement, a sense of euphoria, and an intense desire to seek information.

Once the reality of the diagnosis begins to settle in, however, a period of grieving begins. The grieving process has been identified by Elisabeth Kubler-Ross (1969), from the common responses of terminally ill patients, as occurring in five stages: denial, anger, bargaining, depression, and final acceptance. What will follow is a fluctuation among the various stages. These stages of grieving are experienced by both the ADD and the non-ADD partner.

Many emotions will surface, such as anger, sadness, and confusion. One of the significant issues with which we see the ADD adult struggle is the sense of lost time and lost potential. This sense of loss can be shared by the non-ADD partner.

Some adults may simply decide to discontinue a medication because they feel that they really don't need it, even if others noticed a remarkable change in them. Although their diagnosis has been confirmed, the adult with ADD may enter a state of denial and refuse to pursue further treatment.

In our opinion, the factor that most facilitates acceptance of the diagnosis is the support and understanding of significant others. As the ADD partner moves through the various stages of grieving, he or she may experience disconnection with his or her partner. Paralleling this, the ADD partner's grief is also a part of the non-ADD partner's grieving process. Even when the diagnosis is made, it may be difficult for the non-ADD partner to grasp the importance of the neurobiological implications associated with ADD behaviors. Many non-ADD partners cannot believe that the behaviors exhibited by their partners are not under their partners' control. It is also difficult for the non-ADD partner to refrain from personalizing the anger associated with ADD behaviors, feeling that somehow "it's being done to them." Once the denial has lifted for the non-ADD partner, and there comes a level of acceptance, a shift will occur toward understanding and supporting the ADD partner. However, it usually does not come about easily; often the non-ADD partner may remain angry until his or her anger is heard and validated.

It is imperative for the clinician who is working with the couple affected by ADD to understand the grieving process and its impact on each of the partners. The clinician can reassure the couple that the process is natural, and can help them to identify the specific stage that each is experiencing. As the couple emerges from grief, they will be better able to build a renewed and restored partnership.

CONCLUSION

While dialogue will not in and of itself cure ADD, it will go a long way toward clearing the fog and making life and relating more manageable for the couples who use it faithfully. Although becoming "dialogical" will certainly be a challenge for such couples, if they are to experience relational connection and characterological growth, then they must make dialogue their central way of communicating and handling conflict. They will find that it is a crucial part of ADD treatment simply because the clarity it provides removes a significant amount of stress (and, therefore, confusion) from the ADD sufferer's life and relationship. Dialogue also makes living with someone with ADD more tolerable and pleasant.

We also feel it is extremely important for ADD adults to share their stories, not only with us and their partners, but also with others in the same situation, who will understand and empathize. Thus, we strongly recommend that clinicians encourage their clients with ADD and their partners to seek support groups, such as CHADD (Children and Adults with ADD). An ADD adult with whom I (Kathleen) worked as a volunteer in CHADD told me that one of the most helpful things for him was sharing his story with sympathetic others. The retelling of his experience allowed him to be more in touch with himself and his ADD, and gave him the opportunity to discover that his experience was not so out of the ordinary. Support groups also provide bolstering for non-ADD spouses, who find that they, too, are not alone in their ADD-caused relationship frustrations.

In the course of our treating couples affected by ADD, and from our own experiences as part of a couple where one member has ADD, we have come to realize the challenge that ADD presents in the struggle to maintain connection, intimacy, and growth. The importance of a modified Couples Dialogue for achieving this connection cannot be overstressed. It is also valuable for both the ADD partner and the non-ADD partner to educate themselves about ADD via the many videotapes, books, and seminars available. We encourage our clients to make use of support groups, such as CHADD, to engage in workshops for couples with ADD, and to consider the possibility of coaching.*

Research in the field of ADD is constantly being updated with regard to its cause, subtypes, treatment, and medication. We encourage therapists to continue to become knowledgeable about adult ADD so that they can better help those couples for whom ADD is a factor. Therapists should attend CHADD meetings, where they can learn about the literature, rent videos, and hear guest lecturers. Joining CHADD is a good starting point to learn about and meet local physicians and psychiatrists who prescribe the many medications available to treat ADD, as well as the neurologists or psychologists skilled in doing evaluations for ADD. It is our hope that, by sharing our expertise, we can alert clinicians to the effectiveness of the Imago approach in helping these couples achieve an intimate connection.

BIBLIOGRAPHY

Amen, D. (1995). *Windows into the ADD mind.* Fairfield, Conn.: Mind Works Press.

Barkley, R. A. (1991). *Attention deficit/hyperactivity disorder.* New York: Guilford.

Fowler, R., & Fowler, J. (1995). *Honey are you listening?* Nashville: Nelson.

Goleman, D. (1995). *Emotional intelligence: Why it can matter more than IQ.* New York: Bantam.

Gottman, J. (1994). *Why marriages succeed or fail* (with N. Silver). New York: Simon & Schuster.

Hallowell, E. M., Miller, A. C., & Ratey, J. J. (1995). Relationship dilemmas for adults with ADD: The biology of intimacy. In K. G. Nadeau (Ed.), *Comprehensive guide to attention deficit disorder in adults.* New York: Brunner/Mazel.

Hallowell, E. M., & Ratey, J. (1994). *Driven to distraction: Recognizing and coping with attention deficit disorder from childhood through adulthood.* New York: Pantheon.

---

*A coach is a friend, therapist, or colleague who knows about ADD and is willing to provide encouragement, direction, and reminders. He or she helps the ADD person stay focused on tasks. This can be done in 10 to 15 minutes a day, often by phone (Hallowell & Ratey, 1994, p. 226).

Hartmann, T. (1996). *Beyond ADD: Hunting for reasons in the past and present.* Grass Valley, Calif: Underwood Books.

Hendrix, H. (1988). *Getting the love you want: A guide for couples.* New York: Holt.

Kelly, K., & Ramundo, P. (1993). *You mean I'm not lazy, stupid or crazy?! A self-help book for adults with attention deficit disorder.* Cincinnati: Tyrell & Jerem.

Kubler-Ross, E. (1969). *On death and dying.* New York: Macmillan.

Nadeau, K. (1995). *A comprehensive guide to attention-deficit/hyperactivity disorder in adults.* New York: Brunner/Mazel.

Nadeau, K. (1996). *Adventures in fast forward: Life, love, and work for the ADD adult.* New York: Brunner/Mazel.

Silver, L. B. (1994). *Attention-deficit/hyperactivity disorder: A clinical guide to diagnosis and treatment.* Washington, D.C.: American Psychiatric Press.

Solden, S. (1995). *Women with attention deficit disorder.* Great Valley, Calif.: Underwood Books.

Weiss, L. (1992a). *Attention deficit disorder in adults.* Dallas: Taylor.

Weiss, L. (1992b). *Attention deficit disorder: Practical help for sufferers and their spouses.* Dallas: Taylor.

Weiss, L. (1994). *The attention deficit disorder in adults workbook.* Dallas: Taylor.

Zametkin, A. J., Nordahl, T. E., Gross. M., King, A. C., Senple, W. E., Rumsay, J., Hamburgs, S., & Cohev, R. (1990). National Institute of Mental Health Study. Cerebral glucose metabolism in adults with hyperactivity of childhood onset. *New England Journal of Medicine, 323,* 1361–1366.

Zeigler Dendy, C. A. (1995). *Teenagers with ADD: A parents' guide.* Bethesda: Woodbine House.

Additional Recommended Reading

Latham, P. S., & Latham, P. H., *Succeeding in the workplace—Attention deficit disorder and learning disabilities in the workplace: A guide for success.* Available through JKL Communications, P.O. Box 40157, Washington, D.C., 20016.

Murphy, K. (1995). *Out of the fog: Treatment options and coping strategies for adult attention deficit disorder*. New York: Hyperion.

Wender, P. (1987). *The hyperactive child, adolescent, and adult: Attention deficit disorder through the lifespan*. New York: Oxford University Press.

Whiteman, T., & Novotni, M., Ph.D. (1995). *Adult ADD: A reader-friendly guide to identifying, understanding and treating adult attention deficit disorder*. Pinon Press.

ORGANIZATIONS

CHADD (Children and Adults with Attention Deficit Disorder)
499 NW 70th Avenue
Plantation, FL 33317
305-587-3700

The National Attention Deficit Disorder Association (NADDA)
P.O. Box 972
Mentor, OH 44063

Adult ADD Association
1225 E. Sunset Drive, Suite 640
Bellingham, WA 98226

EDITORS' COMMENTARY

Imago therapy rests on the assumption that couples need to create safety to see and hear each other fully. Once established, safety allows couples to develop an empathic connection, enabling the partners to differentiate and grow to become the unique persons they were meant to be. This chapter asks, "But what if a partner has a deficit in the area of the brain responsible for the creation of safety?" This is the plaintive question of couples affected by attention-deficit disorder (ADD).

Among its other functions, the frontal lobe of the brain gives us the unique capability to think about our thinking—to become conscious of our own thought processes. Of all animals, only human beings can reflect on how accurately we might be seeing the world or imagine how others see us. The incredible sophistication of our frontal lobes enables us to understand beauty and morality and to develop impulse control and character. Yet, as this chapter illustrates, not all of us have perfectly functioning frontal lobes. After years of scientific argument, most clinicians now conclude that there are, in fact, identifiable brain-based abnormalities that cause subtle but significant problems in how we think and react, especially in our relationships. ADD is one of these syndromes, and it can wreak havoc on a couple's relationship.

ADD does not affect a person's intelligence, basic goodness, generosity, or creativity. Rather, because the frontal lobe is understimulated, its ability to monitor and modulate the brain's instinctual and emotional reactions is short-circuited. In conflictual interactions, the partner with ADD often finds himself or herself relinquishing control to the reptilian brain, which is programmed to "kill or be killed." This puts the ADD-affected partner in an adrenaline-stimulated defensive mode, making it very difficult to feel or create safety with their non-ADD partner.

The authors of this chapter write with authority about the relationship problems that ADD poses, since both have dealt with ADD in their own partnerships. They underscore, as do other chapters on Imago work with special populations, the need to be flexible and creative with Imago processes. To ask an ADD partner, for example, to "find your safe place" when he or she is fast becoming flooded with negative emotions is probably asking for the impossible. As Goleman (1995) points out, once flooded, even the "normal" brain needs, at minimum, 20 minutes to calm down. Certainly, there are times when couples, ADD or no ADD, should stick with the Imago process, regardless of how difficult that might be. But in some instances, instead of insisting that an ADD-affected couple stay in dialogue, the therapist would be wiser to suggest that the ADD partner withdraw temporarily in order to use various self-soothing processes that can help the brain regain its composure. ADD symptoms often improve with medication and are helped by the practice of skills, but the ADD will probably rear its head many times over the course of the couple's relationship. Dialogue, as powerful as it might be, does not cure ADD.

It is also important to underscore the unlikelihood of ADD's being the sole cause of the couple's problems. It is common, once a partner is diagnosed with ADD, for couples to blame all their problems on the ADD, which implies that all their problems are caused by the ADD partner. Obviously, one partner's having ADD does not negate the effects of the developmental wounding experienced by the other partner. Quite the contrary: living with ADD has most likely compounded the effects of the earlier wounding suffered by each partner. The therapist needs to focus as much on the non-ADD partner's characterological deficits as on the ADD partner's frontal-lobe deficits. Otherwise, the ADD could erroneously receive all the blame at the expense of the characterological growth of the partners.

As editors, we consider this chapter particularly valuable, because, like many of our readers, we are both married to partners who have been diagnosed with attention-deficit disorder. Our spouses are incredible people: bright, highly creative, spontaneous, and virtuous in many ways we are not. With our partners, we have created intense connection, and with our partners, we have shared fierce struggles, some triggered by our own wounding, others by our partner's ADD symptoms. Like our partners, we have learned the wisdom of waiting, waiting a few moments for brain activity (theirs and ours) to subside, with the understanding that we will later come together to resume our dialogue. In many ways, because of—not despite—ADD, we are fortunate to be married to our partners: with them, we have experienced the transforming power of commitment, of keeping our paddle in the water, no matter how fiercely the waters, or our brains, might rage!

Chapter 13

ADDICTION, COUPLES, AND RECOVERY

Bruce A. Wood

As an Imago therapist, I have developed a method that addresses addictions by including Imago Relationship Therapy with chemical-dependency treatment and a 12-step recovery orientation. It is a technique that evolved from my listening to my clients, trying to find a way to meet their needs when traditional methods did not work.

JOHN AND CAROL

When I first learned about Imago therapy, I was on the staff of an intensive outpatient chemical-dependency program. At the time, one of the cases I managed involved a man who was in treatment for alcoholism. I was also working with his wife, Carol, in the family program.

John, a lawyer in his mid-50s, had come for treatment at his wife's insistence, and because he had experienced periods of sobriety in the past, he was accepted as an outpatient. Ten years earlier, he had stayed sober—perhaps "dry" is the better term—for two years by joining Alcoholics Anonymous (AA). After relapsing, he then had another year of sobriety, followed by another relapse. Each time that John would quit drinking and attend an AA meeting, it was under pressure by Carol. But alcoholics who go to AA meetings to please someone else—someone who thinks they have a problem—will stay sober only if, as a result of their experiences there, the consequences of their drinking become real and important to them. This hadn't yet happened for John.

The program for which I worked required participants to bring to the group sessions written reports of episodes of drinking and drug use, which they would read aloud to the group. The accounts had to include the negative effects of the bout. The listeners would grade the presenter as to how emotionally connected to the consequences of the episodes he or she seemed to be.

The consensus of John's group was that John seemed unmoved by the results he had listed. Although he hadn't stated this explicitly, it was John's wife—not John—who saw his drinking as a problem.

It became clear to me that the techniques we used in this program were not going to be effective with John. There was no threat of job loss to use as leverage; there were no charges for driving while intoxicated. Whatever mental impairment John's alcohol use might be causing, his responsibilities in his law practice were routine enough to get him to retirement age without significant difficulty. Men in their 50s are often more susceptible to arguments about how addiction can cause health problems than are younger men, but John was physically strong and resilient. His children were grown and on their own, and so were able to distance themselves from John's drinking. That left John's wife, Carol.

John's standard response to Carol was, "What more do you want? I'm in treatment. I'm going to AA. I'm staying sober." He was giving her what he had always given her: momentary compliance.

After evaluating John's stance, I gave him the following assignment. He was to relate to Carol each of the drinking episodes he had shared with the treatment group, recounting them to her just as he had to his peers.

At our first treatment session following this assignment, I asked John to report on his homework. He said, visibly shaken, "I did it, but I think we have to stop. Carol was very upset."

I asked, "Did she say she wants to stop?"

"No."

"Then I want you to continue the assignment."

I had coached Carol to avoid responding to John with blaming or shaming statements, but stipulated that she could add any details that he left out.

John's stories triggered a barrage of painful memories and feelings in Carol, who did, in fact, fill in many of the grim details. Typically, a significant other has much more information than the addict has about the effects of the addict's behavior on others. Carol described to John the many consequences of his drinking for his children, consequences of which he had been totally unaware.

John had not known this before because he and Carol had never discovered a way to communicate that wasn't defensive, blaming, and polarizing. Once John felt safe enough to hear Carol's message about his drinking and its effects, he found the motivation to change.

I kept track of this couple for over five years after they left treatment. At my last contact, John was still sober and was actively involved in AA. Carol was continuing her involvement in the Al-Anon family program.

About two years after I treated John, I went into full-time private practice, with a specialty in couples therapy. About half of my practice as an Imago therapist is devoted to working with couples who are struggling with active addiction or recovery issues.

MARCIA AND TONY: ACTIVE ADDICTION

Marcia first came to me for individual therapy. She was distressed over her husband's use of pornographic magazines as an aid to his frequent masturbation. When she discovered that Tony had run up a bill of over $100 in one month for phone sex, she asked to switch to couples therapy. Tony said he was willing to work with me as a couples therapist.

Marcia is a recovering compulsive overeater. She became involved in Overeaters Anonymous (OA) shortly after marrying Tony five years previously. She "put together" about a year's worth of abstinence by adhering to a strict food plan; then, thinking she could manage on her own, she left the program. A short time later, she began binge eating again. When she first came to me, she was again abstaining from compulsive eating by using a food plan. She was also very active in OA.

Marcia knew that Tony was a sex addict who was in denial. Tony, on the other hand, considered Marcia overwhelmingly needy and demanding, and he constantly tried to distance himself from her.

When I work with couples, my first objective is to get the partners on the same side. To do so, I help them establish a "collaborative set." This requires that the couple take joint ownership of their relationship problem and agree to construct solutions together.

Marcia demanded that Tony admit his addiction and become involved in Sex Addicts Anonymous (SA) or Sex and Love Addicts Anonymous (SLA). She said that if he didn't do so, she would leave him. Her threat sounded empty to me, and perhaps also to Tony, but it was nonetheless compelling enough to get Tony into my office.

Marcia's contribution to the problem included her unwillingness to allow Tony to discover for himself whether or not the term "addiction" fit his behavior. From my experience in working with thousands of alcoholics, I know that, on average, it takes between five and seven years from the point of diagnosis to achieve stable abstinence. Some, of course, never get sober. I took a neutral position: we didn't know for sure whether Tony's sexual behavior was due to addiction, to his anger toward Marcia, or to irrational jealousy on Marcia's part. I got them both to agree that we needed to examine together the entire picture of their relationship.

To strengthen their collaborative set, I immediately started having them explore how their frustrations with each other were connected to childhood wounding. I did a guided imagery to help them remember their childhood experiences, and then asked them to share their memories with each other using the Parent–Child Dialogue.

I next gave Tony the assignment of reading Patrick Carnes' (1992) work on sexual addiction, *Out of the Shadows*. I asked Marcia to reflect on her codependency issues, which usually surface for overeaters once they have established abstinence.

Within a short time, although neither was any less frustrated with the other, Tony and Marcia had reframed their problems. They realized that the problems stemmed from childhood wounds, and that, given these wounds, it was not surprising that they both used compulsive behaviors as a refuge from their painful feelings. Tony acknowledged that he might have a sexual addiction and so perhaps needed to enter a 12-step program, although he would rather try to deal with it first on his own.

After less than 10 weeks into the therapy process, I received a message from Marcia saying that they were canceling their appointment. They had had a fight over the weekend, and Tony had announced that he was leaving the marriage.

I was nonplussed over this and decided to wait for another call from them. It came a week later: Tony had relented and at last agreed to start attending a program for his sexual compulsion. However, the couple had also decided that they didn't have enough money to continue therapy at that time.

This is a fairly typical pattern. In confronting any addiction, an individual moves through a series of stages, beginning with precontemplation, followed by contemplation, determination, and, finally, action.

In precontemplation, the addict doesn't consider his or her behavior problematic and so sees no need to change it. Similarly, it's rare for a partner to go into couples therapy before admitting that the other's complaints have some validity. During precontemplation, the addicted partner keeps busy arguing, debating, minimizing, and blaming the other for any problems. The codependent, meanwhile, does the same thing with regard to his or her own behavior. The therapist's task is to move the couple out of this mode and into one of mutual exploration. This requires creating enough safety to allow contemplation, with all the strife and ambivalence it entails, to occur.

During contemplation, therapy focuses on how each partner contributes to the couple's problems. My therapeutic goal is to help partners connect emotionally with the negative consequences of their behaviors. To accomplish this, I point out how their behaviors are incongruent with their self-image, and I work toward increasing their awareness of how their dysfunctional behaviors keep them from achieving their goals. Once the partners make these connections, contemplation yields to a determination to change.

The crystalization of such determination in couples work is often the result of a crisis. This happened in Marcia and Tony's case. Marcia was able to do some honest soul-searching once she gave up insisting that Tony admit he was an addict. Tony, however, hadn't given up being Tony. He was still acting out, although more discreetly. In exasperation, Marcia once again insisted that he change "or else." Tony retaliated by saying, "It's over." Still, enough information had seeped through to him: when asked if he really wanted to break up his marriage over a behavior that he could no longer defend, even to himself, Tony's answer was No.

Reframing the problems, using the dialogue structure, and imparting new information all worked together to enable this couple to break through their impasse and move into the next stage of their recovery and of their relationship.

DIALOGUE AND 12-STEP MEETINGS: A LINK

The Couples Dialogue, with its three steps of mirroring, validation, and empathy, provides the same healing process that all 12-step recovery programs offer to their members.

A speaker in recovery from addiction tells his or her story to the others in the room. The story outline includes (1) what it was like to be in the grip of the addiction; (2) what happened to make the speaker receptive to the recovery process; and (3) what it is like to be in recovery. The listeners are fellow sufferers in various stages of recovery, ranging from prerecovery to long-term abstinence. They respond to the speaker's story by sharing how it applies to their own lives.

Sitting in on a 12-step meeting is like being in a room filled with mirrors. One hears one's stories—stories that others outside the room respond to with blaming and shaming—mirrored back with understanding and empathy.

In fact, one's experiences are mirrored back not only with understanding and empathy, but with a kind of enlargement. Distorted concepts, such as "I can handle just one drink," are exposed as the distortions they are, and with humor. At the same time, no one in the room is an authority, and no one dictates how anyone else's recovery is to be accomplished.

This atmosphere of tolerance and exploration is exactly the opposite of what has characterized many addiction treatment programs during the past 30 years. In the worst of them, counselors would provoke patients to shame one another in the service of "breaking down denial." Studies of outcomes associated with such confrontational tactics clearly show that such methods increase resistance, lead to early dropout from treatment, and are correlated with poor long-term outcome (Miller & Rollnick, 1991).

Neither are these strategies are effective when spouses use them to try to force their partners to give up addictive or codependent behaviors. It is understandable that one partner might become so frustrated with the other's destructive patterns that he or she would resort to heavy-handed tactics. The problem is, those tactics don't work. Therefore, the couples therapist has the task of helping partners give up trying to control each other and instead learn to share their perceptions.

DOREEN AND MICHAEL: EARLY RECOVERY

Early recovery, defined as the first two years or so of working a 12-step program, is generally so demanding that few couples are able to undertake couples therapy during this phase. When they do, it is usually the result of a crisis.

This was what happened in Doreen and Michael's case. Michael was sober and drug-free after having been in AA for a year and a half. He was very active at meetings, attending them daily while sponsoring three newcomers. He was a special education teacher whose work did not end when the school day was over. He was also very invested in raising his three young children, with whom he made sure to spend quality time.

He took care of everyone—except Doreen. During their first session, Doreen explained why she wanted a divorce. Throughout the past year, she had begged Michael to go into counseling with her; he had refused. Now he was willing, but it was too late. She had found another man and had decided to leave Michael. She was tired, and she wanted out.

I asked Doreen if she would be willing to do the good-bye exercise with Michael. In this exercise, one partner says good-bye to the other—good-bye to all the pain, to all the good times, and to all the dreams for their future together. The exercise is designed to move the process of separation forward, if the desire to end the relationship is genuine. But if the person saying good-bye feels ambivalent, the exercise will reveal that ambivalence.

Doreen sat across from Michael and, at my instruction, she looked into his eyes and began, "I want to say good-bye to all the times you stayed out till three or four in the morning without calling. I want to say good-bye to the fights, to the times you said I was a horrible mother, to the times you blamed your using alcohol on my being sexually inadequate. Those times really hurt. I want to say good-bye to the time Jimmy broke his arm and you were too drunk to take him to the hospital. I had to handle it all alone." Doreen continued to pour out the many painful experiences she'd had during her marriage to Michael. Michael listened quietly, but his emotions were clear from the way his eyes welled up with tears.

Next, Doreen was to say good-bye to the good memories of the relationship. She began, "I want to say good-bye to the first time we met, to how you kept coming around, to the way you were so attentive. I want to say good-bye to our excitement when I was pregnant for the first time, to the time we spent together in Lamaze classes, and to your presence at the birth of Jimmy, and then Meg, and then Patrick. Those were very special times." Doreen continued to recall her positive memories; when she paused, I urged her to continue until she had said good-bye to all the good memories.

Doreen sat quietly for a moment, and then said she was finished. "Now, Doreen," I said, "Say good-bye to all the dreams and all your hopes for this relationship that now will never come to pass."

Doreen turned back to Michael and stared at him, but instead of seeing him, she seemed to be seeing her dreams. "I want to say good-bye to . . ." She paused, her voice cracking and tears beginning to stream down her cheeks. "To the dream of us growing old together." Michael, too, began to cry. "I want to say good-bye to the dream of having the kids grow up with both of their parents in a loving home. I want to say good-bye to the dream of having a second honeymoon. I want to say good-bye . . . ." She stopped, looking confused. "But, no! I don't want to say good-bye to all of this. I don't. I don't."

By this point, both of them were sobbing. I guided Doreen into Michael's arms, where he could cradle her. It was the first moment of true connection they had experienced in many months.

This marked the beginning of couples therapy, which Doreen and Michael sorely needed. During one of his bouts of drinking and cocaine use, Michael had had a brief affair. During the past year, desperately lonely, Doreen had started a retaliatory affair with an active alcoholic. The adult child of an alcoholic, Doreen knew enough about the effects of alcoholism on the family to recognize that she, too, engaged in addictive behavior patterns. She agreed to focus on herself instead of on Michael. This meant becoming involved in Al-Anon Family Group meetings and in Adult Children of Alcoholics (ACOA) meetings. Michael, on the other hand, needed to cut back on his AA meetings in order to spend more time with Doreen.

The therapy sessions became a place where the partners could share what they were learning in their separate programs. My focus was on helping them to stabilize and deepen their connection with one another.

I devoted a good deal of time to teaching them and having them practice the validation step of the Couples Dialogue. Validation reinforces differentiation—a crucial task for the addicted couple. In their 12-step programs, Michael and Doreen were learning to identify their distinct feelings, perspectives, and experiences as separate from those of their partner. Validation and the Couples Dialogue helped them stay connected to one another during this important period of differentiation, so that they could continue to grow together even while learning that they were separate individuals with differing needs.

HAL AND EILEEN: LONG-TERM RECOVERY

Now in their late 30s, Hal and Eileen had been together since they were teenagers. They had never married and had no children. Having both come from alcoholic homes, they had drunk and used drugs together throughout their 20s. Each had had about five years of sobriety at the time they came to see me.

Hal owned a motorcycle shop in a blue-collar neighborhood; the couple lived behind the shop. Eileen worked in the shop as well, keeping the books, placing orders, and waiting on customers. Because her job was off the books, she had never paid anything toward Social Security, nor did she have any retirement savings of her own. Hal had always told her, "You don't need to worry about that. I'll take care of you."

Two years earlier, Eileen had begun seeing another man whom she had met in AA, and then moved in with him. Hal was devastated: he promised he would change, and nine months later, Eileen moved back in, breaking off her relationship with the other man. During his separation from Eileen, Hal had formed a friendship with another woman, who was also in AA. Theirs was not a sexual relationship, but one that allowed Hal to talk about his feelings.

It made sense to me that these two partners, who had come together in their youth and thus had never explored other relationships, might try to compensate later on by looking for intimacy outside of their own relationship. Yet, it was over a year since they had reconciled and expressed their desire to make things better, and although they had tried, they didn't seem to know how to do so.

Hal and Eileen were what I call an anger-expressive/anger-sensitive couple. When Hal became angry, he would fight; in terror, Eileen would freeze and tiptoe around Hal's anger.

Of the three basic survival responses—fight, flight, or freeze—two were becoming manifest in front of me. I used this as a lead-in: "If both of you are falling into basic survival reactions, then you must be triggering very powerful survival issues in one another."

Hal had had very little experience with expressing any emotion except anger. At one point, when he indicated his scorn for Eileen's vulnerability, I asked him, "What would have happened to you if you had shown emotions like Eileen's when you were growing up in your family?"

His response was immediate. "I woulda been killed."

Hal had been physically abused by his rageaholic father. When his family members weren't in a rage, they were cold toward Hal. He spent as much time away from his family as possible. Physically large and intimidating, Hal also lived in a tough neighborhood where fighting was a way of life.

He once said, "You know that serial killer called the Ice Man? I saw a show on him once. He said he didn't feel a thing inside. Ice. That's how I feel a lot. Just cold. Nothing, you know?"

However true Hal considered this description of himself, it certainly wasn't the whole story. He had been sober and working on personal growth for five years. Although he still had difficulty in identifying and naming his feelings, they had at least been coming up more frequently.

When Hal and Eileen's dialogue seemed to be going around in circles, I would use "doubling" to get at Hal's emotions. For example, Hal would repeat his complaint, "You say you want a relationship, but you went off and left me for some prick bastard of a pussy."

This is where I would interrupt. "I think I'm hearing an argument you've had over and over. Am I right?"

"Yeah," Hal muttered. Eileen, sitting with arms crossed, nodded assent.

"So let's try something different, because if you keep going on this way, you'll end up where you always end up. Okay?"

"Okay."

"Hal, I'll pretend I'm you, and I'll say to Eileen what I think you might be feeling. When I'm done, take what I've said, and if it fits for you, repeat it to Eileen the way I said it. Otherwise, change it until it fits and say it that way to her. Okay?"

He looked intrigued. "Okay."

I began doubling as Hal: "I really could forgive and forget about the affair you had. It's just that when you put up that wall, when you act cold and angry, I get terrified you're going to leave me again. I don't know how to reach you."

I asked Hal: "Is that about it?"

"Yep."

"Well, you try it. Say it in your words."

Hal looked at Eileen. "It's like he said," he quipped.

"So tell her," I urged, "so she can hear it in your voice and really believe it."

Hal began, "Uh. I'm afraid I'm gonna lose you. There's this wall. I don't know what to do."

The anger-expressive/anger-sensitive couple is dealing with powerlessness. The anger-expressive partner is afraid of being powerless; the anger-sensitive person constantly feels powerless. Like Hal, Eileen had grown up in an alcoholic, rageaholic family; she protected herself by becoming extraordinarily skilled at sensing another's anger, which she'd then respond to by freezing up or pleasing the other—as she did with Hal. With Eileen, my goal was to have her own more of her power. My goal with Hal, on the other hand, was to help him tolerate feelings of vulnerability and powerlessness.

I teach partners to use an "emotional ladder," a series of sentence stems, to go deeper into their experience. For Hal, the series was:

1. "What I'm so angry about is . . ."
2. "What hurts so much about that is . . ."
3. "What's so scary about that is . . ."
4. "What that reminds me of in my childhood is . . ."

For Eileen, we reversed the progression, starting with fear and moving finally to anger. This enabled her to access the anger toward her parents that had been buried for so long. Eileen's process was also helpful to Hal, who could see that his wife's fear, hurt, and anger preceded their relationship: it wasn't only about him.

I had been feeding Hal sentence stems from the emotional ladder to give to Eileen. Eileen's responses led into a Parent–Child Dialogue.

"What this reminds me of from childhood is . . .," Hal suggested to Eileen.

"It's just like the time my mother chased me to my bedroom. I was so scared, I slammed the door and leaned against it with all my weight. I was so scared she was going to hit me or yank my hair. She would do that when she was drunk."

"Hal," I said, "take on the role of Eileen's mother, and let's do a Parent–Child Dialogue."

Hal said to Eileen, "I'm your mother. What do you need to say to me?"

Eileen responded to Hal, "Stop it. Just stop it. You're crazy. Leave me alone."

I worked with Eileen to expand her angry feelings. Eileen's difficulty with anger toward her mother stemmed from the internalized image of her mother as a big, scary, and powerful person. To help her with this, I had Eileen climb on top of the desk and tower over Hal, her as-if mother, while saying what she needed to say. Eileen's work helped Hal develop a sense of empathy for her struggle to emerge as a strong self.

Eileen got stronger. Sometimes Hal liked this; sometimes he didn't. Sometimes he could express his own hurt and fear when he didn't like something. More often, outside the therapy room, he couldn't. The partners often came in feeling polarized, hurt, and angry with each other.

A crisis developed when Eileen decided she wasn't going to give Hal sex on demand. This didn't look like progress to Hal, for whom sex meant love. For several sessions, I could not find a way to help them through this impasse. All my attempts to reframe the problem or to engender empathy were futile.

Around this time, Hal and Eileen participated in a group session I held for four couples struggling with anger issues. All four couples were in 12-step programs. I hoped that, as a result of the experience, each couple would walk away thinking, "We're not so different. Lots of couples have these same problems."

Once, when sharing with the group, Hal alluded to his relationship with Ray, who had started the business that Hal now owned and operated. Ray, retired and living in Florida, still received some income from the business.

Hal described how, when he was about 10 years old, Ray was the only adult to show Hal any respect and understanding. He became a mentor to Hal. He also drew Hal into a sexual relationship.

During our couples work, Hal had passed lightly over this issue. At the group session, however, he spent much more time talking about it; more surprisingly, he was open about the topic with the other men in the group.

"Then," he added, "at the age of 12, I put a stop to it."

"Why was that?" I asked.

"I just had to say No, to stand up for myself."

"You mean," I said softly, "kind of like Eileen is doing now."

I saw many emotions pass across his face in rapid succession. Hal became disoriented. He started to respond a couple of times, but stopped.

Finally, he said, "I guess it could be kinda the same."

When Hal and Eileen came in for their next conjoint session, Eileen was despondent. "For five days after the group, he treated me like a queen. Yesterday he went back to being his old self."

I was elated: I had found the way in. With Hal's ready assent, I brought his relationship with Ray to center stage. His willingness suggested that, perhaps on an unconscious level, Hal had been sending me a message during the group that he was ready to work on this connection between his past and his present.

That connection was complex. I had been focusing on strengthening Hal's ability to tolerate vulnerability. What emerged instead was a memory of a relationship that helped Hal understand how it could be possible to say No and still remain in the relationship, as he had with Ray. It wasn't that Eileen didn't want to have sex with him. Rather, she wanted to change the terms. Just as Hal had renegotiated his relationship with Ray, moving Ray from the role of mentor to that of a peer, Eileen wanted a peer relationship, not a master–servant relationship, with Hal.

My work with this couple lasted approximately two years. When they felt they were far enough along in the process to go the rest of the way on their own, we terminated therapy. I left my door open for them, though, and they came in for a little help about every six months. But they had gained the skills they needed to continue to work on their relationships on their own.

I consider it my job to help couples get to a point where they feel they can do the work by themselves and no longer need me.

CONCLUSION

In Imago terms, active addiction is an exit from a relationship. In my experience, deep-level healing of childhood wounds cannot occur when so much of the addict's energy is devoted to the addiction. So when active addiction is present, I concentrate on helping the couple identify and explore their compulsive behaviors. I then have them share, without blaming or shaming, the impact of these behaviors on themselves and on each other. This offers the best chance of breaking the impasse—the merry-go-round of denial.

In my work with members of 12-step programs, I use many sources as guides. I find basic AA and Al-Anon literature helpful to me and to my clients, and so recommend that all clinicians working with couples become familiar with this literature.

To finish, I quote a passage from AA's "Big Book," *Alcoholics Anonymous* (1976).

> As each member of a resentful family begins to see his shortcomings and admits them to the others, he lays a basis for helpful discussion. These family talks will be constructive if they can be carried on without heated argument, self-pity, self-justification or resentful criticism. Little by little, mother and children will see they ask too much, and father will see he gives too little. Giving, rather than getting, will become the guiding principle. (pp. 127–128)

BIBLIOGRAPHY

Alcoholics Anonymous (1935, 1955, 1976). New York: Alcoholics Anonymous World Services.

Carnes, P. (1992). *Out of the shadows: Understanding sexual addiction.* Minneapolis: Hazelden.

Hendrix, H. (1988). *Getting the love you want*. New York: Holt.

Miller, W., & Rollnick, S. (1991). *Motivational interviewing: Preparing people to change addictive behavior*. New York: Guilford.

EDITORS' COMMENTARY

This chapter discusses how to work with couples affected by addictions by integrating Imago therapy with the principles of 12-step recovery programs. Imago work is, as Bruce Wood points out, highly compatible with 12-step approaches. If a person has been using alcohol and drugs to soothe emotional pain, then by teaching the addict to use, instead, the dialogical processes of Imago therapy, we can offer a way out of the addictive patterns. Of course, it's unlikely that dialogue alone will be enough to help most addicts overcome their addiction. Rather, as the author indicates, Imago techniques can assist the addiction-affected couple to improve the quality of their relationship. This, in turn, can help them strengthen their connection so that, together, they can invest their energy fully in their 12-step programs.

Dialogue can serve a different function during the various phases of recovery. For example, during early recovery, couples can dialogue about the pain of having lived together through years of active addition. Couples who have been in recovery for a longer time can use the dialogue to redefine their relationship and create a relationship vision for the future.

The Intentional Dialogue, when used in the recovery process, has parallels with the fourth and fifth steps of AA's 12 steps. The fourth step instructs the alcoholic to make a searching and fearless moral inventory. In essence, this is encompassed in Imago Relationship Therapy processes: partners are asked to look inward to discover their truths, feelings, needs, and desires. Then, within the safety of the dialogue, they reveal themselves fully to their partner, peeling off the layers of the false self that has long been maintained through the addict's denial.

The fifth step tells persons in recovery to admit the exact nature of their wrongdoings to themselves and to another human being. The dialogue offers an ideal structure for the addicted person to complete this step with the most significant, and probably the most affected, person in his or her life: the addict's partner.

So, the moral inventory accomplished in the fourth step is given voice in the fifth. The dialogue process infuses both steps with safety, allowing the couple to connect on a deeper level than was possible during the active phase of the addiction.

Relapse is part of the process of recovery. Although liberating, living soberly can also be terrifying, especially for the addict who has been using alcohol, instead of the partnership, to deal with the pain and the developmental arrests carried over from childhood. Sooner or later, most recovering persons revisit their false selves, fleeing from the difficulty of growing to again live life protected by the lie of addiction. But if both partners are willing, just once more, to risk becoming vulnerable and open to growth, relapse does not have to spell defeat. It can, instead, be one more marker pointing the way toward recovery.

Addicts who have been in long-term recovery, not to mention the spouses who have gone the distance with them, are truly remarkable people. They have fearlessly revealed their weaknesses to one another and, in many cases, to the world. They see learning about themselves as a lifelong project: for them, the examined life is indeed worth living. As a result, sincerity and wisdom are their hallmarks.

Chapter 14

IMAGO THERAPY WITH SEXUALLY DYSFUNCTIONAL COUPLES

Bonnie Bernell

JOYCE AND TOM

Married for 15 years, it had been almost that long since Joyce and Tom had had good sex. They had not had intercourse at all during the past 12 or 13 years. Both partners were in their late 30s. But they didn't sleep in the same bed, or even in the same bedroom. Joyce avoided sex by working on projects until the middle of the night, long after Tom had retired. Tom avoided sex by going to bed early, well before Joyce did, because, he said, since he got up early, he needed his sleep. Despite the lack of a sexual relationship, however, the couple was struggling to stay together.

Joyce is a bright, attractive woman, but with a multitude of physical complaints; Tom is a self-described "techie type" who typically wears the "Silicon Valley uniform": a T-shirt with his company logo, red pants, Birkenstock sandals, and glasses. He also has long hair and the stubble of a beard. He reported having had problems attracting women since his early teenage years. He'd had one girlfriend when he was in his late teens, but they had never had sex. Still, when Joyce met him, Tom seemed to be everything she ever wanted in a man. She'd previously had miserable experiences with men, feeling that they used her and then left her. Tom, on the other hand, thought Joyce was sexy, and to his delight, she liked almost all the things he did. Although both were virgins when they met, like many couples when they are first together, Joyce and Tom had hot sex, and they had it often. After a seven-month courtship, they married.

Early in their relationship, they accepted each other's quirks, relieved that they would not be spending the rest of their lives alone. But as the months and years passed, resentments began to build. Although Tom earned an excellent salary as a computer engineer, Joyce objected to his long work hours. As for Tom's being a lover, Joyce described him as a "brute" who "needs sex his own way and doesn't care about me," and who furthermore has "long, uncut toenails that gouge me and make me feel like he doesn't care about me." She was further dissatisfied that Tom "rejects vibrators or any other aids that would help me reach an orgasm."

Over the years, as Joyce's physical complaints worsened, she began to work less and less, leading to Tom's bitter characterization of his wife as "unwilling to work." Tom also felt rejected by Joyce, whom he saw as cold, withholding, critical, and distant. He felt that she blamed him for everything. Nevertheless, Tom stayed with her because he imagined that no one else would ever choose him as a sexual partner, much less as a spouse.

There was a profound, deep melancholy about this couple. Joyce looked 10 years older than her chronological age. Tom's body was concave. I sensed that each partner's personal development, and thus the couple's emotional connection and sexual relationship, had been thwarted long before, at an early developmental stage.

Therapy was their last resort. But was it ethical for me to see a couple with these problems? Was it reasonable to promise that their sexual connection could be resurrected, that their relationship could get better? An ethical therapist is required to promote realistic expectations about treatment outcomes. I wanted to offer them the hope of getting what they wanted, but I wasn't certain that such hope was warranted. Tom wanted a physical relationship with Joyce: he wanted to touch, cuddle, and have sexual intercourse. He admitted being terrified of losing Joyce, as he doubted he would ever find another partner. Joyce did want the relationship, but she did not want sex. So how could I move this couple toward mutual goals, if they didn't seem to have any—at least in the sexual area?

The "boiled frog" syndrome, a term used by a valued teacher, Peter Pearson (personal communication), is how I saw this couple's problems. This term refers to issues that sit on the back burner for so long that by the time the couple reaches a therapist's office, all the life has been boiled out of the relationship. In contrast, other couples, when they feel the heat rising, jump up to look for help, while they still have the energy to jump.

When I greeted Joyce and Tom in the waiting room before our first session, they were sitting as far apart as possible with their noses buried in magazines. They walked into my office slowly and sullenly.

During that session, Joyce complained about myriad issues, describing a few in detail. Tom reported having only two frustrations: he wanted to be able to spend money on the things he wanted and he wanted a physical relationship with Joyce.

I immediately asked them to enter into dialogue, beginning with issues unrelated to their physical relationship and sexuality. The deliberate decision to steer them away from their sexual relationship in the initial discussion was based on the assumption that it was an immensely difficult and scary issue for them. Beginning with the easier frustrations in their marriage allowed the couple to develop some confidence and hope, and the motivation to stretch toward working on their impasse issues.

For several sessions, Tom deferred to Joyce, dialoguing about her concerns rather than his own. Whenever she asked for behavior changes, he readily complied. Finally feeling listened and responded to, Joyce was able to contain, listen to, and respond to Tom's issues.

A moderately difficult problem for this couple related to managing their money. Tom wanted to spend money on his own interests, whereas Joyce wanted to save money for a down payment on a house. Through several extensive dialogues, they came up with an inventive and generous solution: they would dedicate set amounts of money from their paychecks for personal, discretionary spending and for their house downpayment fund. If Tom needed more money for a current interest, he would borrow from the family house fund, and pay it back, with interest, within three months. Tom now felt as though his wishes and interests were important to Joyce, important enough to allow this concession; consequently, he was determined to be totally responsible about repaying any money he borrowed. Likewise, because Joyce was getting what she wanted, movement toward buying a house, she was able to go along with what she typically saw as Tom's frivolous and unnecessary purchases. Each felt satisfied and more confident that they had found a resolution for a very difficult problem.

They now seemed ready to dialogue about sexual matters. Soon after Tom initiated the dialogue, Joyce became highly reactive. She cut him off, jumped up from her chair several times, covered her ears, and kept restating how awful Tom had been to her during the first years of their marriage. Tom acknowledged that he had seriously damaged Joyce's trust and feelings of safety with him. But he also felt, he said, that 10 years of celibacy were enough of a penance for him. Because Joyce was unable to listen to Tom at this juncture, he agreed to listen to her. They had the following dialogue.

> **Joyce:**   *Are you willing to listen to me for a change?*
> **Tom:**   *Yes, I'll listen to you.*
> **Joyce:**   *I think you are mean and oversexed. You have hurt me for years and years. You cannot be trusted. In 1989, you said I had to have sex with you. I don't like you, and. . .*
> **Therapist:**   *Try to remember that Tom will be able to hear you more fully, the way I have heard you say you want to be heard, if you speak about your experience, rather than blaming, judging, or attacking him. (To Tom): If you feel criticized by Joyce, simply do your best to mirror her without defensiveness or countercriticism.*
> **Tom:**   *If I hear you correctly, you do not like how I have treated you, and that's why you won't ever again have sex with me. Is that right?*
> **Joyce:**   *No, no! See, he won't do this. It always has to be his way.*
> **Therapist:**   *Try to mirror her again, Tom.*
> **Tom:**   *If I hear you correctly, you do not think I'll listen to you, and you feel that I have been mean to you. Is that right?*
> **Joyce:**   *Yes, but. . . you will never do this right. I don't trust you. I don't like you. I don't care about having sex with you, ever. So there.*
> **Tom:**   *We'll never have sex again.*

Joyce needed Tom to say the exact words she had said, or she did not feel mirrored. I thought she was saying the same thing over and over. Was he being saintly or foolish? After about 20 minutes of this, after he had once again asked, "Is there more?" Joyce started to sob. She cried and cried, finally saying that no one in her entire life had ever listened to her before. Having Tom listen to her in this way made her feel as though she could trust him.

They had made emotional contact, even if just for one moment. But I wondered whether they would continue to move forward in the upcoming weeks. In the following sessions, they continued to make contact, although slowly and awkwardly. When Joyce became afraid that being closer to Tom would lead to her being engulfed by him, she would ward him off with rage and criticism. He would then become terrified that she was abandoning him, so he would pursue her more aggressively. Yet, through it all, they did their best to stay in the process of dialogue. However, the question remained: would all of this lead to any sexual connnection?

It was Tom's turn to initiate the dialogue.

> **Tom:**   *I want to hug you and kiss you. When I hug you, I want to hug you more.*
>
> **Joyce:**   *(to the therapist) I hate this.*
>
> **Therapist:**   *Remember that your reactions come largely from your own experiences, even before you met Tom. He is offering you a new experience, a new possibility. Stay in the process.*
>
> **Joyce:**   *Okay. So, you want to hug and hug and hug. You will never be satisfied with what I give. If I agreed to hug you once this week, next week you'd want two hugs. That is too much. I do not want to hug you.*
>
> **Therapist:**   *Can you let go of your belief that you know what Tom wants better than he does? All you have to do is listen. No one is asking you to agree to do anything else. Your job is to hear Tom and let him know that you get what he is saying.*
>
> **Tom:**   *I love you. I want to be close to you. I want to hug you.*
>
> **Joyce:**   *So, you love me and want to have sex. Is that right?*
>
> **Tom:**   *No. I love you. I want us to be close. I want to be patient with you. I want to hug you.*
>
> **Joyce:**   *You love me and want to hug me. You want us to be close and you say you will be patient with me. Is that right?*
>
> **Tom:**   *Yes.*
>
> **Joyce:**   *(with prompting from the therapist) Is there more?*

Once again, they slowly moved forward. He started to speak more freely and she was able to listen more. In a later session, they were ready to work on Behavior Change Requests.

> **Therapist:**   *It seems as though you both understand one another's experience pretty well. Let's work on developing Behavior Change Requests. Remember, requests must be "smart," that is, specific, measurable, achievable, relevant, and time-limited. They must also pass the "stranger test" and the "dead-man test." Passing the stranger test means that, if a stranger were to walk in and find a note with your request written on it, he or she could give you exactly what you wanted. Meeting the dead-man test means that the request cannot be something a dead person would be capable of doing. In other words, you want to ask your partner to do something; not to stop doing something. A dead man can do that. You cannot know if your partner has stopped doing something, so you can never know if the request has been met. Does that make sense?*

Tom: *Yeah, I get it. Well, my desire is to have sex once, soon, or at least to get close to her. I want to have a normal sexual relationship with my wife. I love her. I want to be close to her.*

Therapist: *(to Joyce) Could you mirror him, please?*

Joyce: *No.*

Therapist: *Please try to hear him. You can choose to give him or not give him what he is asking for. That is always your choice.*

Joyce: *Right. You want sex all the time. Is that right?*

Tom: *No, I want to be close to you. I want to touch you. And, yes, I want sex.*

Joyce: *So you want to have sex. Right?*

Tom: *Yes.*

Therapist: *(to Tom) Your three requests are...*

Tom: *For the next month, every night, I want to lie in bed and cuddle.*

Therapist: *Add some details, such as for how long each night, whether with or without clothes, and with or without the expectation of having sex. Given where you two have been with all this, asking for sex now might be asking too much. But this is your request, Tom, so you decide.*

Tom: *I want this to work and to go forward. So, okay. For the next month, every night for half an hour, I want to lie in bed and cuddle. Afterward, we can do whatever we want, get up, go to sleep, whatever, but I will not expect that we will have sex. Of course, I would like that, but I won't push for it.*

Joyce: *See. He just wants sex. Nothing else will be good enough.*

Therapist: *Breathe. Push your feet into the floor and see if you can ground yourself and soothe yourself. Okay? Mirror what you heard.*

Joyce: *Right; I want to do this. Okay. Your first request, Tom, is that we would cuddle, in bed, naked, for half an hour every night for the next 30 days. Is that right?*

Tom: *Almost. Wearing pajamas, a T-shirt, or whatever would be okay with me.*

Joyce: *It would be okay with you to do this with something on. Right?*

Tom: *Yes. My second request is that we sit and watch television, at least two times a week, for the next month, with my arm around you, and that we look into each other's eyes during every commercial.*

Joyce: *Ugh. No.*

The session continued in a similar vein. But in the end, Joyce agreed to Tom's second request. Then, in the next session:

Tom: *I appreciate the time we had together last night. I appreciate how we could sit with each other, close, with my arm around you, and my kissing you. I loved just watching you.*

Joyce: *You're happy. I'm not. I did it, but I'm not happy.*
Therapist: *(to Joyce) Do your best to listen and mirror.*
Joyce: *You enjoyed what we did. You appreciate our close contact.*
Tom: *Yes. You did just what I asked. I am happy.*

Then it was Joyce's turn to respond.

Joyce: *I know I said I wasn't happy. Actually, the truth is that I am scared, still, that you will leave me. But I liked what we did, too. I felt relaxed. I felt like I could actually give you what you want and still be okay. I hardly ever thought that was even possible.*
Tom: *You are scared, but what we did was okay, too. Is that right?*
Joyce: *Yes. I am frightened. I am worried that I'll never be enough. It is just so hard. Still, I am starting to see what we can do together.*
Tom: *You are still scared, but you are seeing what we are able to accomplish together. Is that right?*
Joyce: *Yes.*

CLINICAL CONSIDERATIONS IN WORKING WITH COUPLES WITH SEXUAL DYSFUNCTION

When working with couples who present with important sexual problems, the therapist has a number of issues to address. The PLISSIT model (Annon, 1974) offers a convenient strategy for determining the level of intervention appropriate for a given couple. This approach is consistent with the clinical protocol of utilizing the "least invasive method" of intervention that is necessary.

In the PLISSIT model:

- *P* stands for *permission*. Some partners, as a result of repressive socialization messages during childhood, have feelings of shame and guilt related to their sexuality. Such partners might simply need, from the therapeutic process, permission to be sexual, to have sexual feelings, and to behave in sexual ways.
- *LI* stands for *limited information*. When one or both partners need additional education about sexually related topics, such as the normalcy of masturbation and sexual fantasies, a psychoeducational approach using, for example, information sharing and bibliotherapy might suffice.
- *SS* stands for *specific suggestions*. Some couples, particularly those with heightened levels of conflict and dysfunction, may need detailed guidance on initiating and maintaining their sexual relationship.

- *IT* stands for *intensive therapy*. Only when one or both partners need to explore issues related to anxiety, depression, recurring frustrations, or childhood wounds should the therapist engage the couple in intensive psychotherapy.

The therapy can be geared to providing each step as needed. Of course, each therapist should determine his or her scope of competence for handling primary sexual disorders, particularly with couples such as Joyce and Tom, with significant dysfunction and distress.

I am strongly in favor of preserving a couple's relationship, particularly when the couple expresses that desire. However, the undercurrent I sensed while working with Joyce and Tom was one of, "We are so far apart, and have spent so many years isolated from each another; we're resigned and worn out. Is all this worth it?" This led me to ask myself the question, "Am I competent to offer what I believe they need?" A couple with the degree of separation that Joyce and Tom experienced would be a challenge for most therapists. A therapist, of course, is not required to accept all couples who apply, but once a therapist agrees to treat a couple, he or she is responsible for offering ongoing and effective care. Thus, couples therapists should look before they leap into treating sexual disorders.

The therapeutic process should focus on developing and expanding emotional as well as sexual contact. Psychoeducation on the relationship between emotional and sexual intimacy can help achieve this dual purpose. Tom and Joyce, for example, held widely disparate views of what sexuality within marriage means. Tom believed that, once he was married, he could have sex whenever and however he wanted it. He thought that Joyce would feel satisfied as long as he took control of their love making and of his having an orgasm. Joyce thought of sex as something you use to get someone to marry you. Because her mother "hated men" and told Joyce that "they only marry for sex," Joyce's negative expectations about sex were confirmed as soon as Tom demonstrated his inexperience and insensitivity. Exploding the sexuality-based myths and fallacies that are deeply ingrained in each partner thus requires examining their beliefs, reactions, and wounds, both emotional and sexual. Dialogue is an ideal intervention. The therapist should also acknowledge the couple's courage in confronting their sexual dilemma. To do so brings to the fore the most vulnerable and potentially shame-based parts of the individuals and their relationship. Normalizing their problems while communicating positive expectations and beliefs about the couple's potential for change can bolster their motivation.

Therapy should include the teaching of communication processes to enable each partner to understand the other's world. Joyce and Tom, as is typical of most couples in conflict, were convinced of the truth of their own positions. Being asked to validate—that is, to express an understanding of how the other could have arrived at the viewpoint he or she maintains—encouraged a shift in each partner's way of seeing things. Validation helped them get used to the possibility that there might be another way to perceive the situation, leading to greater tolerance of their differences.

This does not mean, however, that Tom, for example, needed to agree that what Joyce described was the "truth." For Joyce, knowing that Tom heard her and understood what she experienced helped her feel seen and heard, and led her to feel that he cared about her and her needs.

As for most couples, behavioral change also was crucial. Joyce was able to move closer to Tom only when she knew that if she said "Stop," he would hear her need for him to stop and respond to it. This knowing came through their practice with Behavior Change Requests, by defining and agreeing to specific behaviors. Previously, whenever Joyce asked Tom to behave in a certain way, he either did not hear her, misinterpreted what she said, or failed to follow through on agreements. Predictably, conflict erupted, and each partner felt justified. Once they learned and began to practice processes for clarifying their needs and making commitments to change, they were able to begin to build trust, knowing both what the other partner needed and what the partner was willing to give.

As the therapist strongly supports the partners' couplehood, the partners themselves need to be sustained as well. This involves the therapist's helping each partner to hold on to his or her own perceptions, own world view, and own voice. Schnarch (1997) describes this process as fostering the partners' differentiation, which includes expanding the ability to self-soothe.

Differentiation was a fundamental concern for Joyce and Tom. Staying in true connection with another requires having a sense of self that can maintain itself, regardless of shifts in the relationship. The dialogue between Joyce and Tom allowed each to hear the other and to be heard by the other, which expanded and moved differentiation forward for both of them.

The therapist, too, has internal work to do. Sexuality is a loaded issue for many of us. As in many therapeutic situations, managing one's internal responses to the couple's problems demands careful monitoring of one's judgments of or projections onto the clients.

When considering how to intervene, gender differences must be appreciated. In general, for women, closeness and sharing lead to feelings of sexual arousal; for men, sexual expression allows them to feel close to their partners. It is important for each partner to recognize that what the other partner needs in order to feel sexually aroused and receptive is probably different from one's own needs, and yet is perfectly normal.

An additional and crucial consideration for the therapist is determining when and how therapy should be judged as successful or as a failure. The typical success rate with couples who receive marital therapy is 40 to 50 percent. The criteria for success with a given couple should be defined in advance and in collaboration with the couple themselves, as should the question of whether or when to terminate treatment, if progress is not made.

Regardless of the severity of a couple's sexual dysfunction, it is important to keep in mind that, in general, those who come for therapy are seeking to create a satisfying relationship. Sometimes therapists lose the vision of that larger picture, becoming enmeshed in the technical details of sex therapy or pursuing the goal of enabling the couple to have good sex. The therapist, whether serving as expert or coach (or in whatever role he or she assumes), should consider first and foremost the process between the partners. But clients must also be convinced that the therapist honors their overarching purpose for being in therapy: to discover how to have a good, happy marriage, as each of them so defines that notion. Therapy is not about what I determine would be good for them; it is about what each wants for himself or herself and for the partnership.

Joyce and Tom were able to touch each other emotionally and sexually, if, at times, only lightly and briefly. Although their movement and degree of success might not meet another couple's standards for a satisfying relationship, they greatly reduced the emotional distance between them during their time in therapy. There are, at the very least, new possibilities for their future as a couple. How far they will go, and whether that will be far enough to meet their separate needs, remains to be seen.

But I am hopeful.

BIBLIOGRAPHY

Annon, J. S. (1974). The PLISSIT model. In *The behavioral treatment of sexual problems*. Honolulu: Kapiolani Health Services.

Schnarch. D. (1997). *Passionate marriage*. New York: Norton.

EDITORS' COMMENTARY

Couples' sexual problems come in many varieties. A surprising proportion of distressed couples come to therapy not having had sex in months, or even years. Interestingly, many couples fail to bring up their sexual difficulties until late in the therapy process. Some complain of having sex too infrequently, or too quickly, or in the wrong position. Their sex feels mechanical. He is insensitive; she lies there like a cold fish. He comes too quickly; she doesn't come at all. Because the most important sex organ in the body is the brain, with estimates stating that 95 percent of sexual response is psychological, it's likely that, when partners begin couples therapy, they're going to need some help with their sexual relationship, as well.

As Dr. Bernell points out, to be ethical, couples therapists should consider their ability to address the broad range of sexual problems that can emerge during a course of therapy. Unlike other types of couple distress, sexual dysfunction requires the therapist to have some knowledge of biology. In many cases, specialized training is needed to understand and treat the combination of physiological and psychological factors that affect sexual performance. Even more important, working with sexual complaints requires the therapist to feel comfortable with his or her own sexuality.

As difficult as it might be for the therapist to listen, it is even harder for some couples to verbalize frustrations with their sex life. The couple Dr. Bernell presents feels anxious and shameful about their sexual problems. Wisely, the therapist moved slowly with this couple, allowing them some small victories over their emotional struggles before plunging them into their sexual issues. This gave the couple a sense of confidence in themselves and the dialogue process, leaving them better prepared to deal with their more anxiety-producing sexual concerns.

The problem seen here, that of low sexual desire, is not uncommon among couples. It could be attributed in part to today's high number of two-earner couples, who, by combining two careers and a family, often run out of time and energy— and the desire to have sex. In Joyce's case, past events taught her to associate sex with anxiety and anxiety with death. Therefore, sex with Tom, or even the mention of sex, threw her body into a fight-or-flight response. Joyce's brain needed to learn that sex need not produce anxiety and that, if it did, the anxiety would not kill her. Just like fear of doing something unfamiliar dissipates as we do that thing over and over again, the anxiety associated with sex can, with repeated safety-producing experiences, fade over time. Joyce, for example, at first could barely tolerate talking about sex at all. As the therapist coached Joyce in managing anxiety ("Breathe. Push your feet into the floor..."), Joyce became capable of listening to Tom talk about sex. Later, Joyce was able to hold Tom's hand as they dialogued; then she could give and receive hugs. Although such changes might seem small and painfully slow, they inched the couple down the road toward sexual freedom and enjoyment. True, anxiety accompanied them every step of the way. But anxiety comes along with almost every behavior change we try to make, whether it be listening to our partner's feelings, containing our reactivity, or letting our partner touch us, fully clothed or totally naked.

Chapter 15

VALIDATION AS A FACILITATOR OF FORGIVENESS FOR ADULTERY

Bonnie Eaker Weil with Lisa Kelvin Tuttle

It has been estimated that only 35 percent of the couples in which a partner reveals an extramarital affair remain together (Pittman, 1990). Whether this statistic is seen as being high or low, it is important to our work with couples. First, the fact that any couples withstand such a disruption should perhaps direct us to investigate the glue that holds these partners together, as well as what tears them apart. Second, if an affair is actually a cry for help, the couple has to be guided to overcome this powerful symptom so that they may be enabled to learn communication skills and to create a sense of intimacy, connection, and bonding.

Adultery is a product of *mutual emptiness* in a relationship, and lack of intimacy is a core problem that the affair is masking. On some level, both partners needed the affair in order to ward off intimacy. Success in working with this population depends on the couple's coming to realize that the affair is not the central issue—not the predominant problem in the relationship—but rather a symptom of mutual disconnection and pain. Thus, the goal of therapy should be to assist both partners in accepting and taking responsibility for their equal contributions to the mutual emptiness that serves as a catalyst for an affair. Sharing responsibility for the lack of intimacy puts it squarely on the shoulders of both the "betrayer" and the "betrayed." When partners can envision an equal sign between them, they acknowledge their own contribution and begin to see that the affair was a dysfunctional attempt to stabilize the relationship. Couples should be helped to reframe the affair as a wake-up call and then to use the experience constructively to create a new relationship.

Infidelity also can be what I call an "emotional inheritance." As discussed in *Adultery, the Forgivable Sin* (Eaker Weil, 1994), a predilection for infidelity is often passed along through family behavior patterns. The subject is of particular interest to me because infidelity nearly tore my own family apart, and I can attest that most of my straying clients had an adulterous parent. Taking a thorough family history from both partners as part of the initial therapeutic assessment, with the goal of constructing a detailed family diagram or genogram (McGoldrick & Gerson, 1985) as a tool to explore the multigenerational context of a family, can reveal the incidence of infidelity in past generations. Such knowledge lays a crucial foundation for the couple's therapy in terms of their coming to view the issue as a developmental one. When the genogram (or "cheat-o-gram," as Mel Brooks once called it [personal communication]) does reveal an adulterous family history, this information may play an important role in lessening the blaming of an individual partner—especially when a legacy of infidelity shows up on both partners' diagrams.

A cornerstone of Imago therapy, the Couples Dialogue process (Hendrix, 1988) greatly assists in the reorganization and healing of an adulterous couple's relationship. Its three-part structure—incorporating mirroring, validation, and empathy—makes it a powerful tool for working with couples who have experienced affairs. The dialogue helps in two ways: it helps partners accept mutual responsibility, and it puts an end to the vicious circle of blame and attack. It is also a form of conflict resolution that teaches couples how to be in the present and not live in the past, which is when the affair occurred. Over time, couples who master the dialogue learn to trust again, and this trust encourages them to commit to the continuing process of change. Couples Dialogue, along with the Imago Behavior Change Request process, aids the betrayed spouse in moving from the shattering experience of finding out about the infidelity, through the recovery period, to *forgiveness.*

In this chapter, I present two cases that illustrate how the Couples Dialogue—with a particular emphasis on validation—is a facilitator of couples' forgiveness of infidelity. In both cases, the men were the betrayers; neither initially could give validation, and both wanted the women to go on with their lives and get over the betrayal. (Often the betrayed partner is open to such an expectation and tries to move on in order to avoid confronting all the pain and the shame that go with it.) I also refer to other exercises that enhance a couple's ability to achieve forgiveness, and conclude with a brief overview of these exercises.

When adultery is an issue, it is generally advisable to treat the couple individually as well as jointly. Individual sessions reduce the level of toxicity and calm the system enough to make the mutual sessions more productive. In addition to these individual sessions, I've found it beneficial to assist both partners in working on their family-of-origin issues directly with their parents or other important caretakers, and for the other family members to be present at the couple's sessions, if possible. When face-to-face meetings are not feasible, conference-call sessions can serve this purpose.

THE POWER OF VALIDATION

In order for a betrayed partner to forgive and for connection to be regained in the relationship, the adulterous partner must validate the betrayed partner's pain and rage. Validation is the key both to uncovering the reason for the affair and to the recovery of intimacy and forgiveness. Without validation, there can be no forgiveness, and without forgiveness, continuation of the relationship is nearly impossible.

When the adulterer can validate, the betrayed partner feels heard, often for the first time. The adulterer can then also be heard. All partners betray one another emotionally when they lack the skills to communicate. For this reason, therapy should include helping couples learn and practice the art of dialogue, with a particular focus on validation. They should be coached in using dialogue as their primary way of discussing the issue of the adultery, as well as other challenging topics that arise in their marriage.

OBSESSING, DART THROWING, AND WORKING THROUGH THE RAGE

It is important that the adulterer be able to understand and validate the importance of the betrayed spouse's expressions of anger and need for verbal "dart throwing," which help to discharge his or her rage. When the betrayer can allow verbal darts to be thrown, the betrayed will eventually stop throwing them. It is essential that the adulterer not express anger toward the betrayed while he or she is in the midst of obsessing over the injustice of the affair, as this will short-circuit the healing process. Ranting and raving are part of what the betrayed spouse must do to begin working through the pain and anguish to get to forgiveness. The obsession subsides when the betrayed partner is able to accept the part he or she played in the scenario. It is not a case of "victim" and "bastard."

An exercise I call "lash the lover" is a time-limited, by-appointment-only process in which the betrayed spouse is allowed to ask questions, complain, and obsess. It's important that the "lashing" be time-limited, because the adulterer cannot take it for too long. Still, the more the betrayed is allowed to lash out, the closer he or she moves toward getting over the anger, the grudge holding, and the dart throwing. The emergence of forgiveness begins, which allows, finally, for the betrayed's recovery of sexual feelings for the adulterous partner.

This structured obsessing helps betrayed spouses to review what was happening in their lives around the time the affair was occurring and when it was discovered. Like putting together the pieces of a jigsaw puzzle, it helps them emotionally to reconstruct their experience to make sense of the crisis. In my experience, only when the betrayed spouse is validated by the adulterous partner for obsessing, and only when the adulterer takes responsibility for what he or she has done, can the betrayed see the role that he or she played in the rift and take responsibility for it.

CASE VIGNETTES

Case 1: Karen and David

I had been working with Karen and David for over 18 months at the time of this writing. He, 45, and she, 42, are an outgoing, attractive, intelligent pair. While Karen was pregnant with and giving birth to their third child, David was having an affair with Lani, who was his best friend's wife and his wife's best friend. David initially denied the infidelity, but when Karen threatened to divorce him, he admitted the affair and discontinued it. David had a very hard time understanding why Karen couldn't just get done with it after three months. He said, "The affair's over, so it's just over." It was their mutual desire to change that brought them into therapy.

Although I believe that this couple had ceased to experience true intimacy, they reported that their sex was still great and that they did spend some intimate time together, going to movies, out to dinner, and to the theater.

Their courtship had been a stormy one. David called the shots; if he said "Jump," she would ask, "How high?" Her sense of low self-worth kept her on an emotional roller coaster: "If he loves me, I must be something." She knew that he frequently flirted with other women. Affection and validation were very difficult for David to achieve because he had not seen them in his own family, and he had to struggle very long and hard to work this through. He had never validated Karen in their marriage. Extremely selfish, he had become accustomed to a life centered around him and his needs. He barely participated in the rearing of their children, and was often off playing golf or tennis.

Karen was overly close to her mother, who would intermittently overwhelm Karen with her own problems and then abandon her emotionally. So Karen chose David, a partner who would not suffocate her. However, neither did he satisfy Karen's emotional needs, and inevitably he also abandoned her through his infidelity. David's father was an alcoholic, and David saw no closeness in his family. Although Karen suspects that David's father had committed adultery as well, David's parents deny this. They were once separated (after which David had his extramarital affair), but they are now back together.

Karen also tended to be overly responsible, seeking to win David's love and approval as she had with her mother. She said she had always tried to be the "good girl," but was getting sick of it. After she found out about David's affair, she responded with what is called an overcorrection: she insisted that David take responsibility for the children, she took up golf and tennis, and she left no time for him to retreat to his usual space. She was trying to *be* him, and over time they began to switch roles. Karen was enraged that David had been so self-involved and unable to validate her sense of rejection and pain. "I am going to be for me, me, me, and I am not going to give in to you anymore," she told him.

In response, I made it clear that we had to work on getting the relationship into balance. It wasn't good when *he* was just "me, me, me," and neither was it good when *she* was just "me, me, me." Her reaction was that she wasn't going to be able to validate him because she was supposed to validate herself. She wanted to give "tit for tat," she said. I insisted that, if she wanted the marriage to work, she would have to validate him even if he couldn't validate her. He was learning, as was she, and I didn't want her to judge him for not yet having the skills he needed. She would have to be patient with him regarding his difficulty in validating her experience.

Validation was something they would both need to learn for the sake of their relationship, with or without the affair. In order to teach him to validate, *she* would have to learn to validate.

Although the couple did move successfully through the obsession/dart-throwing stage, it took them quite a while. In numerous sessions, Karen was given license to obsess and question her husband's relationship with his lover. In dialogue, she expressed her fury with him, asking him again and again why he kept telling her she was crazy—why he had invalidated her and denied her when she initially expressed her suspicion of the affair. Initially, the more she kept asking, the more he would respond that she was overreacting. Karen asserted that she was allowed to overreact.

Karen could not resist talking about the affair; she would initiate dialogue about it without first making an appointment with David. She had agreed to limit her obsessing to 5 or 10 minutes, using dialogue, which was about as long as David could handle. He was also allowed to ask for time-outs, provided he agreed to resuming the dialogue later. Whenever Karen refused his requests for time-outs, David found dialogue and validation impossible. This was Karen's way of unconsciously sabotaging David's efforts to change. At times, Karen would use the dialogue and David's self-revelations to punish him. She was afraid that if she were to validate David, it would give him license to rekindle the affair or to remain self-centered and do whatever he liked. David complained that Karen would not do anything they had agreed to in therapy unless he made the first move.

The following transcriptions from two sessions show how difficult it was for this couple to validate each other's experience. In the first interchange, I purposely avoided directing them and keeping them "in process," as I normally would. This gave them the opportunity to vent and define some core issues. In the second session, I intervened more directly, and they were better able to develop a connection.

> **Karen:** *I can't believe you told me I was so paranoid about Lani that I needed a mental hospital. You constantly made me feel the way my mother did. I had to be the good girl, the good wife. I hate you! I want a divorce—not because of the affair, but because of all that invalidation. You should have told me so I would not doubt myself. That slime, Lani, manipulated me, trying to find out if I had any sexual or emotional problems with you. I bought into it and got taken, and then you turned against me and protected her when I confronted you. See if you like the feeling of punishment the way you punished me with my feelings and thoughts, telling me I was crazy. You always tried to convince me I was wrong to feel what I felt. How am I supposed to get over how you don't care about my feelings or what's important to me? It's always you, your needs, your space, your friends. What about me? I want you to pay for what you did to me. I can't forgive because I'm afraid that if I do, you'll just see that as license to treat me like I'm invisible again. I count. I exist! You owe me an apology.*

Why should I do the work when you did this to me? It's a hell of a lot harder for me than for you. All you do is chalk your behavior up to a mistake. I'm the one who is left with the mess. I'd rather leave you so I don't have to do all this work.

David: *I can't take much more of this. I validate you, but it's never enough! You really don't want to forgive me. It's easier to wallow or blame—then you never have to look at your own stuff. We both contributed to the affair. What's your part? I'm not the bastard and you the saint, Karen. I'll do the work, but I'm damned if I do, damned if I don't. Give me a break or let me go. Yes, I made a big mistake, but I'm paying my dues now. I've taken responsibility. You're just punishing me. When does the punishment stop? I love you, but you're killing our love by blaming it all on me.*

Karen: *Well, being close to you is not easy. It doesn't feel safe at all. So I push you away like you did me.*

David: *Then don't put me in a no-win situation and then lambaste me for doing what you say you want. Stop putting a wedge between us. Lani's not in the middle anymore.*

Karen: *I resent having to do all the work when you betrayed me. I was pregnant and you were out having fun. Can't you see why I'm so furious? Try to imagine being in my shoes.*

David: *I can feel it. I just feel so helpless, like I have to fix it but I can't. I don't know how to. Even when I validate you, it doesn't help. You want more and more. I can't measure up. I'm not you. You're not me. I need you to let up and quit badgering me and threatening divorce.*

Karen: *Maybe I want that. Maybe I want to end it so I won't have to feel this anymore. I'll have some control for a change. If you weren't in control, you'd feel what I've felt.*

A second interchange reveals a very different tone.

Karen: *I never felt loved by you or by my mom. I was never good enough for either of you. My mother suffocated me most of the time. Then she ignored me when I most needed her. I feel like that with you too. I don't want you too far away, but I don't want to let you get too close either. Maybe I somehow let this affair happen, so I wouldn't feel so vulnerable with you. Maybe I unconsciously gave Lani to you. I saw in front of my very own eyes what was going on. But when I suspected, you shut me up. I should have trusted my intuition! I didn't trust myself, just like when I was a kid and my mom would tell me how my ideas were wrong.*

David: *I heard you say you've never felt loved by either me or your mom, that you weren't good enough in our eyes. You're wondering if you* *really want to be that close to me, and if, on some unconscious level, you let me go with Lani so you wouldn't feel so vulnerable. Did I get it all?*

Karen: *Mostly. Also that somewhere along the line, I learned to not trust my own intuition. That I knew what was going on but let you convince me I was wrong.*

David: *So even though you knew what was going on, you let yourself be convinced that you didn't, just like your mom talked you out of your own ideas when you were little. You stopped trusting your intuition.*

Karen: *Yes. You got it all.*

Therapist (coaching):   *David, now let Karen hear how her experience makes sense, and let her know you heard the feelings she expressed to you.*

David: *I can hear how painful it must have been when you were growing up, Karen. It must have made it worse when I had the affair and you suspected, but I told you that you didn't know what you were talking about. It makes sense that you would feel abandoned and unloved by the way I treated you. And it makes sense that getting too close to me would be intolerable too, and that maybe you let the affair happen to get some distance from me. I can imagine you have been feeling a lot of feelings—hurt, sadness, confusion, frustration, anger. I can see right now how much hurt I've caused you.*

(Karen, dabbing her tears with a tissue, nods in affirmation).

Therapist: *David, what would you like to tell Karen right now?*

David: *Just that I'm so sorry I wounded you. I want a chance to be the partner you need me to be. Will you give me that chance? And will you try to not make this whole thing my fault?*

Karen: *Damn it, David. Why do you always do that? Just as I'm beginning to feel heard by you, and validated, you say something self-serving and cancel out all the good feelings I'm starting to have. How can I possibly feel safe? It's enraging!*

David: *What do you mean? I was validating you. This is impossible. I do my best to imagine what she's feeling, and she rejects me. All of a sudden, she's the wronged one again and I'm the bad one.*

Therapist: *Tell Karen this directly.*

David: *I get so frustrated. I feel as though I'm validating you, which I want to do, and I begin to empathize with how painful all this is for you. But then you say something that makes me think that only your pain is legitimate. I'm afraid that you'll refuse to see how much pain I'm in, that I'm hurting too.*

Therapist: *Please mirror him, Karen.*

Karen: *If I got it right, you really want to be able to validate my experience, but when you do, you think I'm saying you're the bad one and I'm* *the good one. You're in a lot of pain, too, and you're afraid that I won't acknowledge it. Is that right?*

David: *Yes.*

Karen: *Well, that makes sense to me. I know this is hard for both of us. I can imagine it must be very painful and shaming to feel you're in the role of the bad one all the time. I know you're in pain. Really, I do care about how you're feeling and I promise to hear how you're hurt, too. But, well, it's hard for me to say this, but I guess I'm feeling cheated that we changed the subject from what I was talking about, David.*

Therapist: *David, you will have your turn. Can you give your wife a chance to feel heard and empathized with now? Don't give up.*

David: *Okay.*

Karen: *First, I want to say that it felt really good to hear you tell me you're sorry you wounded me and you want to be the partner I always needed. I know you mean it, David.*

David (taking a deep breath): *Okay. Thank you, Karen. Let's try this again. It makes sense to me why you're still angry and can't forgive me. I did a horrible thing, and it was even worse when I made you feel crazy for having suspicions that you were right about. I can imagine how humiliated, disappointed, and enraged you must feel.*

Karen: *Just hearing you say that makes me feel understood. I want you to help me get over this, and I want to help you, too. It's hard work, but I think we're worth it.*

Toward the end of this session, after some slow progress had been made, David lost patience and said, "Enough is enough. If you don't want to get past this, you'll have to let me know now. If you're not going to forgive me, then we have to move on. I am doing the best that I can." This made Karen realize that it was solely up to her to decide whether or not to forgive him. It struck her that forgiving him would be as much a gift to herself as to David. She finally understood that by punishing him, she was also punishing herself and her children. She then said to David, "I am going to forgive you. I may never forget, but I forgive you, and I do not want you to leave. And if I don't want you to leave, I can't make it miserable for you to stay."

Now, 18 months later, although they are still struggling in therapy, Karen's loving feelings for her husband have returned.

I worked very closely with this couple on issues related to their families of origin. During the period when David was not able to overcome his selfishness or genuinely validate Karen, I encouraged him to do some work with his parents. Through dialoguing with his parents, he began to feel validated by them, which led to his feeling more capable of validating his wife.

At first, David was very defensive, but he gradually softened. He ultimately came to view the affair as a wake-up call to the problems in the marriage. David admitted that he had been in control of the marriage, and he was able to connect his experiences in his relationship with Karen to early childhood wounding.

After many discussions over a year, Karen realized that she had been using the dialogue against David, and that what she really wanted was to connect with and bond with him.

During one session, Karen recognized how her unwillingness to validate David's experience led him to feel overwhelming shame and guilt for what he had done. I explained to her that more adulterers leave their marriages out of guilt than out of a lack of love for their partners. Rather than using her energy to sabotage his progress in therapy, if what she really wanted was for him to leave, she should just tell him right then and there. She replied that she really wanted to forgive him. I explained that she had to take the steps, one of the most important of which was not to use the dialogue process against him.

David learned to validate Karen, and Karen can now validate David. He participates more in rearing the children, making sure that Karen has time for herself. He is supportive of her going to school, which he opposed before out of fear of losing her. David admits that he will never completely understand what Karen has been going through, but he is able to talk daily about the affair and can handle the lashing-the-lover exercise for about 10 minutes at a time. He has found a way to allow her to be upset without feeling that he has to fix it. He is working on some behavior changes that Karen requested, and believes that, someday, they will be able to put all this behind them.

Karen came to take responsibility for her own contributions to their problems. She sees that she had been stopping her own orgasms, her own pleasure and fun, and that by failing to accept responsibility for her part in the problem, she was interfering with the healing process. She admits that she will never completely understand why David couldn't empathize with the way she felt, but it no longer devastates her. She realizes that people do make mistakes, and that the affair had a purpose in their marriage: it served as a catalyst to take on the challenge of learning genuine communication skills, and becoming truly intimate, connected, and bonded.

Once they began to accept one another's limits, these partners were able to use the dialogue process productively. In time, they began to accept the slow pace of progress, knowing that each of them was stretching to the best of his or her ability. They are becoming intimate partners, and they consider themselves best friends.

Case 2: Caesar and Suzy

The second case involved a husband who met with a childhood sweetheart six times a year. His wife found out about his lover when she called home one day and listened to the answering machine.

Caesar and Suzy are in their 50s and have three children. They described themselves as "two ships passing in the night." There had been no validating or empathizing, but instead constant mutual blaming throughout their marriage. They complained of having no intimacy, which probably was due to their poor communication skills.

Suzy could not understand why her husband had taken a lover when she had been available to him all along. It pained her that she and Caesar talked so little and that their sex consisted of "quickies." I explained to them that having an affair with someone whom one saw only six times a year was pseudointimacy. The reason Caesar could be close to his lover was that there was no relationship debris—no problems, no demands, and no expectations. Perhaps Caesar craved intimacy, but he obviously could not handle it on a regular basis. Suzy came to understand that Caesar's fleeting liaisons with his lover were as much a reflection, an avoidance, of genuine intimacy, as was his inability to maintain closeness with her in the marriage.

They loved each other, but as a result of their lack of bonding and connection—which had begun, as is typical, the first six months of their marriage, as they moved from the romantic love phase into the power struggle—both experienced a great sense of loneliness. Caesar's loneliness resulted in his having an affair and in becoming a workaholic; Suzy's loneliness turned her into a gambling addict and a "schoolaholic."

As a child, Suzy had learned to be a good girl in order to avoid being abused. As an adult, she had turned for comfort to her work, her children, and eventually to gambling. Because her serious gambling began around the time Caesar had started having the affair (of which she was not then aware), she says she suspects that her unconscious was picking up on his infidelity.

Both had known emptiness in childhood. Suzy was an abused child who became afraid to ask for what she needed. Caesar was a Holocaust survivor who had lost both parents at an early age. His mother, an overbearing woman, survived the camps but died young. Caesar's father, who was imprisoned for many years, died during the war. Caesar learned not to trust or get close to others.

Like so many couples, each blamed the other for the problems in the marriage, and they had been unable to find mutually satisfying solutions. For this reason, the couple had great difficulty with the dialogue process: both continued to speak without listening to the other, and to rely on criticism and blame. Both saw themselves as the victim, and neither liked being told what to do.

Many of Suzy and Caesar's sessions were spent practicing the Couples Dialogue and its companion process for dealing with anger, the Container Exercise. For couples in the process of overcoming the wounds inflicted by infidelity, anger work must be a core component of therapy. The seven-step Imago Container Exercise is particularly effective in assisting such couples to deal with rage constructively. It was ideal for Suzy and Caesar, as it helped Caesar deal with his pattern of angry reactivity and gave Suzy a safe way to lash out and obsess.

I quickly observed a circular causality to this couple's relating: both had a great need to feel needed, but they were caught in a circle in which they continually rejected each other and thus received the exact opposite of what they wanted. Suzy's air of independence was her defense against the sting of rejection she felt when she expressed her feelings to Caesar. Caesar's angry facial expressions whenever Suzy shared her feelings or asked for something recalled for her the beatings she had received from her mother. Caesar's rejection of her would squelch her dependency needs, and she would withdraw from him further, exiting from the marriage through school and gambling. Caesar's angry reactivity to Suzy's emotionality was his defense against experiencing his own helplessness and pain. He attempted either to smooth over Suzy's painful feelings or to push them away, because they activated his own inner upset. When Suzy acted as though she didn't need him, this fanned his neediness; then, because he experienced his wife as unsafe, he would attempt to assuage his neediness through an affair with a needy lover. Both spouses wanted desperately to go to each other to get their needs met, but neither felt safe enough to do so.

It took a long time for Suzy to recognize the underlying reasons for her husband's affair and to acknowledge that, all along, she had been denying her own neediness. Through the expression of validation and empathy in the Couples Dialogue, they both realized that they had the same childhood wounds, the same needs, and the same desires. Suzy began to validate Caesar's need to be needed, and he began to validate her need to be desired and needed by him.

In one powerful interchange, Suzy told Caesar how much she missed him when he was away. She explained how she had tried for many years to talk to him, to get through to him, whereupon he would become angry and walk out of the room. One time, she said, he almost hit her, and this reminded her of her mother. Through her tears, Suzy said that only gambling gave her solace. Caesar replied that he had been ashamed of her gambling, which made him want to leave her. He said he hadn't realized that he had been distancing himself from her, but thought that, by being a good breadwinner who provided well, he was giving her everything she needed. He now realized that she needed, more than anything else, his time and his love.

Following is some of their dialogue about these issues.

Suzy: *It is only when you are validating me, instead of telling me I am crazy or stupid, or changing the subject, or trying to make me laugh, that I know you are really hearing me. That's when I feel safe with you. Your validation is the most important thing to me. It's through validation that you make me not feel crazy, and it's through validation that I feel you understand me and my needs. I need you to take me seriously. I need you to set time aside to be with me, both before we make love and afterwards.*

Caesar: *Let me see if I got all this. More than anything, you want me to understand your needs and take you seriously, and it's my validating you that makes you feel safe. You also want me to set aside time for you when we make love. Did I get that?*

Suzy: *Yes. Well, specifically, I want you to make time for us to be intimate, to spend more time together before and after we make love, especially afterwards, instead of turning over and going to sleep.*

Caesar: *Oh, okay. You want me to make special time for us when we make love, to be intimate together before and after—not just to turn over and go to sleep, right?*

Suzy: *Right. You got it.*

Caesar: *It makes sense that you want me to validate you, because it makes you feel valued and important and understood by me. It also makes sense that you want me to be a more attentive lover. That's an area of our relationship that has really suffered. I do love you and want you to feel loved by me again in that way. I can imagine that you've felt rejected and lonely by the way I've been with you in bed. You'd feel a lot more cared about and connected to me if I made our sex life and intimacy more important. Did I get it?*

Suzy: *Yes. That felt good. I know there are some things you need from me, too. I know you need me to be there for you, instead of spending all my time with the kids and going to school and working.*

Caesar: *Well, I also feel safe enough to talk to you now. Finally, you're not mad at me all the time, and you're not judging me. You know, I've had a hard life, too. I was a Holocaust survivor, remember. I have been abused, just like you. Getting close to you is very scary. I wasn't even sure I wanted to dialogue with you, because I thought you might use the things you found out about me—my weaknesses—against me.*

Therapist: *Suzy, can you mirror back what you heard Caesar say? If you need him to repeat some of it, that's okay.*

Suzy (silently looking down at her hands, seemingly lost in thought and close to tears):   *I did hear you, Caesar. Just like me, you have had a hard life and were abused. And just like me, you're afraid of getting close. You weren't sure you wanted to dialogue at first, because you were afraid I'd use what I learned about you against you.*

Later in the session, as Caesar began to see his wife as a wounded child, his attitude toward her softened.

Caesar: *I am so sorry—I never realized that I was hurting you. I never realized that I was doing the same thing to you as your parents did. I just could not handle your emotionality. I mean, my mother was so emotionally suffocating, I had to move away from her. So I also felt I had to move away from you. Then I hurt you even more by having the affair. I never knew you felt like a failure. I never knew you cared so much about me. I just figured we were two ships passing in the night—that's why I had the affair. I am so sorry.*

They cried and held one another silently for a while. It was at this point that they began to understand how similar were their wounds, their needs, their fears, and their hopes.

There is an Imago principle that states that the behavior changes one wants most from one's partner are the very ones that are the most difficult for the partner to give. In working on Behavior Change Requests, this couple learned that although it would be difficult for them to stretch into what each other wanted, if they were able to do so, they would be healing the most wounded parts of one another and thereby bringing out the best in both. For example, Caesar had always wanted to be able to share and to be more open, and so he was drawn to Suzy—a natural communicator who was well suited for a career in social work. However, the ways in which Suzy tried to get Caesar to communicate more put tremendous pressure on him. But fortunately, she came to realize that her nagging wasn't enabling Caesar to communicate any better. Further, she saw that she had attracted a man who was always angry; this set up an ideal situation for Suzy to work through and resolve her own anger toward her mother.

By envisioning Suzy as a wounded child, Caesar finally began to understand her needs. He worked hard to listen to her obsessing over his affair. During the six months they were in therapy, Suzy eventually stopped alternating between attacking him and withdrawing from him. Instead, she would say to Caesar, "Please put on your safety vest* and make it safe for me to talk to you." In turn, Caesar became more capable of listening to Suzy without becoming defensive and withdrawing in self-protection.

Suzy needed about three months' worth of obsessing and dart throwing; by then, she felt heard and validated enough by Caesar to be able finally to stop. Caesar was able to end his affair because he was getting his needs met through his marriage. He is continuing to learn how to share his feelings with Suzy, so that when he gets scared, when he feels the need to detach and withdraw, Suzy knows that he is not trying to abandon her, and she doesn't take it personally. Therefore, she can allow him to do whatever he needs to do at the time—achieve some distance or move closer to her—to feel a safe connection with her.

Dialogue helped both partners to become aware of and accept the parts that they had played in the emptiness of their marriage. Caesar gave up the affair, Suzy gave up the gambling, and they committed, first and foremost, to meeting each other's needs. He scheduled at least 10 minutes a day to listen to Suzy talk about herself, her childhood, and her feelings. They began to reromanticize their relationship—having fun together, going for walks, and holding hands. Suzy finally felt connected with and touched by Caesar; Caesar finally felt valued and desired by his wife.

Slowly they're reclaiming the lost parts of themselves as they tear down the walls between them and stretch to heal their childhood wound and the wounds of their marriage. Their struggles to forgive one another and their parents have made each of them more whole as individuals. Their viewing one another as wounded, the affair as a catalyst for their healing, and their marriage as a way to finish childhood, has opened the door to a deeper and more authentic love than they ever had before.

COMMENTARY

These two cases are about love, courage, and, ultimately, spirituality. Both couples came to realize their fullest potential through using the dialogue process to deal with the pain of an affair. The betrayers had to learn that, just because the affair was over for them, it wasn't necessarily over for their wives. They needed to make some serious behavior changes, including the promise of fidelity and regular dialogue. They also needed to allow their partners to be angry with them. When their wives obsessed, these men needed to validate their wives' feelings, instead of withdrawing or distancing. Before learning the dialogue process, the betrayers'

---

*The metaphor of "putting on one's safety vest" taught in the Container Exercise is a device for helping couples visualize themselves as safe and protected from their spouses' verbal attacks in the process of discharging rage.

shame and guilt might have driven them away from their marriages. But through the dialogue, these men were able to share shame and guilt and other feelings in a safe context.

The women who were betrayed also had to do a great deal of stretching. They needed to take responsibility for their contributions to the emptiness of their marriages, and they eventually had to release their partners from guilt and shame. The wives had to acknowledge that they, themselves, had been keeping the affairs alive in their own minds long after they had ended. Both the wives and their husbands had to do their part in rebuilding the damaged trust and safety of their marriage. This involved recommitting to their relationship, becoming a listening and validating partner, and demonstrating caring in ways that were meaningful to their partners.

Both couples have come a long way, yet they still struggle to validate each other consistently. As is commonly the case, the husbands become impatient, wishing their wives would just "forgive and forget" and never bring up the affairs again. Certain times are more challenging, especially the period around the anniversary of the affair. For Karen, this was an impossibly difficult time, which led to a setback in the progress she and David had made. Unable to deal with the feelings and the memories by themselves, the couple returned to therapy.

Ultimately, what made forgiveness possible for these couples was that, at some point, the women accepted the fact that their husbands had made a mistake, and they *decided* to forgive them. Both spouses had to be willing to see each other, and themselves, as human. Through the dialogue, they were able to share the feelings that can build the bridge between the hearts and minds of romantic partners. They must continue to make the decision, every day, to keep their connection intact.

EXERCISES*

The following exercises can be offered to clients as between-sessions work or incorporated into sessions as the therapist sees fit.

Lash the Lover (Time-Limited by Permission of the Adulterer)

The betrayed gets to attack the other object of affections, ask questions, and complain about how this has ruined his or her life. This is the *only* time this can

---

*Lash the lover, discharging anger through letter writing, and the forgiveness acronym are adapted, with permission, from *Adultery, the Forgivable Sin* (Eaker Weil, 1994).

be done, although you can go through the exercise as often as needed, provided you stop when the adulterer has had enough. The betrayer cannot respond, defend, or protect the lover, as he or she usually does, except to answer questions. (This exercise will help relieve the betrayed's anger and fend off obsession. The more you tell, the less they dwell.) *Warning: If you don't play by the rules, you could send your partner back to the lover.*

Caution: Some questions are better left unvoiced, or at least unanswered. Do you really want a graphic description of where and when and how the sex took place? Do you think you will ever be able to erase that picture from your mind?

Don't ever say to the betrayed, "I never loved you, anyway."

If the deceived mate does ask, the deceiver should resist the impulse to seek revenge by boasting—unless he or she doesn't care about ever putting things back together again.

Resist, too, the common impulse to defend your inamorata by saying, "She's prettier—and better in bed!" even if the accusations are unfair or untrue. If you do, you may destroy the foundation of your relationship beyond repair.

For the adulterer, some legitimate questions to expect:

- Who?
- Where—on marital turf?
- How long has this been going on?
- When did you meet?
- Will you stop?
- Do you love this person?
- Will you leave me and marry this person?
- Who else knows?
- Do you still love me?

Discharging Anger Through Letter Writing

Letter writing can be a great way to discharge toxic anger. You must handle anger with care. Hold it in and it can destroy you; let it explode, and it can destroy everyone else you care about. Follow these steps to detoxify your anger before you vent it on your partner. How best to do this? Write letters. Deposit them daily in what one of my professors, Dr. Philip Guerin of the Center for Family Learning, calls a "bitter bank."

You should come up with one of these a day and put it in a folder for your eyes only. Do not mail it or show it to anyone else.

Letter 1: Write only "I hate you, (spouse's name)" as many times as you can—ideally more than 70 times.

Letter 2: Tell your mate how hurt, angry, and sad you are about what happened, how much you hate him or her in response, and that you want to leave. Ask why he or she betrayed you.

Letter 3: Explain how much you love and need your partner and why you can't let go. Describe your fear of abandonment and what life would be like without your mate.

Letter 4: Compose the letter you wish your spouse would send in response. Put in everything you want to hear—apology, rationale, regrets, and penance for the adultery; nice things your partner is going to do to try and make it up to you; what a wonderful, loving person you are (and how much you are loved and missed). Have your spouse beg you not to leave and grovel about how unworthy he or she is; tell you how sorry he or she is to abuse you after all the wonderful things you've done; describe how he or she will ask for forgiveness and recommit to you and your marriage from now on.

Letter 5: Write down any part you may have played in all of this. Address it to your partner—and this time, deliver it. Equalizing the responsibility reduces your anger, obsession, and feelings of victimization. Here, *you* ask for forgiveness.

Letters 6–10: Repeat all the previous letters, but this time address them to the parent from which you are most distant or who hurt you the most with some kind of betrayal—if not adultery, then by being cold, demanding, selfish, or neglectful, or by never being there.

Letters 11–15: Repeat all previous letters, but this time address them to your other parent.

Read your parental letters to your partner. Help him or her understand the relationship of today's hurts to yesterday's. This will dissipate some anger.

You must deposit your letters daily in your file or "bitter bank" for one week to three months, until you feel your anger diminish. Try not to dwell on your anger, however, except in the time set aside every day for banking your bitterness.

Forgiveness Acronym

To reach that state beyond blame and shame, you must pass through the following seven steps, whose initial letters spell FORGIVE. Ask for help again and again, from your parents, grandparents, and siblings, as well as from your mate.

*F*orget your obsession with the affair, no matter how tough it is to let go. This is just another way to put something or someone between you and your partner, another way to avoid intimacy and hide from your real problems.

*O*pen your hearts to each other. Not only the affair, but other damaging secrets as well, need to be revealed. Also discuss your childhood fears and needs and emptiness.

*R*ebuild trust. To do this, the betrayer must not have any contact with the lover. Fight fairly, use conflict positively, share and confide. You will have doubts. Talk about them; don't fixate.

*G*o courting again. Renew your sense of fun, spontaneity, and desire to please each other. Remember the traits that attracted you and cultivate them.

*I*nvite intimacy. Practice a new system of open, honest, full communication. Don't let work or children or in-laws or anything else reinsert itself between you. When your mate is forthright and it smarts, don't criticize—appreciate the honesty. Make it safe to communicate.

*V*alue fidelity. Discuss your permissible limits. Repeat an oral contract to each other regularly, or even draw up a written one.

*E*ncourage embraces. From quick cuddles to prolonged cradling, touching and caressing will help ease the way over the most painful hurdle: sexual healing. People having affairs plan for sexual pleasure. Why shouldn't you?

BIBLIOGRAPHY

Eaker Weil, B. (1994). *Adultery, the forgivable sin*. Mamaroneck, N.Y.: Hastings House.

Hendrix, H. (1988). *Getting the love you want: A guide for couples*. New York: Holt.

McGoldrick, M., & Gerson, R. (1985). *Genograms*. New York: Norton.

Pittman, F. (1990). *Private lies: Infidelity and the betrayal of intimacy*. New York: Norton.

EDITORS' COMMENTARY

When an affair has shattered a relationship, forgiveness is the ultimate goal of the therapy process. Bonnie Eaker Weil holds that before partners can forgive one another, sincere validation must be given not only to the betrayed partner, but to the betrayer as well. Validation is vital to all Imago therapy communication, and it is crucial in cases where there has been an affair. An affair, once revealed, creates severe disruption in the life of a couple with intense emotions being unleashed, emotions that become stronger and more destructive if they are not heard and understood. The betrayed partner's feelings of rage, loss, humiliation, and resentment must be witnessed, honored, and validated by the betrayer. Equally important, the feelings with which the betrayer is struggling—shame, isolation, guilt, and emptiness—also must be validated. Only when validation has come full circle, having been offered and received by both partners, can true forgiveness and healing take place.

Eaker Weil describes the steps she considers necessary for resolving the crisis of an affair. These include anger and obsession, validation, and forgiveness. She also insists on problem reciprocity, by which she means that the betrayer discusses those problems that interfered with intimacy in his or her relationship with the betrayed and thus provided fertile ground for the affair. Such discussion demands stark honesty on the part of the betrayer and deep humility on the part of the betrayed. This type of affair work is usually too ambitious for couples to do without the containing presence of a therapist. However, with the proper support and the couple's intentional movement toward forgiveness, the partners may discover a level of connection that few other couples ever achieve.

The intense pain that an affair causes can end a marriage—it can also fuel a marriage's rebirth. The illusion of romantic love has faded forever. The partners are now faced, ready or not, with the ultimate challenge of marriage: learning to love on an authentic level. And this is what Imago therapy is all about.

Marriage is a crucible (Schnarch, 1991). Those who stay on the journey without straying can learn to deal with the anxieties and tensions of being intimately involved with one other person. The heat that is generated by frustration and conflict, and even by the desire to be with another person, transforms partners as they come to terms with their feelings. An affair is usually a no-growth option. Fidelity is a transformative and growth-producing process. However, if a couple can come to view the occurrence of an affair as a wake-up call—as a painful yet powerful route to a more conscious marriage—their relationship may, with time and renewed commitment, become richer and more rewarding than they would have previously even allowed themselves to hope for.

REFERENCE

Schnarch, D. M. (1991). *Constructing the sexual crucible.* New York: W. W. Norton.

Chapter 16

IMAGO RELATIONSHIP THERAPY AS A SPIRITUAL PATH

Dale Bailey

We are not human beings having a spiritual experience. We are spiritual beings having a human experience.

Tiellhard de Chardin

Although traditional spiritual paths have not focused on the role of intimate committed relationships in the inner life, nowhere can spiritual transformation take place more fully than within such relationships. Only in relationship do we become truly human. Only another human has the potential of constellating so many sides of ourselves, can react so pointedly to our inhuman side, and can bring to consciousness so much of that of which we are unaware. Nowhere else do we have such an opportunity to learn the true meaning of love as in the drive for reunion with that from which we have been separated.

The connection between the spiritual life and relationship is described most succinctly by Martin Buber (1952, p. 125), who says that a human being "becomes most truly a person" in the dialogic meeting with God, the Eternal Thou. Buber regards our spiritual growth as equivalent to our ability to see every person as a thou and as a glimpse into the eternal Thou. When we open ourselves to meeting the other as a thou, we both know the other's essence and we discover most fully who we are. Buber writes, "In the act of true dialogic (I–Thou) relation, man becomes a self. And the fuller its sharing in the reality of the dialogue, the more real the self becomes" (p. 125).

In my work using the dialogue process with couples, I witness spiritual moments. The possibility of entering into the divine dimension is brought to fruition through the dialogue. This happens whether or not religion has been mentioned and whether or not the couple is religious. I have come to understand that such moments of connection have a mystical quality that can transform and heal those involved. Like moments of communion with nature, when one is overcome by nature's beauty, or at times of religious devotion or conversion, when one is overcome by an inner Presence, when partners connect empathically with one another, they may become immersed in a moment of grace. Through such empathic connection, the partners go beyond themselves to join each other in an experience of affective oneness.

This experience is self-transcendent in two ways. One partner, despite disagreeing with the other and being in emotional pain, provides validation and empathy for the other. To do so, he or she must contain and transcend his or her own reactions to understand and empathize with the other's reality. Imago Relationship Therapy calls this "stretching" and growth. The one who receives the validation and empathy not only is calmed and soothed, but is often powerfully moved by a sense of gratitude. For the couple, it is a healing experience. What they receive enables them to transcend themselves in a moment of oneness with their partner, which provides the basis for inner transformation. Transcendence, therefore, has two aspects: to transcend oneself in order to provide empathic connection to the other, thus producing growth; and to transcend oneself in a moment of grace where empathy calms and soothes providing healing. Growth and healing are twin facets of the effects of Imago therapy.

MARK AND ANDREA

Just how growth and healing take place was particularly evident in the case of Mark and Andrea, a couple in their mid-30s who came to me hoping to restore their marriage. Andrea had left their six-year marriage three months earlier, and they were still living separately. She said she had left because she no longer was able to tolerate, among many other things, Mark's inability to provide a stable income, owing to his poor management of his law practice and his bouts of depression. Because Mark now appeared to have improved in both of these areas, and because he clearly wanted her back, Andrea had agreed to work toward rebuilding their relationship.

They were both intelligent, articulate, professional people, but both had been badly hurt in the relationship and were angry, cautious, and suspicious regarding each other. They commited initially to 12 therapy sessions. As is typical at the beginning of Imago therapy, the couple agreed to defer any decision as to whether to stay in the relationship or to leave it until completing the 12 sessions; they would instead simply invest in the work of the therapy process. The purpose of this commitment, as I explained to them, was to relieve any pressure about staying in the relationship while enabling each partner to feel safe that the other part-ner would remain in therapy and work through any difficult issues that might come up.

As they quickly picked up the technique of the dialogue process, their sense of wariness toward each other began to fade. The safety and connection they regained through the dialogue process within the first few sessions were clearly moving for them, and they began to behave toward each other in caring and generous ways. They even began to resexualize their relationship, which was encouraging to both. The romance of the first months of their relationship was beginning to return as a result of stretching beyond their own self-absorption to enter the other's world. Even in the early stage of dialogical interaction, they were experiencing a deeper connection and awareness of the other's presence, which was healing for them.

For Andrea, the major theme of their early dialogues was the anxiety she had felt over what she considered Mark's inability to make and manage a stable income, his moodiness, and his periods of depression. Andrea feared ending up like her mother, whom she viewed as preoccupied with having too little money. Andrea needed to know that Mark was seriously dealing with the issue of their financial stability.

But as this couple's dialogue deepened, for Andrea, the larger and more in-tensely felt issue that surfaced was her feeling of being unseen by Mark. Through-out their relationship, she said, she felt that she had to defer to Mark on almost everything. When they married six years earlier, Andrea had wanted to live in the city, but Mark said it wasn't possible and wouldn't discuss it with her. Mark had insisted that they live in the suburban house in which he'd lived during his previous marriage because it was close to where his ex-wife and children now lived and he had joint custody of the children. Andrea also felt that she had no say in the raising of Mark's children, although she had bonded with the children over the six years she'd been with Mark. She felt that Mark either did not see or would invalidate her wishes and views.

Andrea's experiences with Mark triggered her deep hurt over seeming to be invisible to her parents during her childhood. Her parents, she felt, had been preoccupied with their own lives and hadn't wanted to be bothered with her and her needs. Andrea related an especially painful memory of asking permission to be a cheerleader in high school. Her parents refused to even consider it and dismissed her request outright, then became angry when Andrea was upset.

Mark hadn't heard Andrea tell this story before, nor had he realized how she felt about his behavior toward her. He had made his decisions regarding the family on the basis of what seemed logical to him. From this dialogue, however, he came to understand Andrea's reaction to the way he did things. He was now able to express remorse for his behavior. His deepened awareness of Andrea's experience of being invisible, devalued, and used was profoundly moving to him. With his expression of empathy for her suffering, Andrea melted into tears. Mark immediately moved over to touch her and offered to hold her in her pain. A sacred healing moment had taken place as a result of their deeper connection. Such moments were repeated throughout their sessions.

Mark's difficulties with Andrea were due not only to her having left him, which he could now understand, but also to her wanting to live what Mark considered a singles' lifestyle. Andrea had moved to an apartment in the city and had had a brief affair during their separation. Although Mark believed Andrea's assertion that the affair was over and that she was now committed to working on their relationship, he still felt very mistrustful. In particular, he did not trust Andrea's best friend, whom Mark and Andrea believed was a lesbian, because Mark was afraid that the woman was attempting to seduce Andrea. He didn't trust Andrea's other friends, either; whenever he and Andrea socialized with them, Mark felt disdained, excluded, and humiliated by them, and by Andrea as well. Andrea's insisting on separating from him and associating with her friends exacerbated these feelings.

All of this reminded Mark of his relationship with his mother. He had never felt close to her or as though he were important to her. When he would try to have discussions with her, they always seemed to turn into arguments. She would adopt a disdainful attitude toward ideas he brought up, repeatedly undermining his suggestions and challenging his logic. Mark also felt unacknowledged by her for his outstanding academic achievements, which left him feeling alone and alienated.

The up-and-down progress of the couple throughout the therapy sessions gave evidence of the interlocking nature of their childhood injuries and emotional sensitivities. Shortly after the fourth session, after they had begun to feel safer, closer, and more hopeful with each other, they became reactive toward one another over a typical incident. Andrea told Mark that she planned to spend an evening with her woman friend. Mark said that if she wanted a relationship with him, then it made no sense for her to continue her relationship with such an obnoxious person. Andrea became furious. On the one hand, Mark was pressing her to avoid a relationship that felt threatening to him; on the other, Andrea felt invalidated by Mark because she wanted a relationship that was important to her and posed no threat to her relationship with Mark. When Mark, enraged, demanded that she give up that relationship, Andrea began to cry and told him she wanted to get out of her relationship with him.

During the fifth session, they were able to see how they had triggered each other. Andrea was so moved by her comprehension of Mark's pain, in this instance, that she said that she was willing to limit her contact with her woman friend in ways that felt comfortable for Mark. Through his tears, he expressed deep gratitude for her even suggesting such willingness. They began using other Imago processes to manage their conflict. They learned to do the Container Exercise, which helps couples express rage in a safe manner. They also agreed to fulfill Behavior Change Requests.

Although their relationship once again began to heal, they were constantly triggering each other over events involving Andrea's relationships with her friends. The couple continued to dialogue about these issues, however, and tried to understand and empathize with each other's feelings. By the 10th session, they appeared to be managing their conflicts well by using the dialogue.

As the end of the 12-session commitment drew near, Mark became anxious about what would happen afterward. After another incident involving Andrea's friend, he was unable to stay in the dialogue process and angrily demanded that Andrea give up her relationship with the woman. He also insisted that Andrea give up her apartment in the city and come back to live with him. Andrea found Mark's explosion and demands intolerably painful. Although she had begun to feel much safer with him, she now became convinced that he simply could not see her for who she was. At this point, Andrea decided that she had suffered one hurt too many. During the 11th session, she stated that she would come to the 12th session but felt too much fear and pain to have any hope for the relationship. Mark apologized for having exploded and expressed his desire to continue the therapy process and rebuild their relationship.

Despite the ongoing conflict, struggle, and pain, many healing moments had occurred throughout the previous sessions as Mark and Andrea were able to validate and empathize with each other. But the 12th and last session was particularly moving; it embodied in a special way what has been referred to here as moments of grace. Andrea tearfully reiterated her decision to discontinue therapy. Although she could not argue with Mark's conviction that they ought to go on, she said that she was in such agony that she could not continue. She no longer felt the shred of love for him that she'd been able to feel when they started therapy. Even worse, she couldn't feel "in my own skin around you." She still felt unseen by him, leaving her with a sense of isolation and alienation. It was as though she were "wasting my life, beating my head against a wall." And it was all the more excruciating because it reminded her of the pain of growing up with a feeling of disconnection from her family.

When Mark suggested that Andrea held him responsible for her feelings, Andrea made it clear that she did not, in fact, blame Mark. She said she realized that it was not their relationship that created the state she was in; rather, the relationship was simply a catalyst that triggered her state of being. She now understood that Mark truly did desire to give her what she needed.

Mark responded that the 12 weeks of therapy had not been a waste of time, even if Andrea left the relationship, because both of them had grown. He could now see how he had been overwhelmed by his own defensiveness, and how reactive he'd become over not knowing whether Andrea would stay with him or leave him. He could also now see how difficult it had been for Andrea to give him the absolute commitment he'd been demanding. And seeing that, he said he was willing to give up his expectation that she commit to him; he felt capable of staying in the dialogue process with her for as long as it took for her to feel safe with him. Tearfully, he acknowledged finally seeing the pain he'd caused her, and said he was very sorry for not recognizing this before.

Andrea clearly was moved. She expressed appreciation for Mark's understanding and empathy, and told him she'd experienced a momentary connection with him. But she admitted that a voice in her head was reminding her that Mark had said something similar the last time she'd left him, and he'd been unable to sustain his good intentions once she returned. She said that her newly gained realization of the size of the issue for him helped her to see that it had been "understandably impossible" for him to keep his word. But still, she added, she couldn't trust that the situation would be any different this time. She wanted Mark to know that, although she felt some bitterness, her greater sense was one of gratitude for his understanding and empathy and for his willingness to extend himself for her. She also expressed sadness for causing him pain. This moment of connection enabled her to express empathy for him, as he had for her.

Mark responded, "I tried to tell you this the other night: what came out in my first container exercise was really harsh and angry. I said that I wished that I hadn't met you, that I was ruined; I'd felt hatred for you after Dan [the man with whom she had the affair]. I don't feel that anymore. I don't regret our time together, and I don't think I wasted my life for it. I don't even regret how our splitting up is going to affect the children, because I think I was lucky to have this time with you, and so were they." Mark began to cry. Andrea mirrored and validated him, speaking very softly and gently. She seemed to be experiencing a deeper sense of connection with him than she had for a long time.

Mark then made one final plea that Andrea consider remaining in therapy. He said he wanted to get a better understanding of why his behavior had hurt her so badly, and that perhaps it would help her get the healing she needed. Andrea gently told him that although she was sad that he was in pain over her leaving, she would not continue with the therapy. She was struggling, in her individual work with her own therapist, to deal with all the issues their relationship work had brought so clearly into focus for her. It felt safe and necessary for her to be in therapy on her own, she said, but it was too excruciating to continue this process with him.

COMMENTS

Mark and Andrea left my office with no plans to return. Obviously, they were not going to continue their relationship at that time. However, the therapy had been successful nonetheless. They had both learned to go beyond their own assumptions and to see the other through the other's eyes, rather than their own. They'd come to understand why they were so reactive to each other's behavior. They realized how they brought each other pain, and they felt remorse and empathy toward one another. When they were in dialogue, they connected very well. There were many sacred and healing moments when they were immersed in each other's presence. But this last session, especially, contained moments of grace: their empathic understanding of each other served as evidence of their having transcended their own pain and self-absorption and having moved into the sacred realm of healing and transformation.

I believe that Mark and Andrea's relationship might recommence once Andrea's pain subsides and she can again remember times of feeling connected to Mark. Andrea and Mark are clearly an Imago match, and their unconscious attraction to one another remains. They had experienced deep connection a number of times during the therapy, even moments of self-transcendent spiritual bonding. Whether they continue with their marriage or decide to divorce, they now know what it takes to succeed in a relationship. In addition, their parting will be devoid of the bitterness and recriminations that are so common when partners divorce.

CONCLUSION

In Imago therapy, our psychological and spiritual well-being are understood as dependent on the quality of our connectedness. Instinctually, human beings, like other mammals, are driven toward attachment. We are social beings; being connected is in our nature. We are happiest, healthiest, and function best when we are in a trusting intimate relationship that supports our connectional nature. When this connection is broken, when our relational nature is not supported, we experience pain, unhappiness, and sometimes pathology.

The development of consciousness and self-awareness has, however, complicated, intensified, and magnified our drive for connection. Self-awareness has made human relationships much more complex, because self-awareness renders us, during our emotional development, more vulnerable to psychological injuries, such as shame, guilt, and depression. Psychologically, we must develop a sense of ourselves as differentiated beings. The awareness of our separateness leads also to spiritual dilemmas: questions emerge about the nature of our connection to the rest of creation, questions that reflect our drive for spiritual connection. As St. Augustine (1900) said, "Our hearts are restless until they find rest in Thee." It is this same spiritual restlessness that drives us toward connection with an intimate partner.

In committed adult relationships, the relationship has at least as much power over the individuals in it as the individuals have over the relationship (Mason, 1996). The relationship takes on a life of its own, and the quality of the relationship has a profound impact on the individual partners. It is as though, instead of having a relationship, the relationship has us. We are grasped by it and by its promise; our destiny is intertwined with it and with its health. When the relationship is good, our functioning is supported and enhanced. When the relationship is in turmoil, our sense of well-being suffers.

Our social nature makes our need for connectedness and relationship primary. When we feel disconnected, whether or not we are in a relationship, we suffer a loneliness and alienation that control us. We experience ourselves as needy, and even neurotic, because we feel so obsessed and oppressed by our need. The way people cope with disconnection takes different forms. For instance, we might experience the disconnection with ambivalence: we know how good the connection feels and how much we need it, yet we become extremely frustrated by it (maximizer type). Or we might fear that the connection is hopeless and too painful, and so, clinging to the illusion that we don't need it, we avoid it (minimizer type). But whatever our coping style, ambivalent or avoidant, when we experience a break in connection, we become dysfunctional. If we are ambivalent, we become addicted to people. If we are avoidant, we become addicted to work, power, acquiring things, or achieving goals.

In Imago therapy, romantic love is understood as a drive for reunion that overcomes disconnection. Falling in love is the spirit knocking; we experience ourselves grasped by the spirit, and our souls come alive. We suddenly become more truly ourselves, free of fears and egoistic strivings. It is as if we feel transformed by a force outside ourselves. We break through our defenses and taste the truth of our essence. We experience a healthy glow, which is, in part, drug induced; endorphins and natural amphetamines flood into our bloodstream. We feel known, whole, and complete. There is an awareness that goes beyond the experience of separate subject and object. There is the ecstasy of union. Two become one, at least temporarily. This oneness is clearly not in the physical sense of becoming one body or in the psychological sense of having the same identity. It is a spiritual experience, a realization of and movement toward a larger, more inclusive sense of self. Each completes the other. "He is half part of a blessed man, left to be finished by such a she; and she a fair divided excellence, whose fullness of perfection lies in him" (William Shakespeare, *King John*, Act II Scene 1, lines 439ff.).

Romantic love is a taste of how a loving connection sustains our life. Such ongoing fusion experiences are essential, because they enable us to live a healthy differentiated existence. In that sense, romantic love is realistic. But the exhilaration of reestablishing connection in romantic love has a temporary quality, because it is also based on illusion. Although the partner maintains his or her positive qualities, romantic love fades because we eventually become unable to sustain our denial of negative qualities. To reestablish and maintain a loving connection, couples must learn to cope in constructive ways with the conflict and frustrations their negative traits generate in the relationship. This task requires the courage to face a dark passage reminiscent of what St. John of the Cross (1959) referred to as the "Dark Night of the Soul."

Imago therapy sees the spiritual journey as moving from the sense of an isolated self to a realization of one's connectedness to all that is. This journey takes place through the intimate committed relationship between romantic partners. The quality of a couple's spiritual journey depends on the characteristics of consciousness and intentionality in their relationship. These characteristics move the couple from the temporary state of romantic love, through the dark night of the soul, to the conscious state of love.

The function of Imago Relationship Therapy is to facilitate moments of empathic connection between partners. Rather than help the couple to solve relationship problems, the therapist's task is to help them restore their relationship as a loving connection in which the needs of both partners are met. Problems cannot be solved except in the context of such relationship.

The dialogue is a process of growth and awakening. Meeting the other through dialogue becomes the occasion for awakening us from our self-preoccupations. We meet an other with a world that, no matter how similar to ours, is also very different from ours. As we open ourselves to mirroring the other's communication accurately, we begin to hear the other's perceptions, assumptions, and interpretations, which differ from our own, sometimes strikingly. We begin to hear something new, which makes possible a different understanding, an understanding of the other from the inside—the other's inside. The difference in our realities becomes a new reality to us. When we can momentarily set aside our own reality, we can become awakened to a larger reality, which also includes the reality of the other.

The objective of the dialogue is to create a bridge that is free from the egocentric distortion that keeps one from seeing the other's reality, and from compulsive overadaptation, in which one gives up core aspects of oneself. Across such a bridge, free communication can pass and empathic connection can be established. Such connection permits two human beings intimately to experience themselves, each other, and the current of life that is released in the space between them. Love and meaning unite in a way that not only is personal and relational, but also, in a larger sense, is truly spiritual.

That is why I believe Mark and Andrea's relationship has been a spiritual path for them. As Paul Tillich (1963, pp. 231–237), one of this century's greatest theologians, would say, they have grown in the spirit. Following Tillich's four principles of sanctification, there has been an increase in the couple's awareness, freedom, relatedness, and self-transcendence. They have increased their awareness of the forces active within them. They have increased their freedom from internal compulsions and reactivity. They have enhanced their relatedness by creating moments of connection that break up their self-absorption and self-seclusion, which puts them in greater contact with themselves. And they have consistently transcended themselves in moments of grace. Such self-transcendence is an act of love for the other: it is agape love, a participation in the holy. "To love another person is to see the face of God" (*Les Miserables*).

BIBLIOGRAPHY

Augustine, St. (1900 ed.). *Confessions*. New York: Everyman's, Dutton.

Buber, M. (1952). *Eclipse of God*. New York: Harper.

Mason, R. (1996). Imago, relationships, and empathy. *Journal of Imago Relationship Therapy*, *1* (2).

St. John of the Cross (1959 ed.). *Dark night of the soul*. Garden City, N.Y.: Image Books, Doubleday.

Tillich, P. (1963). *Systematic theology*, vol. III. Chicago: University of Chicago Press.

EDITORS' COMMENTARY

Spirituality is invisible to the naked eye, yet it is overwhelmingly real when we experience it. Imago therapists describe a feeling of awe, a sense of the sacred, when watching couples shift into deep connection during the dialogue. Spiritual experiences often have a "you had to be there" quality, but the aftereffects are unmistakable. For both the couple and the therapist, something new was born, or perhaps reborn, in the therapist's office. What was born or was born anew is the relationship.

Dr. Bailey describes a case in which spirituality emerged from the ashes of a broken relationship. It was not the outcome of the therapy that reflected spirituality; this couple, after all, broke up. But it is when a person is in the most desperate of states, is in the deepest of agonies—in this case, because of the end of a relationship—that he or she is able to surrender the false self. In the birth of the authentic self, the "I" is revealed, and only "I" can encounter, in safety, the "thou" that Buber describes.

Birth is painful. Any woman who has given birth knows the indescribable pain that precedes the sheer joy of having a baby. Yet most women say they would do it all over again. Likewise, when they are in dialogue, partners are giving birth to their relationship. Like a newborn child, a relationship cannot exist unless it is co-created by two people. As a sort of midwife to the birth of the couple's relationship, the therapist needs to attend as much to the baby being born as to the parents giving birth. That "in-between," the space and interface between two committed partners is where spirituality emerges. The eternal thou exists in the interface of two people. Dialogue lets the eternal thou emerge.

Each time a thought, feeling, or revelation is shared by one partner and validated by the other, something sacred has occurred; two people have co-created a reality. According to modern philosophers, such as Ken Wilber, the next frontier is the mind. Couples willing to enter into the fertile field of consciousness are the next explorers on this planet. The Couples Dialogue is like a capsule carrying partners into the noosphere, the far reaches of the mind. By exploring one another, they are exploring their hidden selves. Such exploration brings answers, purpose, forgiveness, and grace.

APPENDIX

KEY WORDS

The following are terms frequently used by Imago theorists and therapists. For more complete explanations, see Luquet (1996) or Hendrix (1988, 1992).

Behavior Change Request (BCR): In this process, the sending partner asks the receiving partner for behavior changes that would decrease the sender's frustrations. The frustration first is stated, and then is recast as a desire; for example, "I hate it when you are late" is restated as "I would like you to be on time." The sending partner then expresses that desire as a measurable, observable, positive, and specific (MOPS) BCR. "I would like you to be on time" becomes, "Twice this week, I would like you to arrive within five minutes of the time you said you would."

Container Exercise: Used on an appointment-only basis, this seven-step process enables the safe expression of anger and rage. In this process, the receiving partner makes himself or herself emotionally safe prior to hearing the sender's feelings. The sending partner then fully expresses feelings of anger and hurt. The sender is encouraged to connect the present feelings with a childhood wound, which activates the receiving partner's empathy. The exercise concludes with the Behavior Change Request, followed by high-energy fun. This is the most sophisticated of the Imago processes, so therapists should be trained or otherwise well prepared prior to conducting it (see a step-by-step description in Luquet's [1996] *Short-Term Couples Therapy*).

Couples Dialogue: The main communication technique of Imago therapy, the Couples Dialogue is a three-step process that ensures intentional and safe communication. In the first step, mirroring, the receiving partner mirrors what the sending partner says, for example, "If I heard you correctly, you said that you get angry when we're at parties and I make jokes at your expense. Did I get that? Is there more?" The sending partner continues to speak and be mirrored until he or she feels understood.

In the second step, validation, the receiving partner validates the sending partner's message. An example of validation would be, "I can understand that. It makes sense to me that you would be embarrassed when I make jokes at your expense." Validation does not necessarily imply agreement; rather, it is understanding and acknowledging the reality and logic of the sender's point of view.

In the third step, immediately following validation, the receiving partner expresses empathy—makes a guess about the sender's feelings: "I imagine you feel belittled, ridiculed, and stupid."

Differentiation: In general, differentiation is a state of recognizing that one is psychologically and emotionally distinct from other persons. In Imago therapy, it is a desirable characteristic that, when related to a couple, could be described as "connected differentiation." Differentiation implies, "I am not you, and you are not me, but I acknowledge that your thoughts, feelings, and actions, although different from mine, are valid." According to Imago theory, healthy differentiation takes place as couples develop their connection through the dialogue.

Emotional Safety: In Imago therapy, emotional safety is a necessary feature of all couple interactions. Initially, couples are taught to create internal safety by centering, finding a "safe place" in their minds, breathing through anxiety, and other techniques. As empathy grows between partners, emotional safety also develops, enabling the couple to dialogue about deeper and more difficult issues.

Empathizing: This is the third step of the Couples Dialogue, in which the receiver reflects back the sender's feelings. "I imagine that would make you feel sad, frustrated, and disappointed" would be a statement of empathy.

Empathy: As defined by Judith Jordan (1991) of the Stone Center, empathy is a twofold experience that includes affective surrender and cognitive structure. That is, empathy involves feeling the feelings of the other, while knowing that the feelings are those of the other, and not of oneself. Empathy entails a momentary overlap between the self and the other, serving as a means of understanding the other.

Holding Exercise: This process places the couple in a holding posture not unlike that of a parent's holding a baby. In this position, the sending partner, who is being held, talks about his or her childhood to the receiving partner, who is doing the holding. The receiver listens with empathy and mirrors back the sender's feelings, for example, "So you felt sad and alone as a child." The goals are to provide a safe context for expressing childhood frustrations and to increase the empathic bond between partners.

Imago Workup: A written exercise, it is designed to help the couple identify how their experiences with childhood caretakers influenced their selection of their romantic partner. Each partner writes down the positive and negative traits of their caretakers, along with unfulfilled desires, frustrations, and positive memories from childhood. This information is used in completing a series of incomplete sentences, which summarize the effects of those childhood memories on adult romantic relationships. (Complete instructions can be found in *Short-Term Couples Therapy* [Luquet, 1996]).

Mirroring: The first step of the Couples Dialogue, mirroring involves the receiving partner's paraphrasing or reflecting back what the sending partner said. This assures both the sending partner and the receiving partner that the sender's message was accurately heard.

Parent–Child Dialogue: In this Imago process, the receiving partner assumes an "as-if" parental persona for the sending partner. The receiving partner poses several questions about childhood to the sending partner, beginning with, "I am your mother/father. What was it like to live with me?" The sending partner responds to the receiver as though the receiver were his or her parent(s). Next, the receiving partner asks the question, "I am your mother/father. What did you need from me that you did not get?" Without commenting or responding, the receiver listens empathically to the sender. The purpose of this process is to enhance empathy in the receiver by allowing the sending partner to safely describe his or her woundedness.

Reptilian Brain: The oldest section of our tripartite brain, the reptilian brain takes care of automatic life-sustaining activities, including heartbeat, digestion, and breathing. It is concerned with physical safety and automatically defends itself against danger, responding with fighting, fleeing, freezing, hiding, or submitting. In Imago therapy, it is assumed that the reptilian brain automatically is activated when partners feel emotionally unsafe with each other.